HC 110 .P6 S8

Sturdivant,

The ghetto m

D1061876

DATE DUE

WITHDRAWN

Demco, Inc. 38-293

THE GHETTO MARKETPLACE

THE GHETTO MARKETPLACE

edited by

Frederick D. Sturdivant

THE FREE PRESS, *New York*

Copyright © 1969 by The Free Press
A DIVISION OF THE MACMILLAN COMPANY

All rights reserved. No part of this book may be reproduced or transmitted in any form or by any means, electronic or mechanical, including photocopying, recording, or by any information storage and retrieval system, without permission in writing from the Publisher.

Collier-Macmillan Canada, Ltd., Toronto, Ontario

Library of Congress Catalog Card Number: 77-81932

Printed in the United States of America

Printing number

1 2 3 4 5 6 7 8 9 10

102929

DEDICATION

To the students who shared in the
ventures in Watts and East Los Angeles
and to the people of those areas
who introduced us to "the other America."

Contents

Preface

This book is about an incongruity in the American economic system. Most observers of the distribution system in the United States are familiar with the highly diverse, efficient, bountiful cornucopia that delivers to the nation the necessities, gadgetry, and playthings associated with its high standard of living. Huge department stores, ubiquitous supermarkets and gasoline stations, and modern suburban shopping centers are, in fact, important symbols of the "American way of life." This book focuses on a less familiar scene: the market-place in the nation's urban ghettos.*

This component of the distribution system stands in vivid contrast to that known to most Americans. It is the system that delivers the standard of living to low-income Anglos, Puerto Ricans, Negroes, Mexican-Americans, and other disadvantaged minority

---

*The term "ghetto" is used in this book to refer to any urban area in which most residents are members of the lower socioeconomic class regardless of whether one racial or ethnic group predominates within the area.

groups. It is a marketplace in which the unwary poor are often the victims of unethical or illegal merchandising practices. It is a marketplace in which the retailers who do try to serve their customers well are faced with such problems as high operating costs and, often, community resentment. It is the marketplace which has served as the focal point of the destructive urban riots of the 1960's. It is in sum, the dark side of American marketing.

The materials that have been brought together for this book deal generally with two aspects of the problem: (1) the characteristics and practices of the consumers and retailers and the nature of their interactions, and (2) the ways in which it might be possible to improve the quality of marketing services rendered to the urban poor. This book is *not* a "definitive" work in the true meaning of that word. Analysis of this problem is too preliminary and too partial to make such claims. What this book attempts to do is to bring together the views of scholars, government officials, politicians, writers from the business press, and other writers who have studied various elements of this problem. It is hoped that this collection and the rather detailed bibliography will not only lead to a better understanding of the plight of the low-income urban consumer and the problems of the retailers who service ghetto areas, but will lead to further research and corrective action.

To the extent that there is any credit due to an editor for bringing together findings and ideas that are largely those of other individuals, this credit should be shared not only with the authors, but with a number of people who have encouraged and assisted in my study of this subject. There are, of course, too many to mention all by name. Among those who deserve special acknowledgment, however, is Robert J. Lavidge, a businessman who not only possesses a social conscience but a commitment to action. He, as chairman, and the other members of the U.S. Department of Commerce Task Force on Commercial Services to Low-Income Urban Areas have served as a source of stimulation and encouragement. Therefore, to Robert D. Buzzell, Blaine M. Cooke, H. Naylor Fitzhugh, Ralph L. Gillen, Walter Hamilton, Robert J. Holloway, Roy C. Parker, and C. Grove Smith, I say "thanks." I am also indebted to George P. Morris, who is now assistant professor of marketing at the University of Southern California, for assisting with the many details of this project while working with me as a graduate assistant. Appreciation is also expressed to Mrs. Nancy Heleman for helping to prepare the manuscript. Acknowledgment should also be made to W. T. Tucker simply for being a refreshingly imaginative and provocative colleague.

Austin, Texas   F. D. S.

Prologue:
Riot Report

Bruce Weber

A Negro woman pushes her shopping cart across a vast parking lot
to a dirty, green, 1957 Chevrolet—already filled with four children,
two of them fighting playfully in the back seat.

She stuffs her merchandise into the car along with the kids—she
can't use the trunk, she explains, because its lid is jammed—and
drives down Central Ave. to her ghetto home, a two-bedroom
structure condemned by the city two years ago. The twenty-nine-
year-old mother lives in Watts, scene of bitter racial violence in
August, 1965.

Sandy Washington shops at discount-minded White Front—not
by choice, but because it is the only major retailer in riot-torn, glass-
littered Watts. She purchases what her monthly welfare budget
allows, and watches for sales. Rarely does she purchase luxury items,
and television sets and hard appliances are definitely out of reach.

Reprinted from "Riot Report," *Merchandising Week* (August 14, 1967),
p. 12, by permission of Billboard Publications, Inc.

"I WON'T GO BACK"

Watts, two years after the explosion, is a depressed business community. Many merchants, burned out and looted two years ago, refuse to reopen. Insurance rates have doubled and tripled in the battle-scarred area.

It's not too early to predict the business future in Watts. "There is none," said Sol Kaplan, who owned a small appliance-TV store. "I'm giving up. I can't afford the high insurance rates, anyway."

Boarded-up stores are everywhere. Fear and bitterness keep merchants from returning, although a few have done so, only to discover Negroes are boycotting "Whitey-owned" establishments.

"I won't go back," shouted Ed Baski, who saw his grocery looted and burned. "I've had it with those people." Baski admits his prices were higher than chain supermarkets, but certainly within the price range of other mama-and-papa stores in the area.

A chain supermarket, gutted two years ago, is not rebuilding either. Today, a vacant lot filled with weeds and a sign remind Watts shoppers of the store that once stood there. "We're not rebuilding," a spokesman for the supermarket chain said. "Why should we? The sign? Oh, that's to remind them [Negroes] of the old store," he said sarcastically.

Watts residents, if they want to shop in a chain supermarket, must travel out of the district and anywhere from seven to ten miles to find a large market.

The Small Business Administration receives few loan inquiries and even fewer applications. "Business is booming everywhere in Southern California—except in Watts," an official said.

White Front stands out in Watts, to be sure: a brick structure without windows and designed to withstand armed insurrection and Molotov cocktails. "The only way this place will burn down now," said a young Negro salesgirl, "is if it's done from the inside."

Why did White Front—which has twenty-two other stores in Southern California—risk rebuilding in Watts?

"We build our stores to service great populated residential areas," an executive with the discount store said. "We have faith in the area and in the people." The store employs Negroes to fill both administrative and sales positions, and keeps its prices steady with other White Front locations.

"That's the trouble," a Negro shopper complained. "This here White Front charges the same prices as the store in Los Angeles. Only difference is we can't afford the prices."

Retail executives at White Front admit sales in "luxury" items in the Watts store are the poorest in the chain. Sales of color television sets and hard appliance items are almost nonexistent.

"It seems shoppers in this store are afraid of the big names like GE or Westinghouse," a salesman explained, "they go for the 'off-brands.' "

A saleslady said Negro shoppers are wary of purchasing "name" items because the "uneducated believe that buying GE or Westinghouse is helping the White power structure."

Larry Brown, a forty-two-year-old Negro merchant, has lived in Watts for eleven years. He has owned a grocery-liquor store for the last eight. Except for minor damage, Brown suffered little in the six-day 1965 riot. Why? "Man, I painted 'Soul Brother' on my store and stood guard day and night."

Brown was lucky. He was able to stand guard. White merchants boarded up their stores, went home, and prayed.

Later, law enforcement officers laughed when Mayor Samuel W. Yorty and former Governor Edmund G. Brown appealed to looters to stop burning and return to their homes. "There are more color television sets in Watts than the rest of Southern California combined," they snickered. "Except for liquor," a police officer said, "they went after stereos and TV's the most."

"BUSINESS NEVER WILL BE THE SAME IN WATTS"

Of the 63 businesses destroyed in Watts, only seven have been rebuilt. Of the six appliance-TV stores gutted during the riots, none have been rebuilt.

"Business never will be the same in Watts," said David J. Solish, vice president of Coin-a-Tune, a jukebox record company. "Good businesses in borderline areas are also feeling the pinch."

According to an official of the Los Angeles County Commission on Human Relations: "The biggest losers are the Negroes. They sacked stores and markets that employed Negroes. Now, many white merchants just laugh when asked if they plan to reopen in Watts."

"Why should I reopen? So it can happen again?" appliance dealer Sol Kaplan exclaimed. "I'm not going to give 'em another chance." Kaplan, who said he gave financial credit to many Negroes at little interest, closed shop one day and was burned out the next. "They even carted away three refrigerators and two freezers, not to mention fourteen television sets and one stereo," he said.

Kaplan, 57, is hoping to sell his property in Watts and reopen in Los Angeles. "I'm too old to fight revolutions," he said. "I'm going to open a small appliance-TV store in Los Angeles and try to forget Watts. To hell with civil rights and all their causes."

"I WAS WILLING TO REBUILD, BUT I COULDN'T GET INSURANCE"

Insurance costs are a major factor in rebuilding the Watts area, according to Richard S. Roddis, California's insurance commissioner. "Insurance costs vary area by area and structure by structure, relative to judgments of risks involved. Insurance costs for some Watts retailers went up about 200 per cent following the riots two years ago."

While "slum area" insurance always has been sky-high, he declared, some rates in urban areas could rise as much as 300 per cent. Policy cancellations and inability to get insurance almost prohibit doing business in the heart of Watts.

"I was willing to rebuild in Watts, but I couldn't get insurance— at any rate," said William Forest, who owned a cleaning establishment. "I complained to my insurance company, but they said I was in a 'high-risk' area and they didn't want my business."

Insurance settlements in the Watts area reached forty-one million, with many claims yet to be resolved. Insurance companies that still allow business insurance admit they have raised rates up to 60 per cent in "higher-risk classifications."

Pacific Indemnity Group rates drugstores, liquor retailers, pawnbrokers, and appliance stores in the high-risk classification. The company extracts a surcharge of $1 per year on $100 of insurance coverage on appliance stores. "The surcharge—on top of high rates —is for fire coverage, and does not include burglary coverage," an insurance company spokesman said.

THE RETAIL COMEBACK IS SLOW

Negro Councilman Thomas Bradley, of Los Angeles, declared: "The proper way to stop racism and return Watts to normalcy includes jobs and job training, inducements to business and industry to return to the stricken communities, federal tax inducements for relocation of firms to Negro areas, and reduction of insurance rates."

Still suffering economically, Watts may prove to be an example to Detroit, Newark, Chicago, and New York City.

What is the business attitude in Watts, two years after the bloody riots?

To the retail community: the comeback is slow, perhaps impossible. To insurance companies: the risk is too high. To Negro residents like Sandy Washington: "We all call the White Front store the Black Front."

Watts, two years later: nothing has really changed.

THE GHETTO
MARKETPLACE

Introduction:
The
Ghetto Marketplace

In one of his essays on life in Harlem, James Baldwin noted that
"Anyone who has ever struggled with poverty knows how extremely
expensive it is to be poor. . . ."[1] A large part of the price paid, of
course, is the taxing of one's spirit. So depressing is ghetto life, in
fact, that a number of writers have treated its residents as victims of
a spiritual death.[2] But in this instance, Baldwin was referring to the
material and measurable cost to the poor in the marketplace. And
the Negro author challenged any skeptical reader who doubted that
the low-income consumer is at a disadvantage to "Go shopping one
day in Harlem—for anything—and compare Harlem prices and
quality with those downtown. . . ."[3]

The high price of being poor is, of course, only one aspect of the
domestic crisis involving the disadvantaged in the United States.
Most of the efforts made by the federal government and various
private organizations and individuals to push back the borders of

See pages 273-274 for all footnotes to this chapter.

the large islands of poverty that remain have centered on unemploy-ment, education, health, and housing. These problems are the most visible and are generally considered to be the most fundamental. Indeed, if society could assure each citizen a good paying job, an opportunity for an education that would equip him to deal with an increasingly complex world, the availability of excellent but reason-ably priced medical care, and adequate housing, the war on poverty would be won. Tangential problems such as inadequate recreational facilities and the lack of access to an effective and reliable market system offering consumer goods and services would be virtually self-corrective. It is for these reasons perhaps that the plight of the low-income consumer and the distributors who attempt to serve them have received relatively little analysis or corrective action: the problem is not viewed as a major one but a problem that will tend to correct itself if the more fundamental problems are solved.

Such an approach is faulty on several counts. Most important among these is the assumption that the more basic problems can be dealt with swiftly and effectively. To even the most casual observer of the war on poverty this is clearly unwarranted optimism. The slow and uneven progress against the enemy must stand as an impressive warning against programs which ignore so-called secon-dary issues on the assumption that rapid progress elsewhere will eliminate the need for direct action. The enemy in the form of antiquated schools, underskilled workers, racial barriers, and the like is simply too firmly entrenched to rout in the face of a limited national commitment.

Another weakness in this approach is the assumption that the conditions facing low-income consumers in the nation's cities are of only minor importance. The Kerner Commission reported that "Significant grievances concerning unfair commercial practices affecting Negro consumers were found in 11 of the 20 cities studied by the Commission."[4] The Commission also stated that "it is clear that many residents of disadvantaged Negro neighborhoods believe they suffer constant abuses by local merchants."[5] The problem was significant enough that "discriminatory consumer and credit prac-tices" were listed among the "deepest grievances" felt by Negroes in the cities which had experienced riots.[6] Indeed, perhaps the most vivid evidence of the seriousness of the problem was the shattered commercial districts left in the wake of the riots. Although the violence thus far has been limited to black communities, the problems of ghetto marketing are to be found in Puerto Rican neighborhoods, low-income Anglo-white districts and elsewhere in the cities. A detailed study of the Mexican-American community in east Los Angeles revealed important parallels with the situation in Watts.[7] To ignore the complaints concerning the market system serving low-income neighborhoods is to ignore a problem that daily affects the well-being of the poor and, rather directly, the well-being of society.

RESEARCH IN THE MARKETPLACE

Ghettos in the United States have been studied from almost every conceivable angle by sociologists, political scientists, economists, demographers, and others; but the marketplace of the ghetto has generally escaped their view. Students of marketing have researched esoteric subjects from brand preferences for bananas to tightly structured mathematical models of distribution systems for undifferentiated raw materials, but until recently the marketing problems of poor areas were largely ignored. Although Baldwin and other writers who have lived in poverty penned scenes of the ghetto marketplace and protested their conditions, it was not until 1963 that the findings of the first systematic analysis of the problem were published. Perhaps the major contribution of this work, *The Poor Pay More* by sociologist David Caplovitz, was that it reminded government officials, businessmen, and researchers that the poor are *consumers*. The middle-class image of American consumers projected through the various advertising media disguises the fact that millions of poor people in the United States must also enter the marketplace and purchase goods and services.

The Caplovitz study of the purchasing practices and experiences of low-income New York families was highly critical of what Caplovitz termed the "deviant market system" of the ghetto. His findings stimulated congressional hearings, a television documentary, and a number of articles in the business press. The subsequent attack on retail institutions during the riots throughout the country, which Caplovitz referred to as "consumer revolts," gave a greater sense of urgency to the problem.

One of the earlier studies to follow Caplovitz's pioneering effort was conducted in Watts and Mexican-American sections of Los Angeles and generally confirmed the sociologist's contention that the poor pay more. The Los Angeles study was more broadly based and considered not only purchases of durable goods, but also prices for other types of goods and the attitudes of the local consumers toward merchants. It concluded that there was a need for a "Better Deal for Ghetto Shoppers" that could best be accomplished by means of a program to alter the economic structure of retailing in such areas by attracting mass distributors to the ghettos.

One of the features of the Los Angeles study was that it recognized the unique problems confronting retail firms in low-income areas. Indeed, Caplovitz in the preface to the 1967 edition of his book was far less harsh on the credit merchant than in the earlier edition.

> I think it is a mistake to see the credit merchant only as a nefarious exploiter of the poor. A more thorough analysis than I undertook in this book would have to examine the economic constraints that operate on these men. In some respects the local merchants charge more for the simple reason that it costs them more to operate. I am not thinking only of the fact that being small businessmen, they cannot buy in bulk the way chain stores and large department stores can. In addition, these merchants frequently have to pay more for the money they borrow and the insurance they need. . . .[8]

A Ford Foundation sponsored study conducted by the Real Estate Research Corporation in Chicago provided the first detailed analysis of the small retailer in disadvantaged areas and identified a number of specific problems which characterized operations in the ghetto.

It was not until the Federal Trade Commission study, *Economic Report on Installment Credit and Retail Sales Practices of District of Columbia Retailers*, was published in the spring of 1968, however, that comparative cost data were available. The FTC research team enjoyed the advantage of having access to the records of both ghetto and non-ghetto stores so that it was possible to determine not only the prices paid by customers, but also the profits made by the retailers. As will be seen in that section of the book, the FTC study not only found that prices were substantially higher in low-income market stores, but that costs were greater and that the makeup of operating costs for these stores differed significantly from their counterparts in general market areas.

While the studies mentioned were generally in agreement concerning the difficulties facing merchants and the higher prices charged consumers for durable goods in the ghetto, studies of food prices produced much more mixed results and stimulated even greater controversy. The findings on this topic range from rather casual observations by journalists to detailed statistical studies by academicians and government researchers.

Hearings before the House Committee on Government Operations produced a number of charges against supermarkets operating in low-income neighborhoods.[9] The Consumer Action Program of Bedford-Stuyvesant surveyed five supermarket chains and found that market basket purchases in their area were up to 6 per cent higher than in Flatbush branches of the same stores.[10] The Ad Hoc Committee on Equal Pricing surveyed prices of ten items in six Safeway stores in Washington, D.C., and claimed that prices in the three low-income area stores averaged 6 per cent higher than in stores located in more prosperous neighborhoods.[11] Charges were also made that supermarkets in poverty areas increase their prices on days when welfare checks are delivered and that the stores stock lower quality meats and produce. On this latter point Deputy Mayor Timothy Costello of New York City testified that "It is in quality particularly that the supermarkets don't come up—supermarkets in the ghetto areas don't come up to the supermarkets in other areas in the city."[12] The Los Angeles study and more recent findings in Detroit[13] had also found price and quality differentials between poor areas and more affluent locations in the cities.

Conflicting findings have been offered by a number of studies, however. In the winter of 1965–66, the Bureau of Labor Statistics priced eighteen items in food stores in Atlanta, Chicago, Houston, Los Angeles, New York, and Washington, D.C. In each city prices were compared for fifteen stores in low-income areas and fifteen stores in more affluent sections. The BLS found no significant differences when the types of stores and quantities of food were held constant.[14] Two independent studies in Philadelphia generally supported the findings of the BLS research, although they differed as to the accessibility of supermarkets to low-income consumers.[15]

To a great extent the lack of consistency in these findings is attributable to problems of research methodology. It is extremely difficult, for example, to make meaningful market basket studies of groceries. The researcher is faced with the problem of devising a market basket whose contents are relevant for low-income Negroes, or Mexican-Americans, or Puerto Ricans that can also be priced in the typical supermarket found outside of the area. A market basket that ignores differences in buying behavior related to special dietary preferences may do little to reflect the actual prices paid for groceries by a given racial or ethnic group. A number of the food pricing studies also can be criticized for failing to take into account differences in quality between ghetto and non-ghetto stores. This is especially true of meat and produce items. Comparative prices have little meaning, of course, if one is pricing "choice" grades of meat versus "commercial" grades, or fresh produce versus wilted and spoiled produce. The limited sample size and lack of objectivity might call into question certain of the testimony brought before the House Committee as well. Because of these methodological problems, studies focusing exclusively on food prices have been omitted from this collection.

THE PROLOGUE AND THE PROBLEMS

In many respects, the article from *Merchandising Week* by Bruce Weber which serves as the Prologue to this book is a microcosm of the problems which characterize the ghetto marketplace. The scenes of Watts, its residents, the retailers, the bitterness, and the stagnation represent many of the elements of the problem that are analyzed by the various articles in the remainder of the book. In general, the writings move beyond the poor-pay-more question and seek to analyze underlying problems.

The most fundamental component of the overall problem, again, is the poverty that afflicts residents of such areas. In the Prologue, the poverty is revealed in both obvious and subtle ways. The old, well-worn Chevrolet with the jammed trunk lid is perhaps the most outward sign of Mrs. Washington's economic state. Those who cash her meager welfare checks are also aware of her limited resources and her dependency on the ineffective county welfare system. Her small purchases, largely devoid of luxury items, also mark her as a disadvantaged consumer in a nation where spending on luxuries is commonplace.

To those unfamiliar with California's urban slums, however,

Mrs. Washington's residence might be misleading. The well-spaced frame houses on Watts' relatively wide, paved streets might pass for working-class neighborhoods in midwestern and eastern cities. Unlike the outwardly revealing tenements of a Bedford-Stuyvesant, the houses in Watts generally require closer inspection to reveal their faulty structures and defective wiring or the city's condemnation notice nailed to the back door. Watts is also atypical in that it is predominantly black whereas nearly 60 per cent of the nation's urban poor are white. But whether the buildings be frame houses or brownstones or the residents black or white, they share the hell that Toyohika Kagawa said "Sweet Heaven sends no miracle to ease." And an important part of the life of poverty Mrs. Washington shares with her neighbors and her counterparts throughout the country are the anachronistic retail communities that serve them.

Weber refers to the retail district in Watts as a "depressed business community." He might also have used the term "depressing." The rubble and glass-strewn vacant lots along 103rd Street, dubbed "Charcoal Alley" following the riots, may, however, be an aesthetic improvement over the pre-riot days. The rows of mom-and-pop groceries, liquor stores, pawnshops, barber shops, beauty salons and the like at least are now broken by open spaces sometimes a block long. In short, whether the areas have experienced a riot or not, the ghetto marketplace hardly resembles the stateliness of the stores in Chicago's Loop or the expansiveness and variety of a regional shopping center. In economic terms, the contrast is basically structural.

The retail community in most slum areas can best be described as atomistic in structure. The largest number of establishments are small, owner-operated concerns. Kenneth Clark, the noted psychologist, has explained that the ghetto "is not a viable community." To a great extent this is because, as Clark notes, "The ghetto feeds upon itself; it does not produce goods or contribute to the prosperity of the city. It has few large businesses. Most of its businesses are small, with what that implies in terms of degree of stability...."[16] Not all of the businesses are small. There are middle-sized establishments generally offering appliances and furniture or groceries. Even some of the door-to-door salesmen might be thought of in this category because of the rather sizable volumes of business they enjoy. But the small stores predominate. Clark notes, for example, that in 1965 there was only one large department store in Harlem, and Mrs. Washington, if she wants to deal with a mass distributor, has but one choice—White Front.

Why are business districts in such areas underdeveloped? There are any number of explanations, but one of the most important is that there are simply too many alternative areas that offer attractive investment opportunities for efficient and well-managed firms. For example, Weber quotes a Small Business Administration official as saying that "Business is booming everywhere in Southern California —except in Watts." Why build a store in Watts if insurance rates are higher? Why open an appliance store in an area where sales of name brand hard goods are reported to be slow at best? Potential retailers also can consider the reputation of an area for having a high crime rate and its implications for burglaries, shoplifting, vandalism, and the like. There are unique problems with employee training and turnover and communication with local consumers.

A consideration that is perhaps more important than any for retail firms contemplating entering Negro areas is the mounting resentment toward outsiders. The predominance of white merchants in such communities is an affront to many black Americans. Malcolm X was an early exponent of that view:

> The American black man should be focusing his every effort toward building his *own* businesses, and decent homes for himself. As other ethnic groups have done, let the black people, whenever possible, however possible, patronize their own kind, hire their own kind, and start in those ways to build up the black races's ability to do for itself. That's the only way the American black man is ever going to get respect.[17]

The bitterness toward white-owned establishments serves as a barrier to entry. Firms which were driven out of Watts by the riots show little inclination to return. The decision to leave the super-market sign standing in the vacant lot where the chain's store once stood is a symbol of the acrimony felt by the other side as well. Or as one owner of a small grocery store who saw it looted and burn-ed, put it, "I've had it with those people."

While Weber's prologue does not specifically mention the problem, one of the aspects of the bitterness between consumers and merchants in the ghetto marketplace is the rise of anti-Semitism.[18]

A substantial number of the merchants in low-income neighborhoods are Jewish; and, therefore, anti-Semitic slogans serve as a handy weapon to hurl at the businessmen. Indeed, the invective "Jew merchant" was spewed at all white merchants in Watts and even some black store owners. Again, Malcolm X explained the perceptions of the militant black people:

> In every black ghetto, Jews own the major businesses. Every night the owners of those businesses go home with that black community's money, which helps the ghetto to stay poor. But I doubt that I have ever uttered this absolute truth before an audience without being hotly challenged, and accused by a Jew of anti-Semitism. . . . I have told them that if I tell the simple truth, it doesn't mean that I am anti-Semitic; it means merely that I am anti-exploitation.[19]

The bitterness and ugliness of the ghetto marketplace is much more profound and complex than can be revealed by simple price comparison studies. Is it any wonder then that "Of the 63 businesses destroyed in Watts, only seven have been rebuilt"?

ATTEMPTS TO SOLVE THE PROBLEM

In spite of the bitterness that exists and the peculiar challenges that confront management in low-income urban areas, it is clear that opportunities do exist in the ghetto. The White Front discount store is but one example of the ability of management to meet the challenges of adapting to ghetto conditions. The three highly respected, white-owned ABC food markets in south central Los Angeles are a monument to imagination and adaptation on the part of an effective management. These examples are a source of encouragement to those who believe that the marketplace in the ghetto can become a viable and effective component of the nation's distribution system.

The drive to improve conditions in the ghetto marketplace has generally taken three directions: consumer protection, encouragement to establish new enterprises, and aid to management. The following are examples of activities in each of these areas:

Consumer protection was one of the major parts of the program of action recommended by Caplovitz in the conclusion of his study. The legal structure of New York was a major target because it so heavily favored the merchant over the consumer. The small print on installment contracts, the use of City Marshalls as collection agents working on commission, the provisions for garnishment and repossession were all part of the legal structure working on the side of the high-pressure credit merchant. The Federal Trade Commission also discovered a serious imbalance in laws related to consumer-merchant rights. The FTC has been active in recommending changes in state and local laws and in encouraging governmental units on those levels to show a greater interest in protecting consumers against unethical merchandising practices.

An interesting example of a private effort in this area is the Consumers Education and Protective Association in Philadelphia. An interracial organization, the CEPA operates without the benefit of grants or other aids from public or private agencies. Its two full-time workers are paid with the low annual dues assessed from the membership. Organized on a neighborhood basis, the organization publishes its own monthly newspaper and uses this medium as well as pickets to bring pressure to bear upon retailers, contractors, savings and loan companies, banks, auto dealers, public officials, or anyone else whom they consider guilty of bilking or otherwise taking advantage of any of their members. CEPA has been highly successful in negotiating settlements and saving its members thousands of dollars. The organization represents a rather exciting and imaginative grass-roots approach to consumer protection.

Encouragement to establish new enterprises in ghetto areas has also been a major objective of groups working on this problem. Among these efforts has been a revitalized program by the Small Business Administration to set up thousands of minority group entrepreneurs in their own businesses. Legislation has been proposed to enable low-income areas to incorporate their own community development corporations to own and manage local businesses. Other legislation has been proposed which would offer tax incentives and investment guarantees to encourage mass distributors to locate in the ghettos. The Ford Foundation has funded an experimental program in Baltimore to enable potential black entrepreneurs to purchase businesses from whites who choose to leave the ghetto. Although other legislation and activities could be cited, the important point is that efforts are under way to revitalize ghetto retail companies.

Aid to management of ghetto businesses is a closely related effort.

Since inefficient and unsophisticated management methods have been blamed for at least part of the higher costs and ill will in the ghetto, several groups have undertaken to assist the management of such businesses. The Interracial Council for Business Opportunity has played an effective role in this area both in Los Angeles and New York. ICBO in effect serves as a clearing house for volunteer consultants from the business and academic community. A number of schools of business throughout the country have patterned programs after the ICBO example. Master's candidates and faculty at such universities as Harvard, Stanford, Howard, Washington, Northwestern, and elsewhere offer their services to ghetto businesses. Various governmental agencies, such as the Small Business Administration, also offer aids to these businesses.

Other programs and activities could be cited, but the important point is that efforts are under way to improve the ghetto marketplace. These and other activities need to be accelerated while the search continues for even more effective methods to correct this flaw in our economic system. It is the premise of this book that the United States cannot afford the luxury of: "Watts, two years later: nothing has really changed."

ONE

THE MARKETPLACE: PARTICIPANTS AND PROBLEMS

An understanding of the operations of the market system in ghetto areas can be gained only by considering the characteristics of the consumers, the retailers who supply them with their goods and services, and the nature of their interactions. The first three articles in this section focus on the attitudes, behavior, and practices of low-income people. These selections are followed by four items that consider the performance of retail firms serving ghetto customers. Following these materials are two selections that treat special problems in the relationship between the merchants and the poor. The final article presents an overview of the marketplace of the poor and proposes a method of improving conditions in this segment of the nation's distribution system.

The first article by Irelan and Besner focuses on the life situation of the poor. It is suggested that a comprehensive understanding of the problems of the poor is necessary before effective solutions can be developed. Although the goals and values of the low-income groups are "typically" American, their powerlessness in coping with their environment leads to an attitude of acceptance of their situation and a reliance on luck to get ahead. The challenge of bringing the poor into the total society so that their dreams can become realistically achievable objectives is viewed as an end that will require years of effort.

Lamale, in a review of historical statistics, shows that the average family has prospered over the last three decades with a decreasing per cent of total spending allocated to the basic necessities of food, shelter, and clothing. She notes, however, that these statistics conceal variations in income and spending associated with different socio-characteristics of families that cannot be treated as a homogeneous group. The number of persons in a family, their total level of income and different patterns of consumption cast doubt on the applicability of average statistics to low-income families.

Richards charges that the definition of a "poverty income" is dependent on the life style of the poor and not simply a figure set by economists. To some extent the low-income consumer's situation is a function of his purchasing practices. In addition, certain characteristics such as limited formal education perpetuate poverty and bad consumer practices. Although the situation of the poor can also be explained in terms of psychological characteristics limiting their ability to overcome environmental problems, some consumer education programs have been successful. Richards suggests that a realistic method of achieving consumer education is an informal approach to teaching financial management.

The preceding articles have reviewed the life style of the poor in coping with their socioeconomic environment. Caplovitz discusses an important part of this environment in a study examining the practices of Harlem merchants in dealing with the poor. To some extent, the characteristics of the low-income consumer—the almost constant reinforcement through advertising of the need to purchase durables, limited income, poor credit position, and a lack of shopping sophistication—facilitate the continued existence of high-cost trade practices. As Caplovitz found, most of the poor are able to make credit purchases. The liberal granting of credit creates a high risk situation for the merchant. However, the deceptive practices of some retailers—such as merchant referral commissions, bait advertising, switch sales, and the sale of used goods as new—cannot be justified on any grounds. These practices represent an intentional exploitation of the poor.

The Federal Trade Commission Report treats installment credit and sales practices of merchants in the District of Columbia and further supports Caplovitz's findings of higher costs to the poor for durable goods. The need for extended and low down payment credit terms by the poor is again reflected in higher cost of credit and product prices. The report also provides information on the cost and profit experience of the retailers studied and reveals that the makeup of costs for ghetto stores differs from that of comparable retail firms in the general market. Net profit on sales are revealed to be somewhat higher in ghetto stores, but net profit return on net worth was considerably lower than for general market retailers.

The Sturdivant and Wilhelm study examines the question of discrimination in the marketplace on the basis of minority group membership as opposed to the economic status of the consumer. The study involved the use of three couples (Anglo-white, Negro, and Mexican-American) who had basically the same credit profile. The couples shopped for identical items in ghetto and non-ghetto stores. The findings indicate that credit charges are a convenient device for exercising discrimination and that although prices were always lower in non-ghetto stores, the minority group shoppers were not free from exploitation when shopping in a middle-class setting.

A review of the findings of a Bureau of Labor Statistics study provides the basis of the article by Groom. This comparative pricing study found that the poor generally pay more for housing, higher food prices in low-income neighborhoods are associated with the dominance of smaller stores rather than discriminatory pricing by food chains, as is often charged, and that the results of price studies of nonfood items are inconclusive.

As indicated in the preceding articles, the ghetto merchant has a major effect on the economic environment of the poor. Some have suggested, in fact, that the merchants have been a principal cause of riots in the black ghettos. *The Wall Street Journal* article reviews the attitudes of both merchants and ghetto residents after the riots and points up some of the problems facing those concerned with improving the ghetto economic environment. Instead of the co-operation needed between merchants and residents in the ghetto, there exists too often a state of fear and resentment. Most merchants claim the riots were not justified and see no reason for further involvement in a hostile community. Some black residents feel that unfair tactics by the merchants have not changed. Walls of concrete and steel have arisen to protect the stores that remain and psychological barriers between merchants and Negroes contribute to a continuing hostile atmosphere that is unattractive to new business.

A special case of retailer-consumer hostility exists between Negroes and Jewish merchants. Jacobs considers the basis for these animosities and the outward manifestations for the growing anti-Semitism in black neighborhoods. It is one of the ironies of the marketplace in the black slums that two minority groups with a history of persecution are becoming increasingly bitter toward each other.

The final article in Part One, by Sturdivant, provides an overview of the findings of a study conducted in Watts and the Mexican-American community in east Los Angeles. The article focuses on the inefficiency of the retail sector of ghettos and points to a number of sources of conflict between merchants and consumers: inflated prices and credit charges, lack of refurbishing and maintenance of stores, and the lack of courtesy toward customers. The paper provides a transition to Part Two by suggesting a possible solution to the problems of low-income marketing. The plan calls for offering incentives to attract efficient and reputable business firms to ghetto areas.

Low-Income
Life Styles

Lola M. Irelan
and
Arthur Besner

Currently, in our national concern for the alleviation of poverty and economic dependency, the need to know and understand what life looks like from the bottom of society is a crucial one. We can induce meaningful change only if we understand the situation where we intend it to occur. It is unlikely, for example, that we can change or reduce rates of dependency and poverty without knowing what the conditions of dependence and deprivation mean to people caught up in them. Nor can we bring any class of people into a different relationship to society without knowing the quality of the existing situation.

Reprinted from *Low-Income Life Styles* (Washington: U.S. Department of Health, Education, and Welfare, Publication No. 14), pp. 1–12.
See pages 274–277 for all footnotes to this chapter.

As yet, knowledge of this sort is fugitive and tenuous. Much needed research has yet to be designed. There are gaps and flaws in the exploratory research which has been done. The findings on hand are suggestive rather than definitive. There is enough known, however, to warrant inventory and judicious application. It behooves us to systematize and use such knowledge as we do have. In the long run, such a step will serve to refine and increase it.

This paper summarizes available findings, largely from studies in the United States, bearing on the approach to life of the poor, the people at the bottom of society's economic ladder. It will discuss the connection between the condition of poverty, the views of man and society which arise there, and the apparent effect of those views on the lower-class version of American goals and values.

LIFE CONDITIONS OF THE POOR

In our society, a continuously low income is directly associated with certain life situations. Poorer, more crowded living quarters, reduced access to education and recreation, occupational restriction to simpler, manual types of work—these and similar characteristics of the very poor are sufficiently obvious to need no underlining. The result of these circumstances is a set of life conditions which is not so obvious. They consist of four general limitations: (1) comparative simplification of the experience world, (2) powerlessness, (3) deprivation, and (4) insecurity. These limitations are, of course, relative. Indeed, they can be discerned only because of the different extent of their existence at the several levels of society.

1. Limited alternatives

The poor, of all the strata in society, have the slightest opportunity to experience varieties of social and cultural settings. Their own setting is one of the least intricacy and flexibility. Throughout life, they experience a very narrow range of situations and demands. Their repertoire of social roles is limited. They seldom participate in any activity which takes them out of the daily routine. They rarely play roles of leadership, or fill any position calling for specialized functioning. On their jobs they confront less complex situations and have fewer, less diverse standards to meet. Socially, they seldom go beyond the borders of kinship and neighborhood groups—people very like themselves.[1]

2. Helplessness

The position of the poor vis-à-vis society and its institutions is one of impotence. They have practically no bargaining power in the working world. Unskilled and uneducated, they are the most easily replaced workers. The skills they do have are minimal, of little importance in productive processes. On the job itself, the very poor man can exercise little autonomy and has small opportunity to influence conditions of work. He is close to helpless even to acquire information and training which would change this situation. He has neither the knowledge nor the means to get it.

3. Deprivation

It is reasonable to suspect that this general condition, almost universally associated with poverty, is felt with particular intensity in American society. Deprivation is, after all, relative. When it is defined as lack of resources relative to felt wants and needs, it is evident that America has one of the greatest gaps between generally accepted goals and the extent to which the lower class can realistically expect to attain them. As a nation, we stress, perhaps inordinately, the value and virtue of high attainment. We expect and applaud efforts at self-improvement and upward social mobility. Commercial advertising attempts to stimulate and increase desire for status achievement. The richness of life in the rest of society is well displayed—on television, in newspapers, on billboards, in store windows, on the very streets themselves. All this, plus awareness that some people have actually succeeded in the strenuous upward move, makes the condition of the unachieving poor one of unremitting deprivation. Their relative deprivation is, perhaps, the condition which more than anything else affects the life-view of the poor. Constant awareness of their own abject status and the "failure" which it rightly or wrongly implies understandably leads to embarrassed withdrawal and isolation.

4. Insecurity

People of low income are more at the mercy of life's unpredictability than are the more affluent. Sickness, injury, loss of work, legal problems—a range of hazardous possibilities—may overwhelm anyone. But to the poor man they are especially fearful. His resources are more sparse. His savings, if any, are quickly expended in any sizable emergency. Certain conditions of his life make emergencies more likely. His work skills are more expendable, sometimes more dependent on seasonal demands. He is more likely to lose his job on short notice. An emergency expenditure of funds may mean the postponing of rent payments and the fear of eviction. He is unable to secure for himself and his family the regular, preventive health measures which would fend off medical emergencies. He often finds that he cannot successfully navigate the channels involved in using public sources of emergency help, such as clinics and legal aid agencies.[2]

LOW-INCOME VIEW OF MAN AND SOCIETY

Constant, fruitless struggle with these conditions is likely to produce estrangement—from society, from other individuals, even from oneself. The wholeness of life which most of us experience—the conjunction of values, knowledge, and behavior which gives life unity and meaning—is less often felt by the poor. They see life rather as unpatterned and unpredictable, a congeries of events in which they have no part and over which they have no control.

Conceptualized as "alienation," this view of life is repeatedly found associated with lower social and economic status.[3] It is multifaceted—despair can be generated and felt in many ways. Generally, however, it seems to have four different forms of expression. The alienation of the poor is graphically seen in their feelings of: (1) powerlessness, (2) meaninglessness, (3) anomia, and (4) isolation.

1. Powerlessness

The objective condition of helplessness in relation to the larger social order leads naturally to the conviction that one cannot control it. The poor are widely convinced that individuals cannot influence the workings of society. Furthermore, they doubt the possibility of being able to influence their own lives. Correspondingly, they are likely to voice such pessimistic views as, "A body just can't take nothing for granted; you just have to live from day to day and hope the sun will shine tomorrow."[4]

2. Meaninglessness

Powerlessness, the feeling of being used for purposes not one's own, usually is accompanied by conviction of meaninglessness. The alien conditions in which an individual may be caught up tend to be unintelligible. He does not grasp the structure of the world in which he lives, cannot understand his place in it, and never knows what to expect from it. Oriented, by need, to the present, he is relatively insensitive to sequences in time. He often does not understand the continuity of past experience and current ones. And, not only does the poor man feel unable to control future events, he cannot even predict them.

3. Anomia

The term "anomie" was originally coined to describe situations in which social standards have been broken down, or have no influence upon behavior.[5] It has subsequently been pointed out that this normless condition is a probable result of the failure of prescribed behavior to lead one to expected goals.[6] The life-view of individuals caught in such a discrepant situation is likely to be cynical, perhaps fatalistic. For example, the poor man who is taught in many ways that economic success is the most desirable thing in life—and then is barred from legitimate means of achieving it—may come to expect that illegal behavior is necessary to reach approved goals. The situation, moreover, induces people to believe in luck. The poor are in no position to comprehend the whole of society's structure and operation, or to understand its dysfunctions. Since they also have little control over it, its impact on them is frequently fortuitous. Understandably, they are quick to credit their difficulties to fortune and chance.[7]

4. Isolation

More than any other segment of society, the very lowest economic stratum is socially isolated. The poor man not only fails to comprehend society or his community, he is out of touch with it. He reads fewer newspapers, hears fewer news programs, joins fewer organizations, and knows less of the current life of either the community or the larger world than more prosperous, better educated people do. Nor do the poor associate among themselves more than minimally.[8] Experiencing separation from society and each other, it is natural for them to feel alone and detached. And feeling no identity, even with each other, they view the world as indifferent and distant— "No one is going to care much what happens to you when you get right down to it."[9]

GOALS AND VALUES

What are the aims of life in such circumstances? In a situation of relative helplessness, knowing themselves worse off than the rest of society, living on the edge of chronic emergencies, and seeing their own circumstances as formless and unpredictable, how do the poor shape their lives? What values do they hold? What goals do they seek? Essentially, they seek and value the same things as other Americans. Naturally enough, since they are American poor, they absorb characteristic American values and preferences. And, just as naturally, the realities of low economic status are visible in the lower-class version of American dreams and designs. The result is a constricted but recognizable variant of society-wide goals and standards.

Increased sophistication of research on lower income and deprived groups is correcting a long-held impression that the poor place no value on occupational and educational achievement. While the poor do have a more modest absolute standard of achievement than do those who are better off, they want relatively more improvement in their condition. They value the same material comforts and luxuries. Psychologically, they seek the securities that appeal to other Americans. They hold, with little qualification, to the same proprieties of social conduct.

Interest in improving one's status, however, seems to have different sources at different social levels. To the middle-class youth, the idea of having a better job than his father is appealing, sometimes absorbing. Such achievement is attractive in itself. A lower-class youngster has more urgent, material reasons for wanting an improved future. His present is painfully unsatisfactory. His urge toward better, stabler occupations is not so much drive for achievement as flight from discomfort and deprivation. It is probably stronger for that difference.[10]

Reality—expenses of education and training, lack of resources— usually keeps less well-off high school students from aspiring to the highest level professions. But, more than their middle-class fellows, lower-class high school students want better jobs than their fathers. They are more likely to value increased income. In significantly greater numbers, they are unwilling to enter the same occupations as their fathers.[11]

Although they may not expect to achieve it, most low-income people value advanced education. It has been found that up to 65 per cent of parents will say they want a college education for their children.[12]

Materially, the lower classes are not satisfied with poor housing or living conditions. High on their list of desirable improvements are better housing and neighborhoods. Inside their homes, they value the same things as the general run of Americans—comfortable and durable furniture, a television set, an array of electrical appliances and, to give life grace as well as comfort, a few ornaments and art objects. Tastes in style are definitely American—modern furniture, colored telephones, pole lamps, systematic color schemes.[13] It some- times happens, as in more affluent circumstances, that materialistic values win out over real human needs. Parents stint on children's clothing to save money for a car. Older children are pressed too early into adult responsibilities because both parents are working away from the home.[14] A woman postpones an operation for herself because the family must have a car or a radio.[15]

In common with other Americans, the lower class enjoys excitement and values the opportunity to escape routines and pressures of day-to-day existence. Spectator sports, television, visiting—all are valued leisure-time pursuits.[16]

Probably the most basic value held by the poor is that of security. Even more than "getting ahead," they value "getting by," avoiding the worsening of an already unstable situation.[17] They are unwilling to take risks, and seek security rather than advancement—also a frequent pattern in economically better-off segments of the popu- lation.[18]

The moral code of the very lowest class is a moot subject. It has been said that they have an entirely separate set of moral and ethical values. They have also been described as subscribing so fully to the general American code that they are frustrated by it.[19] The most realistic conception seems to be that which credits them with an adapted version of society's rules of behavior. They value stable marriages, perhaps even more highly than do middle-class Americans. They do not, however, reject out of hand other forms of sex partnership. A sliding scale seems to exist, whereon a good common-law marriage is valued less than legal union, but more than a transient arrangement. Illegitimacy is not devalued to the extent that it is elsewhere. Legitimate families are the ideal, but there is also some merit ascribed to the parent who acknowledges and supports children born out of wedlock.[20]

LIFE THEMES

The anomaly of life at the poverty line is evident. When people live in conditions of such obvious helplessness, when they are themselves so aware of their condition as to feel alienated and apart from society, how can they retain, much less implement, the values of that society?

The apparent answer is reinterpretation. Paths to achievement, to security, to any goal—the very quality of the goal itself—are refracted by the lower-class view of life. They are interpreted in the light of what the poor man considers to be facts about life. The help-lessness which he feels, the insecurity he experiences, the meaningless-ness of life—all have their effect upon the way he lives and behaves.

There are four distinctive themes peculiar to lower-class behavior, all apparently the result of a deprived, alienated condition: fatalism, orientation to the present, authoritarianism, and concreteness.

The genuine powerlessness experienced by the lower class is the source of persistent fatalistic beliefs. The natural counterpart of feeling helpless is belief in uncontrollable external forces. The attitude is reminiscent of belief in fate. People cannot avoid what is going to happen to them. Resignation is the most realistic approach to life.[21] Even when optimism is expressed, it is likely to be in terms of the working of chance—"A poor person should never give up hope; there's always a chance that a lucky break will put him on top."[22] This attitude acts as a definite brake on occupational and educational aspirations, and retards health care. In various other ways fatalism minimizes efforts to cope with deprivation and its consequences.

Hand in hand with fatalism goes a persistent tendency to think in terms of the present rather than the future. It is, after all, fruitless to pay attention to the distant future or try to plan life when fortune and chance are considered its basic elements. Also, when so much of one's resources must be expended simply to survive the present, little is left over for the future.[23] Results of this ad hoc orientation are pervasive. It handicaps people for the planning required in systematic economic improvement. It works against the frugality and rainy-day planning which could offset economic dependency. In the home, it results in child-training in terms of immediate reward and punishment. Children quickly evince their own present-time thinking. This low concern for future goals has been shown to be related to low academic achievement[24]—and the cycle continues.

The authoritarian theme is a strong underlying factor in interpersonal relationships of the poor. Generally defined, it is the embodiment of belief, more prevalent in the lower classes than elsewhere, in the validity of strength as the source of authority, and in the rightness of existing systems. It seems to arise from simplification of life experiences, in which one learns to prefer simple solutions to problems, and from constant subordination of the poor. Authoritarianism is incarnate in the habit of classifying people as either "weak" or "strong," in belief that deviance or disobedience should be severely punished, and in reliance on authority, rather than reason, as the proper source of decisions. It has traceable effects on family relations, child-rearing patterns, and relation to community institutions—schools, clinics, the police, welfare agencies, even to churches.[25]

Concreteness, stress on material rather than intellectual things, is a believable but little-discussed theme of lower-class life. It is natural to people preoccupied by material problems. It shows itself in verbal patterns, in distrust of intellectualism, and in occupational values.

The concrete verbal style of the poor has been well-documented.[26] It is characterized by less abstraction, fewer concepts, more frequent reference to concrete objects and situations, and a less discursive manner. It includes fewer generalizations, relies less on intellectual processes than on observation, and is more tied to the world of immediate happenings and sensations.

Consistent with its patterns of speech, the lower class inclines to withhold its admiration from "egg-heads," reserving it instead for the practical, down-to-earth man of action. What counts is not abstract, intellectual pursuits, but the hard tangible products of action. Results are important.[27]

This pragmatic orientation has a vital effect upon the occupational values of the lower classes. They have been found, at as early an age as ten years, to value occupations for more tangible rewards rather than for intellectual or emotional ones. That is, a boy will aspire to a certain profession because of what it offers in terms of money and prestige rather than the nature of the work itself.[28]

SUMMARY AND IMPLICATIONS

Our lower-income population is insecure and comparatively powerless in relation to the rest of American society. Realizing their submerged position, they have come to feel apart from society rather than part of it. From their own helplessness, they have generalized to the belief that most of life is uncontrollable. They are convinced of their own impotence so that, while they accept typical American values they are frequently lethargic in trying to attain them.

It would be incautious, in view of the sparseness of our knowledge, to say what program implications such knowledge has, or what techniques of improvement are most likely to succeed. But it would be irresponsible to close this discussion without underlining the precautions it suggests:

1. The entire life situation of the poor must be considered if any part of it is to be changed. Their attitudes arise in no vacuum but are logical results of real circumstances.

2. Lower-class citizens must be brought off the periphery into the structure of the community. Nothing which the community does for them can be durably effective until they are a functioning part of the community.

3. Energetic patience must prevail. The alienated adult cannot be completely reeducated. His children can be somewhat swayed. But it is with his grandchildren that one can really have hope.

How the Poor
Spend Their Money

Helen H. Lamale

A cartoon which appeared before the Election last fall showed the
President patting his head with his left hand, labeled "Prosperity,"
and rubbing his stomach with his right hand, labeled "Poverty."
The caption said, "It's easy once you get the hang of it . . .!" Getting
"the hang of it" is the problem which confronts anyone who under-
takes to discuss and evaluate levels of living among the poor. It can
only be done within the framework of the levels and manner of living
of the total population. It requires an understanding of how radically
these levels of living have changed—in recent years and since the
mid-1930's when widespread national interest was last focused on
the problem of poverty. The significant differences in size, age, and
other characteristics of families, their participation in the labor force,
and place of residence, which have accompanied the greatly improved

Reprinted from "How the Poor Spend Their Money," Herman P. Miller (ed.),
Poverty American Style (Belmont, California: Wadsworth Publishing Company,
Inc., 1966), pp. 150–61, by permission of (Mrs.) Helen H. Lamale, Chief,
Division of Living Condition Studies, Bureau of Labor Statistics, U.S. Depart-
ment of Labor.

economic status of families, are all important considerations in appraising levels of living among the poor today. Poverty in the midst of prosperity is quite different from poverty in the midst of general economic depression. A few historical statistics on consumer income and expenditures will give perspective to this discussion of current levels and distributions of income, spending, and saving.

MID-1930 TO 1950

Between the mid-1930's and 1950, average current expenditures of employed city-worker families increased almost 60 per cent after allowance for the price increases over the period. The proportion of their total spending used for food, shelter (including fuel and utilities), and clothing declined from a little more than 70 per cent in 1934–36, to a little less than 60 per cent in 1950. Expenditures for household operation, house-furnishings and equipment, medical care, recreation, and automobile purchase and operation in 1950 were all two to more than three times their level in the mid-1930's. Net increases in expenditures for personal care, education, and tobacco all exceeded the 60 per cent average increase in total goods and services. The net increase in food expenditures, though considerably less than the average for all goods and services, was still substantial—30 per cent. Food consumption surveys, conducted by the Department of Agriculture in the late 1940's, reported a marked improvement in the nutritional adequacy of diets—some of it through the improved processing of foods, e.g., enriching of white bread and flour. Current shelter expenses of renters and homeowners had a net increase of 26 per cent from the mid-1930's to 1950, and payments on mortgage principal and down payments on homes averaged four and a half to five times their mid-1930 level—reflecting the increase in homeownership among city-worker families from 30 to 45 per cent. The period was characterized by expanding use of insurance and credit to cover current living expenses.

THE GAINS OF THE 1950's

These improvements in the level of living continued in the 1950's. In 1960–61, urban families and single consumers (hereafter referred to as families) spent an average of $5,390 for current annual living expenses. After allowance for price increases over the decade, this bought about 14 per cent more in goods and services than in 1950. Since their average "real" income (after taxes and price change) was up 22 per cent, they used only 91 per cent of their after-tax income for current consumption in 1960–61, as compared with 97 per cent in 1950. The widened margin between income and current expenditures enabled families to increase their gifts and contributions, to put more in personal insurance, and to save more than in 1950.

The improvement in the level of living of the average family during the decade is also indicated in the continued reduction in the per cent of total spending allocated to the three "basics," food, shelter (including fuel, etc.) and clothing, and to food alone. For urban families, the relative importance of spending for the three "basics" declined from 57 to 53 per cent, and for food from almost 30 per cent in 1950, to 24 per cent in 1960–61. These indications of improvements in the level of living observed for the average family also occurred throughout the income distribution and among families of different size, age, occupation, and place of residence. Failure to recognize these changes over the past two decades can lead to understatements of our progress in reducing poverty and misunderstanding with respect to the nature and extent of the present need.

LEVELS AND PATTERNS OF LIVING IN 1960-61

The average income after taxes of all nonfarm families—urban and rural—was $5,634, and their expenditures for current consumption goods and services averaged $5,145 in 1960–61. These averages, however, conceal wide variations in income and spending associated with different sociocharacteristics of families. They also conceal wide variations in consumption levels actually achieved by various groups in the population after allowing for differences in consumption needs associated with differences in family size, age, and composition. For example, about 45 per cent of one-person families had incomes under $2,000, while only 7 per cent of all families of two or more persons had such incomes. On the other hand, the budgetary requirements of one-person families, most of whom are elderly, are only about 37 per cent of those of a four-

TABLE 1. Summary of Family Expenditures, Incomes, and Savings, by Family Size at Selected Income Levels

Total Nonfarm United States, 1960–61[1]

FAMILY SIZE AND ANNUAL MONEY INCOME AFTER TAXES

	1 person $1,000–1,999	2 persons $2,000–2,999	3 persons $2,000–3,999	4 persons $3,000–3,999	5 persons $4,000–4,999	6 or more persons $5,000–5,999	Families and single consumers $6,000–7,499
Family characteristics:							
Number of families in sample	523	520	356	149	150	164	1,854
Families in universe							
Estimated number (000)	2,403	2,415	1,691	702	676	752	7,994
Percent in size class	29.4	15.5	18.3	8.4	12.5	15.1	15.4
Average:							
Family size	1.0	2.0	3.1	4.1	5.1	7.0	3.7
Money income before taxes	$1,493	$2,603	$3,324	$3,695	$4,748	$5,734	$7,513
Number of full-time earners	.4	.3	.6	.7	.8	.9	1.0
Age of head (years)	65.6	60.1	42.8	38.7	37.3	38.9	42.9
Education of head (years)	8.2	8.0	8.9	9.2	9.6	9.7	11.3
Number of children under 18 years	—	.1	1.0	2.0	3.0	4.7	1.6
Percent:							
Homeowners, all year	42	57	42	41	52	62	67
Auto owners, end of year	15	57	68	77	84	88	92
Nonwhite	18	13	20	19	15	17	6
With children under 18 years	—	13	77	95	100	100	66
With persons 65 years and over	64	56	19	10	5	7	10
Avg. income, expenditures & Savings:							
Money income after taxes and other money receipts	$1,485	$2,543	$3,211	$3,648	$4,564	$5,624	$6,779
Net change in assets & liabilities	−119	−217	−235	−383	−95	−75	+173
gifts and contributions	1,664	2,861	3,651	4,411	5,147	6,021	6,875
Account balancing difference	−60	−101	−205	−380	−488	−322	−269

[1]For definitions, see *Consumer expenditures and Income*, BLS Report No. 237–93, and Supplement 3-part A to BLS Report No. 237–38, U.S. Department of Labor

person younger family. To allow for these variations, the following discussion of current levels and patterns of living is based on the income and spending patterns of families of different size which are equivalent to those of four-person families with after-tax income of $3,000 to $4,000, as reported in the BLS Survey of Consumer Expenditures in 1960–61. All nonfarm families of two or more persons in 1960–61 averaged 3.6 persons and had income and expenditures approximating those of families with incomes after taxes of $6,000–$7,499. This is the income class used for comparison with the selected "equivalent low-consumption" classes. (See Tables 1 and 2.)

1. Food expenditures

The per cent of total spending used for food is a commonly accepted measure of relative levels of living of various groups in the population—the lower the percentage, the higher the level of living. This has been found to be a reasonably valid measure provided the population groups being compared are generally homogeneous with respect to family characteristics and other factors related to food expenditures, including the relation of food prices to prices of other goods and services.

In 1960–61, food expenditures of nonfarm families, on the average, accounted for 24 per cent of total current consumption expenditures; they represented the same proportion of total spending of families in the $6,000–$7,499 class. (See Table 3.) This was approximately 5 percentage points lower than for all urban families in 1950.

In the selected low-consumption classes in 1960–61, the per cent spent for food varied from 27 per cent for three-person families to 31 per cent for families of six or more persons. This is about the same, or slightly less than the per cent spent for food by the average urban family in 1950.

Food expenditures as a per cent of total spending for families with incomes under the selected classes ranged from 29 per cent for one-person families to 34 per cent for families of six or more persons, a level approximately the same as that of employed wage- and clerical-worker families of two or more persons in 1950.

Although comparisons of the per cent spent for food give an idea

TABLE 2. Details of Family Expenditures, Insurance, Gifts and Contributions, Value of Items Received without Expense and Home-Produced Food, by Family Size, at Selected Income Levels

Total Nonfarm United States, 1960–61

FAMILY SIZE AND ANNUAL MONEY INCOME AFTER TAXES

	1 person $1,000–1,999	2 persons $2,000–2,999	3 persons $2,000–3,999	4 persons $3,000–3,999	5 persons $4,000–4,999	6 or more persons $5,000–5,999	Families and single consumers $6,000–7,499
Expenditures for current consumption	$1,554	$2,659	$3,436	$4,139	$4,773	$5,542	$6,177
Food, total	449	737	941	1,140	1,393	1,733	1,493
Food prepared at home	352	661	812	966	1,208	1,525	1,209
Food away from home	97	76	129	174	185	208	284
Tobacco	20	59	83	95	112	98	117
Alcoholic beverages	17	30	37	39	48	64	103
Housing, total	668	877	1,029	1,151	1,323	1,510	1,782
Shelter	372	422	478	494	557	626	803
Rented dwelling	262	247	301	290	279	237	256
owned dwelling	105	166	165	194	271	381	502
other shelter	5	9	12	9	7	8	45
Other real estate	1	2	2	2	11	1	5
Fuel, light, refrigeration, water	132	195	202	224	285	309	292
Household operations	108	150	181	225	236	261	341
Housefurnishings and equipment	55	108	166	207	234	314	341
Clothing, clo. materials and services	87	165	309	413	499	608	641
Personal care	42	80	110	132	150	168	176
Medical care	121	270	240	320	260	318	398
Prepaid care	32	66	63	70	71	91	107
Recreation	31	63	109	142	168	194	258

	$18	$25	$25	$29	$30	$41	$56
Reading	18	25	25	29	30	41	56
Education	1	6	22	39	20	42	59
Transportation	86	280	487	560	659	681	696
Automobile	56	242	447	520	621	624	892
Other travel and transportation	30	38	40	40	38	57	77
Other expenditures	14	67	44	79	111	85	125
Personal insurance, total	27	82	133	191	246	317	391
Social security, government and private retirement	10	34	49	92	131	158	219
Gifts and contributions, total	84	120	82	82	128	162	307
to persons	40	63	35	30	53	50	151
to organizations	44	57	47	52	75	112	156
Value of items received without expense	133	151	188	201	206	251	211
Food	15	14	14	27	20	16	12
Housing	47	42	47	47	41	54	37
Clothing	19	31	46	53	79	79	65
Transportation	11	7	14	11	8	13	11
Medical care	24	40	34	40	20	62	39
Other	17	17	33	23	38	27	48
Value of home-produced food	4	30	30	36	48	36	15

TABLE 3. Percentage Distribution of Expenditures for Current Consumption, by Family Size at Selected Income Levels

Total Nonfarm United States, 1960–61

	1 person $1,000–1,999	2 persons $2,000–2,999	3 persons $2,000–3,999	4 persons $3,000–3,999	5 persons $4,000–4,999	6 or more persons $5,000–5,999	Families and single consumers $6,000–7,499
Per cent distribution							
Expenditures for current consumption	100.0	100.0	100.0	100.0	100.0	100.0	100.0
Food	28.9	27.7	27.4	27.6	29.2	31.3	24.2
Food prepared at home	22.7	24.9	23.6	23.4	25.3	27.5	19.6
Food away from homes	6.2	2.8	3.8	4.2	3.9	3.8	4.6
Tobacco	1.3	2.2	2.4	2.3	2.4	1.8	1.9
Alcoholic beverages	1.1	1.1	1.1	.9	1.0	1.2	1.7
Housing total	43.0	33.0	29.9	27.8	27.7	27.2	28.8
Shelter	23.9	15.9	13.9	11.9	11.7	11.3	13.0
Rented dwelling	16.9	9.3	8.8	7.0	5.9	4.3	4.2
Owned dwelling	6.7	6.3	4.8	4.7	5.7	6.9	8.1
Other shelter	.3	.3	.3	.2	.1	.1	.7
Fuel, light, refrigeration, water	8.5	7.3	5.9	5.4	6.0	5.5	4.7
Household operations	7.0	5.6	5.3	5.4	4.9	4.7	5.5
Housefurnishings and equipment	3.5	4.1	4.8	5.0	4.9	5.7	5.5
Clothing, clo. materials & services	5.6	6.2	9.0	10.0	10.5	11.0	10.4
Personal care	2.7	3.0	3.2	3.2	3.1	3.0	2.8

Medical care	7.8	10.2	7.0	7.7	5.5	5.7	6.4
Prepaid care	2.1	2.5	1.8	1.7	1.5	1.6	1.7
Recreation	2.0	2.4	3.2	3.4	3.5	3.5	4.2
Reading and education	1.2	1.2	1.3	1.6	1.0	1.5	1.9
Transportation	5.5	10.5	14.2	13.6	13.8	12.3	15.7
Automobile	3.6	9.1	13.0	12.6	13.0	11.3	14.4
Other travel and transportation	1.9	1.4	1.2	1.0	.8	1.0	1.3
Other expenditures	.9	2.5	1.3	1.9	2.3	1.5	2.0
Sum of food, shelter (incl. fuel, etc.) and clothing	66.9	57.1	56.2	54.9	57.4	59.1	52.3
Value of items received without expense as a per cent of total current consumption expenditures:							
Food	1.0	.5	.4	.7	.4	.3	.2
Housing	3.0	1.6	1.4	1.1	.9	1.0	.6
Clothing	1.2	1.2	1.3	1.3	1.7	1.4	1.1
Medical Care	1.6	1.5	1.0	1.0	.4	1.1	.6
Other	1.8	.9	1.4	.8	.9	.7	.9
Total[1]	8.6	5.7	5.5	4.9	4.3	4.5	3.4

of the relative level of living of various groups in the population at a given time and improvements in levels of living over time, they give no clue as to the quality of living with respect to the content and nutritional adequacy of diets which such food expenditures may provide. For this, expenditures must be compared with food plans which provide nutritional adequacy at different cost levels. Such food plans have been developed and published by the U.S. Department of Agriculture (USDA) for four cost levels—Economy, Low-Cost, Moderate-Cost, and Liberal.

In the 1960–61 BLS survey, the annual food expenditures of nonfarm families in the $6,000–$7,499 class averaged $1,493, or $404 per family member. *In the selected low-consumption classes*, food expenditures ranged from $449 for one-person families to $1,733 for families of six or more persons, or from $449 to $248 on a per-family-member basis. These averages were well within the range of 1961 costs for the USDA Low-Cost Food Plan, as estimated for different types of families within size classes and across regions.

Family size	Annual average food expenditure in "low-consumption" classes	Approximate range in annual cost of USDA Low-Cost Food Plan	
1 person	$ 449	$305 to	$ 450
2 persons	737	450 to	865
3 persons	941	615 to	1,260
4 persons	1,140	760 to	1,630
5 persons	1,393	885 to	1,960
6 or more persons	1,733	995 to	2,240

2. Per cent of the "Basics"

Like the per cent spent for food, the per cent of total spending allocated to the three "basics"—food, shelter (including fuel and utilities), and clothing—is often used as a measure of relative levels of living. This is based on the assumption that these three expenditure categories are "necessities" and that spending for other goods and services is discretionary. Although the distinction between necessary and discretionary spending is by no means as clearcut today as it was several decades ago, the per cent spent for the three "basics" still furnishes some insights into relative levels of living of different groups in the population.

As previously mentioned, the per cent spent for food, shelter, and clothing by urban families dropped from 57 per cent in 1950 to 53 per cent in 1960–61; nonfarm families in the $6,000–$7,499 income class in 1960–61 used 52 per cent of their current spending for these "basics." Families in the selected low-consumption classes spent from 55 to 59 per cent, except for one-person families who used 67 per cent of their total spending for these three "basics." The proportion spent for food, shelter, and clothing by these low-consumption families in 1960–61, was approximately the same as that spent by the average urban family in 1950. Also except for one-person families, families with incomes under those of the selected low-consumption classes, used from 58 to 63 per cent for food, shelter, and clothing in 1960–61—about the same as spent by wage- and clerical-worker families of two or more person in 1950.

The per cent of total spending used for clothing, both by families in the selected low-consumption classes and with incomes below this level, varied widely across family-size groups—from 6 to 5 per cent, respectively, for one- and two-person families to 11 per cent for six or more-person families, compared with 10 per cent at the $6,000–$7,499 income level where the average family size was 3.7 persons. The relatively low clothing spending of these one- and two-person families is, in part, a reflection of their age which averaged sixty to seventy years in these family-size and income classes.

The per cent spent for shelter also varied widely across family-size classes—from about one fourth of total current expense for one-person families to about one sixth for families of six or more persons in the selected low-consumption classes; and from one third to one sixth of total current spending, respectively, for families with lower incomes.

However, this pattern of spending for shelter, by families of different size at low-consumption levels cannot be appraised apart from an appraisal of their combined expenditures for shelter and transportation and the pattern of home and auto ownership, which vary widely among families of different size at low-consumption levels, and incidently, among geographical regions and between large cities, small towns, and rural nonfarm areas. When transportation expenditures are added to shelter, the combined expenses represented about 37 per cent of total current expense for one-person families at both the selected low-consumption level and those with incomes under that level. For other family-size classes, the per cent spent for shelter and transportation varied between 29 and 34 per cent, compared with 33 per cent for all nonfarm families with incomes of $6,000–$7,499. Homeownership in the selected low-consumption classes ranged from 41 per cent for four-person families to 62 per cent for families of six or more persons, and auto ownership from 15 per cent for one-person families to 88 per cent for families of six or more persons. In the $6,000–$7,499 income class, homeownership was 67 per cent and auto ownership, 92 per cent.

The quality of the housing occupied by these low-consumption families cannot be discerned from the available tabulations of the BLS survey data. Generally, the space provided and the condition of owned dwellings are better than those of rented dwellings, and better inside than outside metropolitan areas for low-income families, as reported in the 1960 Census of Housing. In 1960, about one third of all U.S. families (Census definition) with income under $3,000 lived in housing that was dilapidated or lacked plumbing (i.e. hot and cold running water, or private toilet, or bathing facilities inside the structure), compared with about one fourth living inside metropolitan areas and about one half of "under $3,000 income" families living outside metropolitan areas. Thirty per cent of all U.S. low-income owners, compared with 42 per cent of renters with income under $3,000, were living in such housing. For owners and renters with income over $3,000, only 6 and 13 per cent, respectively, occupied such housing.

Although the household inventory data obtained in the BLS survey have not yet been tabulated by level of income and tenure, the high average level of ownership by all urban families of such items as vacuum cleaners (70 per cent), televisions (84 per cent), washing machines (66 per cent), refrigerators (81 per cent), etc., makes it evident that a majority of all nonfarm families at the selected low-consumption levels, particularly homeowning families, have these items.

The presence of a telephone in the home, or substantial expenditures for such service, is also a clue to the nature of the household inventory. In 1960–61, 81 per cent of the families in the selected equivalent low-consumption classes reported expenditures for telephone and telegraph services which average $63 annually per family buying, compared with reports of such expense by 97 per cent of all nonfarm families with incomes from $6,000 to $7,499, and with annual average expenditure of $101 per family buying.

The great variety of expenditures for shelter, transportation and household equipment, coupled with differences in patterns of home and auto ownership among various types of families in different localities, raises serious doubts as to how "discretionary" such spending really is for families at low economic levels.

3. Discretionary spending

Most discussions of the buying habits of the poor eventually get around to the question of whether the poor are spending their incomes for "luxuries" at the expense of "necessities"; and its corollary—whether they pay more for their purchases than do higher income families. Undoubtedly, some poor families, like some rich families, spend foolishly, and there is much evidence that poor families are often victims of unfair selling practices. On balance, however, the 1960–61 survey data seem to indicate that families at the lower end of the income scale were buying the same goods and services as the average family, but at a rate and/or price level commensurate with the difference in their financial status. For example, 6 per cent of the selected low-consumption families bought refrigerators at an average cost of $176, compared with an average of $266 for the 8 per cent of families in the $6,000–$7,499 class who bought. For washing machines, the comparable figures were 7 per cent at $140, and 9 per cent at $197; for vacuum cleaners, 4 per cent at $68, compared with 9 per cent at $85.

Average expenditures per family buying for many items represent multiple purchases of such items during the year, for example, women's shoes, and thus are not unit prices. They do, however, seem to reflect the same buying pattern with respect to purchases of the average family, as data for household durables. About three fourths of the low-consumption families reported expenditures for women's shoes which averaged $18 per family buying, compared with 88 per cent of the families at the $6,000–$7,499 level buying at an average expenditure of $31.

The data also show pretty much the same pattern of relationships between the buying of low-consumption families and the average family for such diverse items as: meals out, snacks, laundry and cleaning sent out, auto purchase (reflecting both new and used car purchases), men's haircuts, purchase and care of pets, and televisions.

4. What about Use of Credit and Insurance

In addition to their expenditures for current consumption, families in, and below, the equivalent, low-consumption classes typically made some payments into health and life insurance. Social Security or retirement funds, and made some gifts to persons outside the family and contributions to religious, welfare, and other organizations.

Families in the low-consumption classes spent about one fourth to one third of their total medical care expenditures for insurance, compared with about one fourth of total medical care expenditures for insurance by families at the average level. Forty-eight per cent of the low-consumption families spent an average of $111 for life, endowment, annuity, etc. insurance (excluding veterans and group insurance deducted from pay), compared with 71 per cent of the $6,000–$7,499 income families at $198 for those buying.

Gifts and contributions to organizations ranged from $44 for one-person low-consumption families to $112 for families of six or more persons, compared with $156 for families at the $6,000–$7,499 level.

Nonfarm families on the average, had an annual net savings (increase in assets or decreases in liabilities) of $177 in 1960–61. Fifty-two per cent of the families reported an increase in savings; 42 per cent, a decrease; and 7 per cent, no change. Families in all size classes both in and below the selected "low-consumption" classes reported net decreases in savings. At the selected low-consumption levels, these ranged from a $75 deficit for families of six or more persons to $383 for four-person families. Available tabulations of the data do not show the per cent of savers and dissavers in these equivalent low-consumption classes, but the data for all U.S. nonfarm families indicate that some families at all current money income levels managed to save during 1960–61, as the following summary shows:

After-tax income	Average net change in assets and liabilities	Per cent of families reporting:		
		savings increase	savings decrease	no change
All nonfarm families	$ 177	52	42	7
Under $1,000	−495	15	59	26
$1,000–$1,999	−181	28	48	24
2,000– 2,999	−173	39	49	12
3,000– 3,999	−203	42	50	8
4,000– 4,999	−36	53	44	3
5,000– 5,999	+31	57	40	2
6,000– 7,499	+173	62	37	2
7,500– 9,999	+461	66	33	1
10,000–14,999	+963	68	31	1
15,000 and over	+4,788	77	20	3

HOW ADEQUATE ARE THE LEVELS OF LIVING OF THE POOR?

Throughout this discussion, I have tried to introduce some qualitative appraisal of the expenditures of families at the lower end of the economic scale, e.g. food expenditures, comparison with 1950 and the average pattern, etc. However, there is much yet to be done before any real appraisal can be made of the adequacy of the levels of living of the poor today. Basic research tools, such as standard budgets and equivalence scales, need to be extended and brought up to date. No real appraisal of adequacy can be made without consideration of the wide variations in prices and living costs which exist between regions and between different types of places within regions. Analysis of family spending and saving for welfare purposes is, primarily, microeconomic research. Statistically, as well as conceptually speaking, "poverty has many faces."

Consumer Practices
of the Poor

Louise G. Richards

To the economist, being poor means having an income below a certain figure—a figure that represents the minimum amount necessary for a decent life in America today. To the behavioral scientist, being poor means a number of characteristics found to be associated with low income: patterns of family life, health care, education, and general outlook on life. To the poor person himself, however, being poor may mean different things depending on how his money is spent. This report is a summary of research findings on those consumer practices. The report covers not only how money is spent

Reprinted from "Consumer Practices of the Poor," Lola M. Irelan (ed.), *Low-Income Life Styles* (Washington: U.S. Department of Health, Education, and Welfare, Publication No. 14), pp. 67–86.
See pages 277–280 for all footnotes to this chapter.

by the poor, but also what kinds of behavior—shopping, methods of payment, and the like—go along with income disbursement.

Few would quarrel with the judgment that an income of $3,000 is too low for a family to live on today. Hardly anyone would suggest that even the best consumer practices would solve the problem of poverty. Many would agree, however, that good consumer practices might alleviate some of the worst aspects. Knowledge of actual practices of the poor can suggest new areas for education and action.

One writer on the topic of consumer practices of the poor has concluded that they are irrational in their buying behavior.[1] Some of the evidence for that conclusion is included in this report. To indict poor consumers as irrational is too simple an explanation, however. Moreover, it provides no handles for action. Much of the evidence for irrationality should be considered in the light of other explanations that make equally good sense. The particular social and demographic characteristics of the poor must be taken into account. The inflexibility of low income per se must be kept in mind. And, finally, the possibility that apparent irrationality may stem from the very conditions of poverty must be dealt with. These explanations will be discussed more fully in a later section.

For practices to be labeled as irrational there must be a standard for judging their rationality. Many people would subscribe to the idea that there are good, common-sense rules for stretching income. Many of those who knew poverty during the Thirties, and those who have known severe reverses since then, would avow that such rules helped them keep their heads above water in difficult times.

Most common-sense rules of financial management are applications of the idea that everyone naturally tries to get the best living for the least money. Recent thinking on the topic includes the idea that psychological satisfactions can be added to material ones in arriving at a calculus of values. It is probably true, however, that low-income consumers can seldom afford outlays for emotional satisfactions, except perhaps in choices of low-cost items. Thus, the traditional rules are probably more pertinent today to the low-income consumer's situation than to that of higher income groups with their larger margins for discretionary purchases.

Very simply, the traditional rules for good consumership can be stated as follows:

1. Spend first for necessities and last for luxuries. Although many individuals disagree on how to classify specific goods, few would dispute that food, shelter, basic articles of clothing, and health should have priority over recreation and other categories of expenditure.

2. Buy the best quality of goods for the lowest price. This means that costly extra features—high styles, nonseasonal treats, store services, and above all, the cost of installment buying—should be avoided. In order to follow this rule, a person needs to shop widely and keep up with information about goods, prices, and sources.

3. Another rule stems from recognition of the fact that it is not easy to suppress desires for luxury goods and extra features: Budget small incomes carefully and plan purchases in advance. If possible, one should save for (or insure against) future emergencies to prevent insolvency.

4. Another rule covers the thousand-and-one suggestions for home production of needed goods: Try to get what is needed or wanted without spending money, or by spending only for raw materials. Home preservation of food, home sewing, self-building and self-repairing of homes, are a few of many recommended money saving practices.

5. Take advantage of certain benefits available to persons with limited incomes. Surplus food (and Food Stamps), legal aid, scholarships, day care for children, public housing, and medical and dental clinics are examples of such benefits provided through legislation or private funds.

Most detailed advice to consumers could be put under one of these five rules. Together they provide a backdrop for viewing actual consumer practices of the poor. In reporting the findings, these five rules will be referred to specifically. Before turning to those findings, we need to review what is known about the different kinds of people that constitute the poor population today, and the different kinds of studies that provide the facts.

POPULATION CHARACTERISTICS OF THE POOR

Several writers have pointed out that the poor as a group are neither homogeneous nor strictly representative of the population as a whole.[2] The *majority* of low-income families are white, nonfarm, and headed by a male between twenty-five and sixty-five years old. Compared with the general population, however, poor families tend to include more nonwhites, fewer earners, more families with female heads, larger families, and more old or young persons. The poor more often reside in rural farm areas or in cities (and less often in rural nonfarm or suburban areas). Above all, poor people have completed fewer years of schooling than the rest of the population. Almost every family or individual below the poverty line can be characterized by at least one of these facts. These differences between the poor and the general population are important in interpreting research findings about their consumer habits.

SOURCES OF FINDINGS

Two broad areas of research were drawn upon in this report. One area includes the economic surveys of consumer expenditures, savings, and debt made by government agencies and by business— a relatively old and well-established research activity. One continuing survey of this type, the Survey of Consumer Finances[3] has been concerned also with certain attitudes and expectations of consumers.

The second research area includes those studies that examine specific consumer practices, the why's and wherefore's of consumption. The most recent comprehensive study in this area is Caplovitz' *The Poor Pay More.*[4] Caplovitz' study provides information on types of stores used, methods of payment for goods, attitudes toward merchants and installment buying, and aspirations for future purchases on the part of a group of low-income families in New York City. Other studies provide facts about the decision-making process, the different sources of consumers' knowledge, and the participation of husbands and wives in financial planning. Also included is a summary of findings from studies of the working-class wife.[5] (Although many working-class families are by no means poor—and vice versa—this summary is the only recent one available on social class differences in taste.)

When possible, we report the practices of families whose incomes are less than $3,000, and indicate how their practices differ from families with higher incomes. When available figures were not broken at the poverty line, we report merely the differences between lower and higher income groups.

CONSUMER PRACTICES

Turning now to consumer practices in the framework of the above-mentioned rules for good consumership, here is the evidence:

1. Do Low-Income Families Buy Necessities First, and Luxuries Last?

For the most part, "Yes." When consumer goods and services are classified according to their survival value (beginning with Food and ending with Recreation), the poor spend more of their income than others do on the basic needs. When goods are classified as durables (automobiles, equipment, furniture, and the like) and nondurables, we find that the poor, on the average, do not buy durables as frequently as higher income families do. When we look at the poor who do purchase one or more durable goods in a given year, however, we find that a startingly high proportion of their income is spent for those goods.

One weak spot in the poor family's purchasing behavior appears to be this overspending on durable goods. Since most durable goods are relatively expensive items, it is not hard to see why the purchase of a durable good makes heavy inroads on a small income. Moreover, it is difficult to judge whether or not a given durable good should be considered a luxury for a poor family. (One could argue that an automatic washing machine is not a luxury for a large family in which the mother's time is at a premium.) However, when purchasing families with incomes less than $2,000 spend almost half of their income on durable goods, we need to look for an explanation.

The durable goods that take the largest bites from poor families' incomes are large household appliances and radios, television sets, and phonographs. These are household items that can be considered part of the standard package of American consumption. According to one writer, these home items are especially significant to working-class wives who aspire to the role of the modern, efficient American housewife. Also, of course, much effort and money are devoted to the advertisement of these and other items in the standard package. The poor are no less vulnerable than others are to persuasive selling. Such pressure may be particularly hard for the Negro poor to resist, since traditionally they have been denied access to other forms of social status.

There are other, less subjective factors in the purchase of durable goods than role image and vulnerability to advertising. Young families and those with large numbers of children spend more on durables, regardless of income. Since the poor include propor tionately larger numbers of young, large families, we can attribute some overspending to heavier need in newly formed households with more demand for labor-saving devices. Another factor in some poor neighborhoods is the incidence of merchandising practices that result in higher prices than those found for the same goods in middle-income shopping areas.

We have made some general statements about how the poor spend their incomes, and have provided some brief explanations of the patterns found. Some of the findings that support those statements are given below.

a. CATEGORIES OF SPENDING. Food shelter, and medical care take larger shares of the poor family's consumer dollar than they do in families with higher incomes, on the average. Clothing and transportation take smaller shares, on the average. Household operation (including furnishings and equipment) and other expenses (recreation, personal care, and education) take about the same share as in higher income families.[6]

The above findings compare average proportions spent annually by different income groups, whether all families in a group made purchases in the category or not. In a given year, most families do buy food, shelter, and at least a few articles of clothing. They probably also pay at least one medical fee. We know from other data that in a given year fewer low-income families make purchases of automobiles, furniture, and household appliances. What is the share of income spent by poor families who do purchase a major durable in a given year?

Among those in the lowest income group (under $2,000) who bought a major durable in 1962, an average of 48 per cent of their income was spent on such purchases. In the next higher income group ($2,000 to $4,999), the share was 28 per cent. These percentages are high compared with the shares of income spent by the poor on "needs," and startlingly high compared with the shares spent on durables by families in other income groups. (In the category that included median family income ($6,000 to $7,499) in 1962, the share spent for durables was only 14 per cent.)[7] The durables that take the largest shares of poor families' income are large household appliances and radios, television sets, and phonographs. High consumption of these same items, and furniture, is reported in Caplovitz' study of low income families in New York: 95 per cent owned television sets, 63 per cent owned phonographs, and 41 per cent owned automatic washers.[8]

b. EFFECTS OF CLASS AND ETHNIC VALUES. The special importance of household appliances, television, and furniture to the working class was discussed in some detail in Rainwater's analysis of the working-class wife. According to that author, appliances and furniture mean something different to working-class wives from what they mean to middle-class wives.[9] The difference in values is a subtle one, but may be an important contribution to overspending.

Working-class wives' lives revolve around home and housework to a greater extent than the lives of middle-class wives. The working-class wife knows that housework is inevitable, and she dreams of a home (especially a kitchen) that symbolizes the role of the modern, efficient American housewife. She also tends to associate the new with the beautiful. The middle-class wife, on the other hand, is interested in labor-saving appliances that free her as much as possible from the role of housewife so that she may enjoy the social, intellectual, and aesthetic pleasures of upper-middle-class life. These differences suggest that the working-class wife sees household durables as an end in themselves, rather than merely as means to other ends.

One sociologist describes another pattern of spending in terms of the symbolic value of certain products. Negroes underspend in four major areas—housing, automobile transportation, food, and medical care. On the other hand, a number of Negro women are more interested than white women in "high fashion," even in the Under-$3,000 income group. And Negro families report buying Scotch whisky, a high-status drink, twice as often as white families do.[10] One theorist writing on the subject of "conditions for irrational choices" suggests an explanation: Irrational choice making occurs when "something . . . [is] . . . repressed among a large number of individuals in a specific segment of our society with a distinctive subculture."[11]

c. THE EFFECT OF YOUTH AND SIZE OF FAMILIES.   In one analysis of frequency of purchase of selected durables, it was found that the rate for young married couples with incomes under $3,000 increases after birth of their first child, whereas the rate for couples with incomes over $3,000 decreases.[12] Caplovitz' study also showed that family size among his low-income public housing tenants affects durable goods' ownership (or aspirations for ownership) regardless of the size of income.[13]

These facts and the much cited findings by Caplovitz about high-priced durables in poor neighborhoods provide the evidence of our answer, "Yes, but . . ." to the question on whether the poor spend their incomes on basic needs. We do not want to leave the impression that the poor are profligate spenders on special goods, however.

There is some evidence that they do not have much desire for all kinds of special purchases. In one nationwide study, their desires for "special expenditures" were found to be less frequent than those expressed by middle and upper income families.[14] Although poor families may not dream of as many new purchases as other families do, they appear to be eager to acquire the standard package.

2. Do Low-Income Shoppers Try to Get the Best Quality for the Lowest Price?

Available evidence indicates that the answer is "No." Lower income consumers are not more deliberate in their shopping, more wide-ranging in their search for good buys, more price conscious, nor more informed on the characteristics of products than families with higher incomes. If anything, they are less apt to carry out those practices than others. Neither are low-income consumers more apt to buy used articles, to buy "separate items," nor to pay cash for their purchases.

On three counts, poor people do exhibit more economical practices. They tend more often to negotiate special deals on durables, especially through relatives or friends. The *very* poor tend to buy goods on sale more often than others. And, although there is just as much use of credit by low-income families as by others, fewer of the poor have installment or mortgage debt. Among those who do have installment debt, however, the effect on family solvency may be ruinous.

On the basis of strict rationality, one would expect low-income consumers to be more deliberate, searching, price-conscious, and informed than high-income consumers. The low level of education of many poor people goes a long way in explaining why they are not, and indeed, why they fall below other income groups in the frequency of some of these activities. Knowledge of the immense variety of goods on the American market is not easily acquired. Expecially in the case of appliances, knowledge of technical features is highly specialized. Knowledge of the intricacies of credit agreements or consumer rights is not easy to acquire, either. The best that a poorly educated person can do, perhaps, is to rely on a known dealer, buy what a relative has bought, or try to negotiate a special deal. These are the very practices that many poor families follow.

Research findings also suggest that shopping practices are affected by length of exposure to urban American ways. The Puerto Ricans are an example of a newly arrived group that prefers traditional, personal stores rather than more bureaucratic, price-competitive outlets, and so do Negro migrants from the rural South. It is reasonable to expect that the longer people live in proximity to modern, depersonalized outlets, and the more they are exposed to knowledge about the urban world (through education or experience), the more often they will conduct wide-ranging searches of stores, and be price-conscious.

One reason for lower frequency of installment or mortgage debt among the poor is their ineligibility for loans under legal credit requirements. It is also possible that some poor families actually prefer not to be in debt. Among those families who are in debt for installment purchases, however, there is a large percentage of young, large families. Again, the pressing needs of this group probably account for some of the extremes of insolvency found among the poor.

The findings that support these views are:

a. DELIBERATION IN BUYING. In a nationwide sample of families, the poor were found to be neither higher nor lower than others on a scale of deliberation in durable goods purchases. On three deliberation activities in the scale, however, they were less active than others: They were less circumspect in seeking information, less concerned about the several features of the item and somewhat more dependent on brands. The poor families were no different from others in the extent of their enjoyment of "shopping around," an attitude found to be positively related to high deliberation.

Extent of formal education was more strongly associated with deliberation in buying durables than was income, in the study described above. The higher a person's level of education, the more he or she tended to score high on the deliberation scale. An interesting exception was in buying sport shirts, however: The less well-educated were more deliberate. Thus, the extent of deliberation may be influenced in some groups by the type of purchase.[15]

b. SHOPPING SCOPE. Several findings point to the tendency of the poor to use nearby stores rather than distant ones, and to prefer personal buying situations (the peddler as an extreme form), rather than "bureaucratic," impersonal ones. The poorest housing tenants in the New York Study used independent neighborhood stores, chain stores, and peddlers more frequently than department stores or discount houses, for buying durable goods. Among these low-income families, it was the poorest who had the narrowest shopping scope. And it was those who bought from the neighborhood stores or peddlers who paid more for the goods, especially for television sets.[16] In a Chicago study, the personal buying situation also was found to be more appealing to the upper-lower-class than to the lower-middle and upper-middle classes.[17]

In a study of urban families in Wisconsin, the preference for independent and neighborhood stores (rather than chain stores) was related to motives concerning the store and its personnel, rather than to motives concerning price, and was more typical of rural migrants to the city than of natives or urban migrants.[18] Caplovitz also found narrow shopping scope more typical of those who had been a short time in New York or any other city, and more typical of those with less education. He found, for example, that the Puerto Ricans in the study were narrower in shopping scope than Negroes or whites.[19]

Another factor in shopping scope, according to Rainwater, is the discomfort felt by working-class women in "downtown" stores:[20] ". . . [Clerks] . . . try to make you feel awful if you don't like something they have told you is nice and they would certainly think it was terrible if you told them you didn't have enough money to buy something."

c. INFORMATION ABOUT PRODUCTS. According to several studies, formal education appears to be the key characteristic of the informed consumer. Income is slightly related to use of consumer rating magazines (the poor use them less often), but education is strongly related.[21] Education is also clearly related to consultation of any kind of reading material (including advertisements) as a source of information about products.[22]

These are formal channels of communication about products, and it is not surprising that those with skills and experience in formal communication are more active. Those with little education do make more use of relatives (though not necessarily more use of all other people) as a source of information about durable goods. Relatives were found to be a fruitful source of information for poorly educated people in decisions on a model for a subsequent purchase of a durable. Other interesting differences between those with lower and higher levels of education have been found. In one study, the latter tended to buy a different model from the one seen at someone's house, whereas the former more often bought the same model.[23] In another study, high-income persons were found to be more critical of features of goods, including obsolescence.[24] Education apparently induces a more critical attitude and less reliance on reference groups in the choice of consumer goods.

d. PURCHASE OF USED GOODS AND SEPARATE ITEMS. The tendency of low-income families in New York to buy new appliances and furniture (especially sets) was mentioned by Caplovitz,[25] but no nationwide data are available to confirm this finding. The only nationwide figures found on the purchase of new versus used items concern automobiles; the evidence is clear that the poor tend less often to buy new autos and more often to buy used ones.[26]

On the topic of buying sets of furniture and other items sold as preselected groupings, one unpublished study indicates that low-income households purchase living room suites less often than higher income households. No difference was found in frequency of purchase of other kinds of sets by income group. There was a slight tendency for low-income respondents in that study to *prefer* suites, and some other types of sets, however, compared with respondents in higher income households.[27]

If lower class consumers do tend consistently to prefer sets of furniture to separate pieces, two factors may be at work; one cultural, and one economic. There may be a true class difference in taste for the strictly harmonious room: More interest on the part of the working class.[28] It is possible also that low-priced sets may be more numerous than separate items in furniture outlets located in poor neighborhoods.

e. USE OF CREDIT AND INSTALLMENT BUYING.   Half or more of the poor families over the nation use consumer credit of some kind. (81 per cent of the New York City tenants in Caplovitz' study used it.)[29] Poor families nationwide who had installment debt in 1962, however, were a smaller proportion—between one fourth and one third of all families below the poverty line. This proportion can be compared with half or more families with higher income who had installment debt in 1962.[30]

Mortgage debt is also carried by a smaller proportion of the poor than of higher income families over the nation—only about one fourth of the former owed on mortgages in 1962, compared with half or more of families in higher income brackets. Another kind of debt—money owed to doctors, dentists, and hospitals—was owed by a small proportion of poor families (about 17 per cent), and this proportion is similar to that reported for families with higher incomes.[31] It is not so much whether poor people buy on credit, however, as what it does to their financial situation that interests us. The ratio of debt to annual income is considerably higher for the poor than for others—about twice as high as the ratio among better-off families.[32] (Also, debt is clearly responsible for a shaky financial status in many poor families, as described in the section below.)

There is conflicting evidence on whether the poor actually prefer buying on credit. On the one hand, findings from a nationwide study show that in general low-income consumers do approve of installment buying.[33] On the other hand, the majority of Caplovitz' respondents said they thought that credit is a bad idea, although some felt that buying on time is easier than trying to save cash for large purchases.[34]

Only persons with high income or a college education are well informed on the real cost of credit, according to one nationwide study.[35] Added to this fact are two others reported in the New York City study: (1) Credit costs were higher for goods bought in the very sources that many poor families use—peddlers and neighborhood dealers; and (2) A majority of the families did not know where to go if they should be cheated by a merchant. Thus, many factors seem to converge in making installment debt an especially pressing problem for the poor.

3. Do Low-Income Families Budget their Incomes and Plan their Purchases?

One proof of good financial management in families—whether or not they manage to stay solvent—suggests that poor families do not score very well. Few have many assets, and a sizable minority have negative net worth. (In other words, these families' debts exceed their assets.) Poor families who are insolvent are not complacent about it, however.

As a group, the poor save very little and are not often covered by insurance. Moreover, when they do save or invest, they tend to be less "modern" in their pattern of saving than higher income groups. Also, their views on the value of life insurance are more traditional.

The central place of installment debt in many poor families' insolvency was described earlier. Regardless of kind of debt, cultural factors may affect this proclivity to be in debt. Solvency as a moral obligation is not strong in all cultures. Thus, we might expect differences among ethnic groups in tightness of control over family finances. We might also expect changes in ethnic groups' state of solvency as they acquire education and higher status occupations in the American setting.

Again, education is an important factor in explaining low efficiency of planning among the poor. Education can affect not only the amount of knowledge one has about financial matters, but also one's mode of thinking about money. The ability to think of money as a long-range, abstract value, rather than as concrete visible amounts, may allow educated consumers to weigh purchases and income more effectively. For the concrete thinker, it is easy to "Buy now" with a small portion of the weekly paycheck, and hard to see in advance how difficult it will be to "Pay later."

Hardly anyone would expect families on $3,000 or less income to save or buy insurance. Furthermore, since there are high proportions of families with no major earners among the poor (as high as 72 per cent in the Under-$1,000 group), savings and insurance plans supported by employers or unions are often out of reach.

Below are some of the facts behind this general picture:

a. INSOLVENCY. In 1962, 17 per cent of those in the lowest income quintile had negative net worth. In these families, debts exceeded assets, whether those assets were savings or merely the value of their own houses and autos.[36]

Negroes and Puerto Ricans in the New York City study were more often insolvent than whites, regardless of age and family size and good or poor consumer practices. Among Negroes, the debt component of the debt-income ratio was greater in the highest income group, while the opposite was the case for whites and Puerto Ricans. When those same groups were classified according to occupational groups, however, the racial difference decreased in importance. Negroes in white collar jobs or in business were more likely to be out of the red than those in unskilled or semiskilled jobs.[37]

Low-income families are not unconcerned about money or about the state of the family's finances, however. In the New York City study those families who were relatively insolvent were much more likely to mention financial worries than solvent families, and more likely to mention financial worries than other types.[38]

b. EFFICIENCY OF PLANNING. In a Minneapolis study of planning, income per se was found to be less important than education in predicting "planfulness of actions" and efficiency in decision making, in eight areas of family life. Also related to these qualities of consumership were certain attitudes characterized as developmental, modern, manipulative, prudential, and optimistic. On this basis, we would expect persons who are nondevelopmental (i.e., more material, traditional, fatalistic, impulsive, and pessimistic) in viewpoint to be less efficient. Among those same families, successful consumership was also related to good family agreement on roles, and good communication in the family.[39]

A certain kind of efficiency is practiced by many working-class wives, but it may not be the best method in the long run. According to Rainwater, the wife in the working-class family tries very hard to exert control over the outgo of cash income.[40] Her style of control often resembles the old "sugar bowl" method, in which small amounts are doled out until the cache is gone. One workingman's wife described the process as follows: ". . . if I have a little extra money then I buy something. If I don't have any money, I just don't buy any clothes for that time, or nothing extra. I like it that way. I always know where I am."

c. SAVINGS AND INSURANCE.   The nationwide figures on extent of saving show that nearly 50 per cent of those in the Under-$3,000 income group had no savings in 1962, compared with 28 per cent or less of those in higher income groups.[41] In the New York City study, 68 per cent were found to have no savings.[42] Low-income persons in general are also less often covered by insurance, either medical, hospital, or life insurance.

The kind of saving most often preferred by low-income families is the low-risk, noninvestment type that can be easily liquidated. Those who think of investing at all think of real estate, farms, or business, rather than stocks, bonds or insurance. Low-income persons who consider life insurance think of it as a source of funds for terminal medical and burial expenses, in addition to support for dependents in case of death.[43]

The avowed purposes in saving differ for low-income families. Their reasons resemble the traditional view that one should try to secure the future against emergencies. Poor families who save, or would like to save, usually mention one reason—they want to save for old age or retirement. Although middle-income families mention this reason too, they also say that they want to save for purchases such as vacations or autos.[44]

4. Do Low-Income Families Meet Some Needs Through Home Production?

Evidence on home production by the poor is sparse, but what there is points to less, not more, production in two areas: food growing, and home repairs. However, since these types of home production are also affected by the extent of home ownership (known to be lower among the poor), these facts about the effect of income must be considered tentative.

In the one study consulted, it was interesting to note that those with the highest average amount saved through home production had training beyond high school (though not a college degree). Those with twelve grades of school or less, and those with a bachelor's degree or more, were below average in amounts saved through home production.[45]

Those findings bear out our hunch that many home production activities will not be attempted, nor be successful, unless someone in the family has had special training or experience in these skills. Often, expensive tools and understanding of technical instructions are necessary for the success of a home project. This means that the poor, and the poorly educated, may be unable to improve their situation very much through this means.

5. Do Low-Income Families Take Advantage of Consumer Benefits Available to the Poor?

The existence of many successful programs in legal aid, medical and dental clinics, and similar facilities, testifies to the variety of ways the poor could cut their cost of living if they took advantage of them. A summary of evaluations of so many diverse programs cannot be included in this report. Many experienced workers would agree, however, that there is need for greater coverage or utilization. The unmet health needs, the legal predicaments of the poor, and the great educational losses of poor children, are cases in point.

Whether coverage is adequate or not, the lack of full success by established programs often is justifiably attributed to apathy on the part of the people who need them most. Apparently, it is not enough to offer the service. It has to be carefully planned to conform to attitudes, schedules, and locales of potential recipients. Also, the availability of the service has to be communicated directly and simply, and the preliminaries have to be carried out quickly and smoothly. Thus, we must conclude that the poor do not use these resources to the full for easing their income situation.

ADDING THE SCORE

How do consumer practices of the poor compare with the recommended rules of financial management? On almost every count, we have found that the poor fail to use what many would call the rational solution:

1. Although they spend most of their income on basic needs, those who buy durable goods make serious inroads on their incomes.

2. Most do not use more deliberation, consult more sources, or shop more widely, to get the best buys. Instead, many depend on known merchants or relatives for judgments of what to buy.

3. Few have savings of any size; most do not have life insurance; and only about half are covered by medical insurance.

4. It is doubtful whether many carry out home production activities to supplement cash purchases.

5. Many probably do not make full use of the programs established to provide services and goods free or at reduced rates.

Explanations of some of these apparently irrational consumer practices can be found in the special needs and characteristics of concentrated subgroups of the poor. We have mentioned the concentration of young, large families, in connection with the problems of durable goods purchases, heavy installment debt, and insolvency. We have also mentioned the concentration of recent migrants (from within or outside the United States), in connection with findings about narrow shopping scope and preference for personal treatment in stores. A third group, one that undoubtedly includes many more of the poor, consists of those with little formal education. The lack of education shows up as an important factor in low level of knowledge about the market and the economy, and in inadequate conceptual tools for planning and making decisions.

Other kinds of explanations point to objective conditions (in sociological terms, to the social structure) that account for existing consumer practices by the poor. Three examples of such conditions are: the credit system, with its risk-cost formula and inexorable penalties that work against the poor; merchandising practices in some low-income area stores; and the fluctuating nature of employment in occupations followed by many low-income earners.

One purely economic explanation also deserves attention: the effect produced by low income, per se. The size of an income determines to some extent whether any "economies of scale" can be employed by a family. A small income has to be disbursed in smaller amounts than a large income, regardless of the different ways families now spend incomes. Thus, low-income families can less often take advantage of low prices for quantity purchases. On the other hand, some products and services are available in standard units that cannot be divided into smaller ones. Thus, large outlays (such as one month's rent in advance) are greater disturbances to a small than to a large income.[46] Since there is less possibility for flexibility in the disbursement of a small income, there is more possibility of imbalance.

Finally, we come to the psychological explanations proposed by a number of writers for explaining consumer practices of the poor. Among the traits or values that are said to dispose the poor to behavior different from the middle and upper classes are: an attitude of fatalism; a preference for immediate gratification of impulses; a low level of aspiration and low need to achieve; an unclear view of the higher social structure; a concrete style of thinking; and over-concern with security.

Often the psychological differences attributed to the poor are discussed as if they were "givens,"[47] in much the same way as the idea of irrationality seems like a "given." However, these same differences are discussed by other writers as possible outcomes of objective social and economic conditions of the lower class.

One set of research findings indicates, for example, that a child's preference for immediate gratification is related to the absence of a father in the home. Another finding indicates that continued delay in reward can induce this same preference in children.[48] In a like vein, it has been said that "splurges" by lower class people are natural reactions to past deprivation and insecurity about the future.[49] Still another writer argues that low ambition in the lower class is more apparent than real: Lower class people have ambition, but since it is unrealistic for the poor to aspire to the same goals as the middle class, their goals only seem less ambitious.[50] Thus, we have explanations that range from the social characteristics of the poor, through purely economic and purely psychological factors, and finally back to the environment of the poor. What does all this mean for planners of programs to improve their consumer practices?

At first glance, the problem seems to be so severe, and the explanations so deeply rooted in far-reaching social problems that it may seem futile to attack it at all. It is instructive, however, to look at some consumer programs that have been successful, and at some recommended programs based on the New York study. Examples of recent successful programs are described in some detail in the 1965 report of the President's Committee on Consumer Interest, "The Most For Their Money."[51] Recommendations based on the New York study are found in the final chapter of Caplovitz' book.[52]

In general, the successful programs and the recommended actions employ unorthodox, "backdoor" methods that capitalize on the very differences in the poor that we have described. They may use informal methods of education carried out locally in poor neighborhoods. They may attack problems of financial management indirectly through appeals to material interests rather than by teaching abstract principles. They may provide for intervention at the top in dealing with problems that stem from rigidities in the market itself. Finally, they may concentrate efforts on special groups of the poor who seem particularly vulnerable to buying mistakes or insolvency.

If the apparent irrationality of poor consumers can be dealt with in these realistic ways, we have some hope of softening the worst efforts of a hand-to-mouth existence.

The Merchant
and the
Low-Income
Consumer

David Caplovitz

The visitor to East Harlem cannot fail to notice the sixty or so furniture and appliance stores that mark the area, mostly around Third Avenue and 125th Street. At first this may seem surprising. After all, this is obviously a low-income area. Many of the residents are on relief. Many are employed in seasonal work and in marginal industries, such as the garment industry, which are the first to feel the effects of a recession in the economy. On the face of it, residents

Reprinted from "The Merchant and the Low-Income Consumer," *The Poor Pay More* (1963), pp. 12–30, by permission of The Free Press.

This chapter is based in part on an unpublished research report by Wolfram Arendt and Murray Caylay.

See pages 281–284 for all footnotes to this chapter.

of the area would seem unable to afford the merchandise offered for sale in these stores.

That merchants nevertheless find it profitable to locate in these areas attests to a commonly overlooked fact: low-income families, like those of higher income, are consumers of many major durables. The popular image of the American as striving for the material possessions which bestow upon him both comfort and prestige in the eyes of his fellows does not hold only for the ever-increasing middle class. The cultural pressures to buy major durables reach low- as well as middle-income families. In some ways, consumption may take on even more significance for low-income families than for those in higher classes. Since many have small prospect of greatly improving their low social standing through occupational mobility, they are apt to turn to consumption as at least one sphere in which they can make some progress toward the American dream of success. If the upper strata that were observed by Veblen engaged in conspicuous consumption to symbolize their social superiority, it might be said that the lower classes today are apt to engage in *compensatory consumption*. Appliances, automobiles, and the dream of a home of their own can become compensations for blocked social mobility.[1]

The dilemma of the low-income consumer lies in these facts. He is trained by society (and his position in it) to want the symbols and appurtenances of the "good life" at the same time that he lacks the means needed to fulfill these socially induced wants. People with small incomes lack not only the ready cash for consuming major durables but are also poorly qualified for that growing substitute for available cash—credit. Their low income, their negligible savings, their job insecurity all contribute to their being poor credit risks. Moreover, many low-income families in New York City are fairly recent migrants from the South or from Puerto Rico and so do not have other requisites of good credit, such as long-term residence at the same address and friends who meet the credit requirements and are willing to vouch for them.[2]

Not having enough cash and credit would seem to create a sufficient problem for low-income consumers. But they have other limitations as well. They tend to lack the information and training needed to be effective consumers in a bureaucratic society. Partly because of their limited education and partly because as migrants from more traditional societies they are unfamiliar with urban culture, they are not apt to follow the announcements of sales in the newspapers, to engage in comparative shopping, to know their way around the major department stores and bargain centers, to know how to evaluate the advice of salesmen—practices necessary for some degree of sophistication in the realm of consumption. The institution of credit introduces special complex requirements for intelligent consumption. Because of the diverse and frequently misleading ways in which charges for credit are stated, even the highly educated consumer has difficulty knowing which set of terms is most economical.[3]

These characteristics of the low-income consumer—his socially supported want for major durables, his small funds, his poor credit position, his lack of shopping sophistication—constitute the conditions under which durables are marketed in low-income areas. To understand the paradox set by the many stores selling high-cost durables in these areas it is necessary to know how the merchants adapt to these conditions. Clearly the normal marketing arrangements, based on a model of the "adequate" consumer (the consumer with funds, credit, and shopping sophistication), cannot prevail if these merchants are to stay in business.

On the basis of interviews with fourteen of these merchants, the broad outlines of this marketing system can be described. This picture, in turn, provides a backdrop for the more detailed examination in later chapters of the marketing relationship from the viewpoint of the consumer.

MERCHANDISING IN A LOW-INCOME AREA

The key to the marketing system in low-income areas lies in special adaptations of the institution of credit. The many merchants who locate in these areas and find it profitable to do so are prepared to offer credit in spite of the high risks involved. Moreover, their credit is tailored to the particular needs of the low-income consumer. All kinds of durable goods can be obtained in this market at terms not too different from the slogan, "a dollar down, a dollar a week." The consumer can buy furniture, a TV set, a stereophonic phonograph, or, if he is so minded, a combination phonograph-TV set, if not for a dollar a week then for only a few dollars a week. In practically every one of these stores, the availability of "easy credit" is announced to the customer in both English and Spanish by large signs in the windows and sometimes by neon signs over the doorways. Of the fourteen merchants interviewed, twelve claimed that from 75 to 90 per cent of their business consisted of credit and the other two said that credit made up half their businesses. That these merchants extend credit to their customers does not, of course, explain how they stay in business. They still face the problem of dealing with their risks.

The Markup and Quality of Goods

It might at first seem that the merchant would solve his problem by charging high rates of interest on the credit he extends. But the law in New York State now regulates the amount that can be charged for credit, and most of these merchants claim they use installment contracts which conform to the law. The fact is that they do not always use these contracts. Some merchants will give customers only a card on which payments are noted. In these transactions the cost of credit and the cash price are not specified as the law requires. The customer peddlers, whom we shall soon meet, seldom use installment contracts. In all these cases the consumer has no idea of how much he is paying for credit, for the cost of credit is not differentiated from the cost of the product.

Although credit charges are now regulated by law, no law regulates the merchant's markup on his goods. East Harlem is known to the merchants of furniture and appliances in New York City as the area in which pricing is done by "numbers." We first heard of the "number" system from a woman who had been employed as a bookkeeper in such a store. She illustrated a "one number" item by writing down a hypothetical wholesale price and then adding the same figure to it, a 100 per cent markup. Her frequent references to "two number" and "three number" prices indicated that prices are never less than "one number," and are often more.

The system of pricing in the low-income market differs from that in the bureaucratic market of the downtown stores in another respect: in East Harlem there are hardly any "one price" stores. In keeping with a multiprice policy, price tags are conspicuously absent from the merchandise. The customer has to ask, "how much?," and the answer he gets will depend on several things. If the merchant considers him a poor risk, if he thinks the customer is naïve, or if the customer was referred to him by another merchant or a peddler to whom he must pay a commission, the price will be higher. The fact that prices can be affected by "referrals" calls attention to another peculiarity of the low-income market, what the merchants call the "T.O." system.

Anyone closely familiar with sales practices in a large retailing establishment probably understands the meaning of "T.O." When a salesman is confronted with a customer who is not responding to the "sales pitch," he will call over another salesman, signal the nature of the situation by whispering, "this is a T.O.,' and then introduce him to the customer as the "assistant manager."[4] In East Harlem, as the interviewers learned, T.O.s extend beyond the store. When a merchant finds himself with a customer who seems to be a greater risk than he is prepared to accept, he does not send the customer away. Instead, he will tell the customer that he happens to be out of the item he wants, but that it can be obtained at the store of his "friend" or "cousin," just a few blocks away. The merchant will then take the customer to a storekeeper with a less conservative credit policy.[5] The second merchant fully understands that his colleague expects a commission and takes this into account in fixing the price.[6] As a result, the customer who happens to walk into the "wrong" store ends up paying more. In essence, he is being charged for the service of having his credit potential matched with the risk policy of a merchant.

As for the merchandise sold in these stores, the interviewers noticed that the furniture on display was of obviously poor quality. Most of all, they were struck by the absence of well-known brands of appliances in most of the stores. To find out about the sales of better-known brands, they initially asked about the volume of sales of "high-*price* lines." But this question had little meaning for the merchants, because high prices were being charged for the low-quality goods in evidence. The question had to be rephrased in terms of "high-*quality*" merchandise or, as the merchants themselves refer to such goods, "custom lines." To quote from the report of these interviews:

It became apparent that the question raised a problem of communication. We were familiar with the prices generally charged for high-quality lines and began to notice that the same prices were charged for much lower quality merchandise. The markup was obviously quite different from that in other areas. The local merchants said that the sale of "custom" merchandise was limited by a slow turnover. In fact, a comparable markup on the higher quality lines would make the final price so prohibitively high that they could not be moved at all. A lower markup would be inconsistent with the risk and would result in such small profits that the business could not be continued.

The high markup on low-quality goods is thus a major device used by the merchants to protect themselves against the risks of their credit business. This policy represents a marked departure from the "normal" marketing situation. In the "normal" market, competition between merchants results in a pricing policy roughly commensurate with the quality of the goods. It is apparent, then, that these merchants do not see themselves competing with stores outside the neighborhood. This results in the irony that the people who can least afford the goods they buy are required to pay high prices relative to quality, thus receiving a comparatively low return for their consumer dollar.

In large part, these merchants have a "captive" market because their customers do not meet the economic requirements of consumers in the larger, bureaucratic marketplace. But also, they can sell inferior goods at high prices because, in their own words, the customers are not "price and quality conscious." Interviews found that the merchants perceive their customers as unsophisticated shoppers. One merchant rather cynically explained that the amount of goods sold a customer depends not on the customer but on the merchant's willingness to extend him credit. If the merchant is willing to accept great risk, he can sell the customer almost as much as he cares to. Another merchant, commenting on the buying habits of the customer, said, "People do not shop in this area. Each person who comes into the store wants to buy something and is a potential customer. It is just up to who catches him."

The notion of "who catches him" is rather important in this economy. Merchants compete not so much in price or quality, but in getting customers to the store on other grounds. (Some of these gathering techniques will shortly be described.)

Another merchant commented rather grudgingly that the Negroes were beginning to show signs of greater sophistication by "shopping around." Presumably this practice is not followed by the newer migrants to the area.

But although the merchants are ready to exploit the naïvete of their traditionalistic customers, it is important to point out that they also cater to the customer's traditionalism. As a result of the heavy influx of Puerto Ricans into the area, many of these stores now employ Puerto Rican salesmen. The customers who enter these stores need not be concerned about possible embarrassment because of their broken English or their poor dress. On the contrary, these merchants are adept at making the customer feel at ease, as a personal experience will testify.

> Visiting the area and stopping occasionally to read the ads in the windows, I happened to pause before an appliance store. A salesman promptly emerged and said, "I know, I bet you're looking for a nice TV set. Come inside. We've got lots of nice ones." Finding myself thrust into the role of customer, I followed him into the store and listened to his sales pitch. Partway through his talk, he asked my name. I hesitated a moment and then provided him with a fictitious last name, at which point he said, "No, no—no last names. What's your first name? ... Ah, Dave; I'm Irv. We only care about first names here." When I was ready to leave after making some excuse about having to think things over, he handed me his card. Like most business cards of employees, this one had the name and address of the enterprise in large type and in small type the name of the salesman. But instead of his full name, there appeared only the amiable, "Irv."

As this episode indicates, the merchants in this low-income area are ready to personalize their services. To consumers from a more traditional society, unaccustomed to the impersonality of the bureaucratic market, this may be no small matter.

So far, we have reviewed the elements of the system of exchange that comprise the low-income market. For the consumer, these are the availability of merchandise, the "easy" installments, and the reassurance of dealing with merchants who make them feel at home. In return, the merchant reserves for himself the right to sell low-quality merchandise at exorbitant prices.

But the high markup on goods does not insure that the business will be profitable. No matter what he charges, the merchant can remain in business only if customers actually pay. In this market, the customer's intention and ability to pay—the assumptions underlying any credit system—cannot be taken for granted. Techniques for insuring continuity of payments are a fundamental part of this distinctive economy.

Formal Controls

When the merchant uses an installment contract, he has recourse to legal controls over his customers. But as we shall see, legal controls are not sufficient to cope with the merchant's problem and they are seldom used.

REPOSSESSION.   The merchant who offers credit can always repossess his merchandise should the customer default on payments. But repossession, according to the merchants, is rare. They claim that the merchandise receives such heavy use as to become practically worthless in a short time. And no doubt the shoddy merchandise will not stand much use, heavy or light. One merchant said that he will occasionally repossess an item, not to regain his equity, but to punish a customer he feels is trying to cheat him.

LIENS AGAINST PROPERTY AND WAGES.   The merchant can, of course, sue the defaulting customer. By winning a court judgment, he can have the customer's property attached. Should this fail to satisfy the debt, he can take the further step of having the customer's salary garnisheed.[7] But these devices are not fully adequate for several reasons. Not all customers have property of value or regular jobs. Furthermore, their employers will not hesitate to fire them rather than submit to the nuisance of a garnishment. But since the customer knows he may lose his job if he is garnisheed, the mere threat of garnishment is sometimes enough to insure regularity of payments.[8] The main limitation with legal controls, however, is that the merchant who uses them repeatedly runs the risk of forfeiting good will in the neighborhood.

DISCOUNTING PAPER.   The concern with good will places a limitation on the use of another legal practice open to merchants for minimizing their risk: the sale of their contracts to a credit agency at a discount. By selling his contracts to one of the licensed finance companies, the merchant can realize an immediate return on his investment. The problem with this technique is that the merchant loses control over his customer. As an impersonal, bureaucratic organization, the credit agency has recourse only to legal controls. Should the customer miss a payment, the credit agency will take the matter to court. But in the customer's mind, his contract exists with the merchant, not with the credit agency. Consequently, the legal actions taken against him reflect upon the merchant, and so good will is not preserved after all.

For this reason, the merchant is reluctant to "sell his paper," particularly if he has reason to believe that the customer will miss some payments. When he does sell some of his contracts at a discount, his motive is not to reduce risk, but rather to obtain working capital. Since so much of his capital is tied up in credit transactions, he frequently finds it necessary to make such sales. Oddly enough, he is apt to sell his better "paper," that is, the contracts of customers who pay reguarly, for he wants to avoid incurring the ill will of customers. This practice also has its drawbacks for the merchant. Competitors can find out from the credit agencies which customers pay regularly and then try to lure them away from the original merchant. Some merchants reported that in order to retain control over their customers, they will buy back contracts from credit agencies they suspect are giving information to competitors.[9]

CREDIT ASSOCIATION RATINGS. All credit merchants report their bad debtors to the credit association to which they belong. The merchants interviewed said that they always consult the "skip lists" of their association before extending credit to a new customer.[10] In this way they can avoid at least the customers known to be bad risks. This form of control tends to be effective in the long run because the customers find that they are unable to obtain credit until they have made good on their past debts. During the interviews with them, some consumers mentioned this need to restore their credit rating as the reason why they were paying off debts in spite of their belief that they had been cheated.

But these various formal techniques of control are not sufficient to cope with the merchant's problem of risk. He also depends heavily on informal and personal techniques of control.

Informal Controls

The merchant starts from the premise that most of his customers are honest people who intend to pay but have difficulty managing their money. Missed payments are seen as more often due to poor management and to emergencies than to dishonesty. The merchants anticipate that their customers will miss some payments and they rely on informal controls to insure that payments are eventually made.

All the merchants described their credit business as operating on a "fifteen-month year." This means that they expect the customer to miss about one of every four payments and they compute the markup accordingly. Unlike the credit companies, which insist upon regular payments and add service charges for late payments, the neighborhood merchant is prepared to extend "flexible" credit. Should the customer miss an occasional payment or should he be short on another, the merchant considers this a normal part of his business.

To insure the close personal control necessary for this system of credit, the merchant frequently draws up a contract for weekly payments which the customer usually brings to the store. This serves several functions for the merchant. To begin with, the sum of money represented by a weekly payment is relatively small and so helps to create the illusion of "easy credit." Customers are apt to think more of the size of the payments than of the cost of the item or the length of the contract.

More importantly, the frequent contact of a weekly payment system enables the merchant to get to know his customer. He learns when the customer receives his paycheck, when his rent is due, who his friends are, when job layoffs, illnesses, and other emergencies occur—in short, all sorts of information which allow him to interpret the reason for a missed payment. Some merchants reported that when they know the customer has missed a payment for a legitimate reason such as illness or a job layoff, they will send a sympathetic note and offer the customer a gift (an inexpensive lamp or wall picture) when payments are resumed. This procedure, they say, frequently brings the customer back with his missed payments.

The short interval between payments also functions to give the merchant an early warning when something is amiss. His chances of locating the delinquent customer are that much greater. Further-more, the merchant can keep tabs on a delinquent customer through his knowledge of the latter's friends, relatives, neighbors, and associates, who are also apt to be customers of his. In this way, still another informal device, the existing network of social relations, is utilized by the neighborhood merchant in conducting his business.[11]

The weekly payment system also provides the merchant with the opportunity to sell other items to the customer. When the first purchase is almost paid for, the merchant will try to persuade the customer to make another. Having the customer in the store, where he can look at the merchandise, makes the next sale that much easier. This system of successive sales is, of course, an ideal arrangement—for the merchant. As a result, the customer remains continuously in debt to him. The pattern is somewhat reminiscent of the Southern sharecropper's relation to the company store. And since a number of customers grew up in more traditional environments with just such economies, they may find the arrangement acceptable. The practice of buying from peddlers, found to be common in these low-income areas, also involves the principle of continuous in-debtedness. The urban low-income economy, then, is in some respects like the sharecropper system; it might almost be called an "urban sharecropper system."[12]

THE CUSTOMER PEDDLERS

Characteristic of the comparatively traditional and personal form of the low-income economy is the important role played in it by the door-to-door credit salesman, the customer peddler. The study of merchants found that these peddlers are not necessarily competitors of the store owners. Almost all merchants make use of peddlers in the great competition for customers. The merchants tend to regard peddlers as necessary evils who add greatly to the final cost of purchases. But they need them because in their view, customers are too ignorant, frightened, or lazy to come to the stores themselves. Thus, the merchants' apparent contempt for peddlers does not bar them from employing outdoor salesmen (or "canvassers," as they describe the peddlers who work for one store or another). Even the merchants who are themselves reluctant to hire canvassers find they must do so in order to meet the competition. The peddler's main function for the merchant, then, is getting the customer to the store, and if he will not come, getting the store to the customer. But this is not his only function.

Much more than the storekeeper, the peddler operates on the basis of a personal relationship with the customer. By going to the customer's home, he gets to know the entire family; he sees the condition of the home and he comes to know the family's habits and wants. From this vantage point he is better able than the merchant to evaluate the customer as a credit risk. Since many of the merchant's potential customers lack the standard credentials of credit, such as having a permanent job, the merchant needs some other basis for discriminating between good and bad risks. If the peddler, who has come to know the family, is ready to vouch for the customer, the merchant will be ready to make the transaction. In short, the peddler acts as a fiduciary agent, a Dun and Bradstreet for the poor, telling the merchant which family is likely to meet its obligations and which is not.

Not all peddlers are employed by stores. Many are independent enterprisers (who may have started as canvassers for stores).[13] A number of the independent peddlers have accumulated enough capital to supply their customers with major durables. These are the elite peddlers, known as "dealers," who buy appliances and furniture from local merchants at a "wholesale" price, and then sell them on credit to their customers. In these transactions, the peddler either takes the customer to the store or sends the customer to the store with his card on which he has written some such message as "Please give Mr. Jones a TV set."[14] The merchant then sells the customer the TV set at a price much higher than he would ordinarily charge. The "dealer" is generally given two months to pay the merchant the "wholesale" price, and meanwhile he takes over the responsibility of collecting from his customer. Some "dealers" are so successful that they employ canvassers in their own right.[15] And some merchants do so much business with "dealers" that they come to think of themselves as "wholesalers" even though they are fully prepared to do their own retail business.

Independent peddlers without much capital also have economic relations with local merchants. They act as brokers, directing their customers to neighborhood stores that will extend them credit. And for this service they of course receive a commission. In these transactions, it is the merchant who accepts the risks and assumes the responsibility for collecting payments. The peddler who acts as a broker performs the same function as the merchant in the T.O. system. He knows which merchants will accept great risk and which will not, and directs his customers accordingly.

There are, then, three kinds of customer peddlers operating in these low-income neighborhoods who cooperate with local merchants: the canvassers who are employed directly by the stores: the small entrepreneurs who act as brokers; and the more successful entrepreneurs who operate as "dealers." A fourth type of peddler consists of salesmen representing large companies not necessarily located in the neighborhood. These men are, for the most part, canvassers for firms specializing in a particular commodity, e.g., encyclopedias, vacuum cleaners, or pots and pans. They differ from the other peddlers by specializing in what they sell and by depending more on contracts and legal controls. They are also less interested in developing continuous relationships with their customers.

Peddlers thus aid the local merchants by finding customers, evaluating them as credit risks, and helping in the collection of payments. And as the merchants themselves point out, these services add greatly to the cost of the goods. One storekeeper said that peddlers are apt to charge five and six times the amount the store charges for relatively inexpensive purchases. Pointing to a religious picture which he sells for $5, he maintained that peddlers sell it for as much as $30. And he estimated that the peddler adds 30 to 50 per cent to the final sales price of appliances and furniture.

UNETHICAL AND ILLEGAL PRACTICES

The interviewers uncovered some evidence that some local merchants engage in the illegal practice of selling reconditioned furniture and appliances as new. Of course, no merchant would admit that he did this himself, but five of them hinted that their competitors engaged in this practice.[16] Several of the consumers we interviewed were quite certain that they had been victimized in this way.

One unethical, if not illegal, activity widely practiced by stores is "bait" advertising with its concomitant, the "switch sale." In the competition for customers, merchants depend heavily upon advertising displays in their windows which announce furniture or appliances at unusually low prices. The customer may enter the store assuming that the low offer in the window signifies a reasonably low price line. Under severe pressure, the storekeeper may even be prepared to sell the merchandise at the advertised price, for not to do so would be against the law. What most often happens, however, is that the unsuspecting customer is convinced by the salesman that he doesn't really want the goods advertised in the window and is then persuaded to buy a smaller amount of more expensive goods. Generally, not much persuasion is necessary. The most popular "bait ad" is the announcement of three rooms of furniture for "only $149" or "only $199." The customer who inquires about this bargain is shown a bedroom set consisting of two cheap and (sometimes deliberately) chipped bureaus and one bed frame. He learns that the spring and matteress are not included in the advertised price, but can be had for another $75 or $100. The living-room set in these "specials" consists of a fragile-looking sofa and one unmatching chair.[17]

The frequent success of this kind of exploitation, known in the trade as the "switch sale," is reflected in this comment by one merchant: "I don't know how they do it. They advertise three rooms of furniture for $149 and the customers swarm in. *They end up buying a $400 bedroom set for $600 and none of us can believe how easy it is to make these sales.*"

In sum, a fairly intricate system of sales-and-credit has evolved in response to the distinctive situation of the low-income consumer and the local merchant. It is a system heavily slanted in the direction of a traditional economy in which informal, personal ties play a major part in the transaction. At the same time it is connected to impersonal bureaucratic agencies through the instrument of the installment contract. Should the informal system break down, credit companies, courts of law, and agencies of law enforcement come to play a part.

The system is not only different from the larger, more formal economy; in some respects it is a *deviant* system in which practices that violate prevailing moral standards are commonplace. As Merton has pointed out in his analysis of the political machine, the persistence of deviant social structures can only be understood when their social functions (as well as dysfunctions) are taken into account.[18] The basic function of the low-income marketing system is to provide consumer goods to people who fail to meet the requirements of the more legitimate, bureaucratic market, or who choose to exclude themselves from the larger market because they do not feel comfortable in it. As we have seen, the system is extraordinarily flexible. Almost no one—however great a risk—is turned away. Various mechanisms sift and sort customers according to their credit risk and match them with merchants ready to sell them the goods they want. Even the family on welfare is permitted to maintain its self-respect by consuming in much the same way as do its social peers who happen not to be on welfare.

Economic Report on Installment Credit and Retail Sales Practices of District of Columbia Retailers

Federal Trade Commission

This report presents the results of a survey of installment credit and sales practices involving household furnishings and appliances in the District of Columbia. The purpose of the survey was to obtain a factual picture of the finance charges, prices, gross margins and profits, legal actions taken in collecting delinquent accounts, and the assignment relationships between retailers and finance companies.

Reprinted from *Economic Report on Installment Credit and Retail Sales Practices of District of Columbia Retailers* (Washington: Superintendent of Documents, 1968), pp. ix–xvi and 1–24.

See pages 284–286 for all footnotes to this chapter.

The survey covered those D.C. retailers of furniture and appliances having estimated sales of at least $100,000 for the year 1966. The 96 retailers providing data had combined sales of $226 million, which represented about 85 per cent of the sales of furniture, appliance, and department store retailers in the District of Columbia.

I
USE OF INSTALLMENT CREDIT BY D.C. RETAILERS

Sixty-five retailers with combined sales of $151 million indicated regular use of consumer installment sales contracts. The remainder sold only for cash or on a regular or revolving charge account basis. This report focuses primarily on retailers using installment contracts. These retailers were classified into two groups: those appealing primarily to low-income customers and those appealing to a more general market.

D.C. stores varied widely in their use of installment credit. Some general market discount appliance stores made very few sales on credit. At the other extreme, a number of low-income market retailers sold entirely on installment credit.

Installment credit was used much more extensively by retailers selling to low-income consumers than by retailers selling to other consumers. Low-income market retailers used installment credit in 93 per cent of their sales. The comparable figure for general market retailers was 27 per cent.

CUSTOMER CHARACTERISTICS OF LOW-INCOME MARKET RETAILERS

A sample of installment sales contracts and credit applications was analyzed to identify the customer characteristics of low-income market retailers. The analysis revealed substantial differences between customers of the low-income market retailers and all residents of the District of Columbia. The average family size was larger— 4.3 persons compared to an average of 3.5 persons for the District of Columbia. Almost half of the families of customers in the sample had five or more members. The median family income during 1966 of the sample customers was $348 per month. This is very low considering the larger than average size of the families. The Bureau of Labor Statistics recently estimated that the maintenance of a moderate standard of living for four in Washington, D.C., requires a monthly income of $730.

Most customers were engaged in low-paying jobs. The largest proportion, 28 per cent, were Service Workers, such as waitresses and janitors. Second in importance were Operatives (including such occupations as taxi drivers and laundry workers). Laborers and Domestic Workers also represented a significant share of the sample. Together, these four major occupational groups accounted for 75 per cent of the customer sample. In comparison, only 36 per cent of the general population in the District was classified in these low-paying occupational groups. There were thirty-one welfare recipients in the sample, accounting for 6 per cent of all customers in the sample. There were also a number of customers in the sample dependent on social security, alimony, support payments, and income received from relatives.

A review of credit references noted in the 486 contracts subjected to detailed analysis revealed that 70 per cent indicated no credit references or references with low-income market retailers only. Only 30 per cent of the customers of this retailer, therefore, had established credit with general market retailers.

GROSS MARGINS AND PRICES OF LOW-INCOME MARKET RETAILERS

The survey disclosed that without exception low-income market retailers had high average markups and prices. On the average, goods purchased for $100 at wholesale sold for $255 in the low-income market stores, compared with $159 in general market stores.

Contrasts between the markup policies of low-income and general market retailers are most apparent when specific products are compared. Retailers surveyed were asked to give the wholesale and retail prices for their two best-selling models in each product line. These price data are typical of the large volume of products sold by each class of retailer.

For every product specified, low-income market retailers had the highest average gross margins reported. When similar makes and models are compared, the differences are striking. For example, the wholesale cost of a portable TV set was about $109 to both a low-income market and a general market retailer. The general market retailer sold the set for $129.95, whereas the low-income market retailer charged $219.95 for the same set. Another example is a dryer, wholesaling at about $115, which was sold for $150 by a general market retailer and for $300 by a low-income market retailer.

OPERATING EXPENSES AND NET PROFITS OF RETAILERS SURVEYED

Despite their substantially higher prices, net profit on sales for low-income market retailers was only slightly higher and net profit return on net worth was considerably lower when compared to general market retailers. It appears that salaries and commissions, bad-debt losses, and other expenses are substantially higher for low-income market retailers. Profit and expense comparisons are, of course, affected by differences in type of operation and accounting procedures. However, a detailed analysis was made for retailers of comparable size and merchandise mix to minimize such differences.

Low-income market retailers reported the highest return after taxes on net sales, 4.7 per cent. Among the general market retailers, department stores had the highest return on net sales, 4.6 per cent. Furniture and home furnishings stores earned a net profit after taxes of 3.9 per cent, and appliance, radio, and television retailers were the least profitable with a net profit of only 2.1 per cent on sales.

Low-income market retailers reported an average rate of return on *net worth* after taxes of 10.1 per cent. Rates of return on net worth varied considerably among various kinds of general market retailers. Appliance, radio, and television retailers reported the highest rate of return after taxes, 20.3 per cent of net worth. Next in order were furniture and home furnishings retailers with 17.6 per cent and department stores with 13 per cent on net worth.

ASSIGNMENT OF INSTALLMENT CONTRACTS

Low-income market retailers typically held their installment contracts and did not assign them to finance companies or banks. Only one fifth of the total contracts were assigned by low-income market retailers. Among general market retailers, appliance stores assigned almost all (98 per cent) of their contracts to finance companies and banks. General market furniture stores assigned somewhat more than half of their contracts (57 per cent). Among the retailers surveyed, only the department store category involved no contract assignment.

FINANCE CHARGES ON INSTALLMENT CONTRACTS[1]

There is considerable variation in the finance charges of D.C. retailers of furniture and appliances, particularly among the low-income market retailers. Most of the retailers surveyed determined finance charges in terms of an "add-on" rate based on the unpaid cash balance. When calculated on an effective annual rate basis, finance charges of general market retailers varied between 11 per cent and 29 per cent, averaging 21 per cent when contracts were assigned and 19 per cent when retailers financed their own contracts. Finance charges by low-income market retailers imposing such charges ranged between 11 and 33 per cent per annum, averaging 25 per cent on contracts assigned to finance companies and 23 per cent on contracts the retailers held themselves.

One low-income market retailer made no separate charge for installment credit. All of his finance charges were, in effect, included in the purchase price. Other low-income market retailers kept finance charges below the actual cost of granting credit. This practice of absorbing credit costs can give the illusion of "easy" credit, but the customer may be paying a great deal for such installment credit in the form of much higher prices.

JUDGMENTS, GARNISHMENTS, AND REPOSSESSIONS BY RETAILERS

One of the most notable facts uncovered by the study relates to the frequency with which a small group of retailers utilized the courts to enforce their claims with respect to installment contracts. Eleven of the eighteen low-income market retailers reported 2,690 judgments in 1966. Their legal actions resulted in 1,568 garnishments and 306 repossessions. For this group, one court judgment was obtained for every $2,200 of sales. In effect, low-income market retailers make extensive use of the courts in collecting debts. While general market retailers may take legal action as a last resort against delinquent customers, some low-income market retailers depend on legal action as a normal order of business.

CONCLUSIONS

Installment credit is widely used in marketing appliances and home furnishings to low-income families. Often these families purchase durable goods, such as furniture, television sets, and phonographs, through the mechanism of "easy" credit. Low-income market retailers specialize in granting credit to consumers who do not seek or are unable to obtain credit from regular department, furniture, or appliance stores. As a group, low-income market retailers made about 93 per cent of their sales through installment credit.

The real cost of this "easy" credit is very dear, however. Primarily it takes the form of higher product prices. Credit charges, when separately stated, are not notably higher than those imposed by general market retailers. Though some low-income market retailers imposed effective annual finance charges as high as 33 per cent, others charged much less or nothing at all. Markups on comparable products, however, are often two or three times higher than those charged by general market retailers.

The findings of this study suggest that the marketing system for distribution of durable goods to low-income consumers is costly. Although their markups are very much higher than those of general market retailers, low-income market retailers do not make particularly high net profits. They have markedly higher costs, partly because of high bad-debt expenses, but to a greater extent because of higher salaries and commissions as a per cent of sales. These expenses reflect in part greater use of door-to-door selling and expenses associated with the collection and processing of installment contracts.

The high prices charged by low-income market retailers suggest the absence of effective price competition. What competition there is among low-income market retailers apparently takes the form of easier credit availability, rather than of lower prices. Greater credit risks are taken to entice customers. Insofar as the problem for low-income consumers is availability of credit, merchants who sell to them focus on this element.

The success of retailers who price their merchandise on such a high markup in selling to low-income families leads inevitably to the conclusion that such families engage in little comparative shopping. It would appear that many low-income customers lack information or knowledge of their credit charges and credit source alternatives, or of the prices and quality of products available in general market retailing establishments. To the extent that door-to-door sales techniques are utilized, such families frequently make crucial purchases without leaving the home and without seeing the products they commit themselves to buy. The fact that low-income market retailers emphasize the use of door-to-door salesmen both reflects and encourages such behavior. The Commission is well aware that door-to-door selling, as well as home-demonstration selling, provides an opportunity for deceptive and high-pressure sales techniques. Moreover, such selling methods are also very high-cost methods of distribution. It would appear, therefore, that the low-income consumers who can least afford mistakes in their buying decisions face two serious problems when they are confronted with a door-to-door or home-demonstration sales approach—(1) the high cost of this sales technique will ultimately be borne by the purchaser, and (2) the opportunity for high pressure or deceptive selling is great, thus discouraging comparative shopping and enhancing the probability that the consumer will agree to purchases he would otherwise not want.

While public policy can help solve the problems of low-income consumers, legislation alone may not be sufficient. Legislation aimed at disclosure and regulation of finance charges will help low-income as well as other consumers make more rational buying decisions. Intensified programs on both state and federal levels to eliminate all deceptions and frauds in the advertising and oral representations of the terms of sale and credit charges will also help to ensure that their money is spent advantageously. The poor, to a considerable extent, however, are not sophisticated shoppers. Many cannot afford the luxury of "shopping around" because their potential sources of credit are limited. Others, because of inadequate consumer education or lack of mobility, simply do not engage in comparison shopping.

Thus, in attempting to deal with the phenomenon of the poor paying more for consumer goods, every effort should be made to improve consumer counseling. Many customers continue to buy from low-income market retailers even though they have sufficient income to qualify for credit at stores selling for less. Greater community effort in consumer education is needed.

Beyond the matter of education is the question of credit availability. Many low-income families are quite capable of making regular payments. They should have the option of making payments on reasonably priced merchandise. Local community effort in the development of effective credit sources could contribute materially to freeing individuals from dependence on "easy" credit merchants.[2] Moreover, perhaps general market retailers can take steps to make it easier for low-income families to apply for and receive credit. Some retailers have already found that they can do so economically. Various community business organizations might consider ways of more actively encouraging low-income families to seek credit from retailers selling for less.

Increased competition for the patronage of low-income consumers would go a long way toward resolving many of the problems confronting them in the low-income market. Public policy should consider the various ways by which new entrants could be encouraged into these markets to increase the competitive viability of these markets.

While the availability of credit is perhaps the major reason why low-income families purchase from the low-income market retailers, it is only logical to conclude that the sales techniques of these retailers are also an important factor. Low-income market retailers have every incentive to continue these techniques since their risk of loss is substantially reduced by their virtually unopposed access to judgment and garnishment proceedings to enforce payment or secure repossession. The 2,690 actions taken by eleven low-income market retailers in 1966 suggest a marketing technique which includes actions against default as a normal matter of business rather than as a matter of last resort. At present, in the face of default, creditors can seek both repossession and payment of the deficiency, including various penalties. It may be appropriate to require creditors to choose one or the other of these legal remedies, and not to have the option of pursuing both courses simultaneously. Repossession would then fully discharge the merchant's claim. It is equally necessary to ensure that purchasers receive *actual* notice of any such proceedings and have legal counsel available to defend them in court. Perhaps, consideration should also be given to some form of negotiation before a court-appointed neighborhood referee as a compulsory prelude to a default judgment.

It is apparent that the solution to the problem of installment credit for the poor requires a variety of actions. A requirement that finance charges be clearly and conspicuously stated is a necessary but not a sufficient solution to the problem of installment credit for those consumers who are considered poor credit risks and are unsophisticated buyers. Among the complementary steps which might be considered are the following: (1) make reasonable credit more accessible; (2) provide counseling services which will encourage customers to practice comparison shopping; (3) equalize the legal rights of buyers and creditors in installment credit transactions; (4) encourage additional businesses to enter the low-income market; and (5) intensify consumer protection activities on both federal and local levels to eliminate all fraud and deceptions in the advertising and offering of credit.

II

INTRODUCTION

As part of its continuing activities in the field of consumer protection, the Federal Trade Commission has undertaken a broad program to eliminate deception in the sale of goods and services through installment credit. Such deception can be a serious problem for consumers from all income groups. Abuses in the use of installment credit may fall most heavily, however, on the poor and disadvantaged. For this reason, the Commission felt it would be useful to obtain more detailed information about the use of installment credit by low-income consumers.[3] Such information will provide valuable assistance in planning future consumer protection activities.

This study is intended to provide objective information about installment credit practices, good and bad, as they affect consumers in the District of Columbia. A specific purpose is to compare the practices of retailers of furniture and appliances who sell primarily to a low-income market with those who sell to a more general market.

It should be made clear that the study is limited in scope. It does not attempt to provide information about all aspects of the operations of low-income market retailers. For instance, the quality and durability of products is not directly examined in this study. Nor is the matter of selling methods dealt with in detail. While these are interesting areas of investigation, it was not feasible to cover them in this report. The study focuses primarily on the following points:

1. Per cent of sales made through installment contracts.
2. Gross margins of retailers.
3. Comparative prices charged by low-income market and general market retailers.
4. Amount of finance charges.
5. Relationships between retailers and finance companies.
6. Legal actions taken by retailers on delinquent installment contracts.
7. Characteristics of a low-income market retailer's customers.

TYPES OF RETAILERS AND MERCHANDISE INCLUDED IN THIS STUDY

All retailers in the District of Columbia with estimated sales of over $100,000 per year who sold furniture and appliances were surveyed by the Federal Trade Commission. Several retailers were excluded because they had gone out of business since the survey period or were unable to provide usable information. Table 1 shows the total 1966 sales of retailers included in the survey. As a basis for comparison, 1963 *Census of Business* total sales for the District of Columbia are also shown. The survey data are for a later period, 1966, but it is unlikely that there has been much change in sales during the intervening years. Furniture and appliance sales of retailers located in the District of Columbia have not been growing rapidly because of an increasing trend toward use of shopping centers outside the District.

TABLE 1. Comparison of 1966 sales of survey retailers with sales reported in 1963 Census of Business for the District of Columbia

SURVEY RETAILERS, 1966:

Type of retail store	U.S. Census total sales, 1963 ($000)	Number of retailers	Total sales, all retailers ($000)	Number of retailers	Total Sales, retailers offering installment credit ($000)	Number of retailers	Total sales, retailers not offering installment credit[1] ($000)
Department stores (SIC 531)	$186,439	6	$144,864	3	$91,361	3	$53,500
Furniture and other home-furnishings stores (SIC 571)	50,442	59	51,255	38	33,929	21	17,326
Appliance stores (SIC 572, 573)	29,912	31	29,693	24	25,677	7	4,016
Total	266,793	96	225,812	65	150,970	31	74,842

[1] Includes stores using revolving credit arrangements; 30-, 60-, 90-day credit arrangements; and stores operating on a cash basis. Source: F.T.C. Survey; 1963 Census of Business, vol. III, pt. 2, pp. 110–15.

The survey included 96 retailers with combined sales of $226 million. This approximates 85 per cent of the 1963 Census total sales of appliance, furniture, and department store retailers in the District of Columbia. Sixty-five retailers with combined sales of $151 million reported that they regularly used installment sales contracts. The remaining stores used revolving credit plans, charge accounts, or sold their merchandise only for cash. Of the $75 million in sales by this group, three large department stores accounted for $54 million. These department stores sold furniture and appliances through revolving credit arrangements.

Although revolving credit is a significant element in the retail credit market, to simplify data collection and analysis this study focuses primarily on installment credit contracts. It is difficult to collect data on revolving credit because such accounts are usually continuing arrangements. Balances may be carried for years, with regular payments offset by periodic purchases. Also, a variety of goods in addition to furniture and appliances are financed by department stores under revolving credit arrangements. The exclusion of revolving credit greatly simplifies the analysis in this report and there is little reason to believe that it creates any substantial bias in the results.

Further tabulations included in this report are based on returns of retailers who used installment contracts. Appropriate mention will be made whenever applicable of the practices of other retailers not using such contracts.

The survey revealed considerable variation among stores with respect to the percentage of sales made on installment credit. Some discount appliance stores made very few sales on installment credit or none at all. At the other extreme, a number of retailers sold almost entirely on installment credit. In addition, other factors such as gross margins or "markups" varied widely among stores. To analyze differences in credit practices, retailers surveyed were classified in various groups.

One means of classification was by type of establishment, i.e., department store, appliance store, or furniture store. Type of store did not, however, appear to be the most crucial element in determining credit practices. A second method of classification was by income of customer, i.e., low-income market retailers versus general market retailers. Since direct data were not available on income of customers served by various stores, two criteria were used to identify retailers serving low-income customers: (1) location of store and (2) advertising practices. As a first approximation, retailers located in or adjacent to low-income residential areas were considered to serve low-income customers primarily. Identification of low-income residential areas was done on the basis of 1960 Census data. In general, it was relatively easy to identify whether or not stores were located in low-income areas.

The District of Columbia is characterized by a wide variation in family income. Additionally, there is a close relationship between geographic sections within the city and income level. The most extensive source of demographic information on the District and the surrounding metropolitan area is the 1960 *Census of Population*. Data are provided for 124 individual Census tracts within the city. While incomes were substantially higher in 1966, the period covered by this survey, the relative positions of different areas probably has not changed greatly since 1960. The principal exception would be the Southwest Washington urban renewal area. The distribution of family incomes within the District of Columbia is indicated below:

1959 income	Per cent distribution	1959 income	Per cent distribution
Under $2,000	9.4	$10,000 to $14,999	13.7
$2,000 to $3,999	18.5	$15,000 to $24,999	5.7
$4,000 to $5,999	22.2	$25,000 and over	2.3
$6,000 to $7,999	16.0		
$8,000 to $9,999	12.2	Total	100. 0

Source: 1960 *U.S. Census of Population*, vol. 1, pt. 10, p. 54.

There is also a definite geographic pattern in income distribution within the city. For the city as a whole the median income was $6,000. However, of the 124 Census tracts, sixteen had median incomes of less than $4,000 in 1959. Ten of these tracts were located in the compact section of Northwest Washington which is often referred to as the Cardozo area. Four were in the southwest section of the city, one in the southeast, and one in the northeast. In con- -trast, fifteen Census tracts had median incomes over $10,000 per year. All were located in a contiguous group west of Rock Creek in the upper northwest area of the city.

Low-income market retailers were, for the most part, located in what could be described as neighborhood shopping areas in or adjacent to low-income areas. A characteristic of low-income market stores is that they are unlikely to draw any substantial volume of business from the more affluent sections of the city or from the suburbs.

The classification of stores as low-income market retailers was established not only by location but also on the basis of advertising practices. It is possible that a store could be located in a low-income area yet sell to a more general market through citywide advertising. Leading Washington newspapers and radio stations which appeal to all income levels, rather than specifically to low-income groups, were checked and no retailers engaged in extensive advertising to the general market were included in the low-income market group.

Thus, stores finally classified as low-income market retailers had to meet two qualifications: location in a low-income area and absence of significant citywide advertising directed to a general market. Eighteen retailers met these criteria. While classification of stores into the two groups, low-income market retailers and general market retailers, involved some arbitrary decisions, the basic differences between practices of the two groups are quite clearcut.

Of the eighteen low-income market retailers, fourteen could be described as furniture stores; two as appliance stores; and two as miscellaneous merchandise stores. These distinctions did not appear particularly important for purposes of analysis, however, and the low-income market retailers were treated as a combined group.

VARIATIONS IN INSTALLMENT CREDIT SALES

A striking characteristic of low-income market retailers is the high proportion of their total sales accounted for by installment contract transactions. Table 2 indicates that installment credit transactions accounted for 92.7 per cent of the total sales of the eighteen low-income market retailers. In contrast, installment credit accounted for only 26.5 per cent of total sales of general market retailers. Most of the low-income market retailers made more than 90 per cent of their sales through credit; none of the general market retailers had such a high proportion of installment credit sales. Many of the general market retailers in fact had the bulk of their sales accounted for by cash transactions or by noninstallment credit.

TABLE 2.   Value of installment contracts as a per cent of sales, District of Columbia retailers, 1966

| | | | INSTALLMENT CONTRACTS | | |
Type of retailer	Number of com-panies	Net sales ($000)	Value ($000)	Per cent of total	As Per cent of net sales
Total	65	$150,970	$45,251	100.0	30.0
Low-income market retailers	18	7,874	7,296	16.1	92.7
General market retailers	47	143,096	37,955	83.9	26.5
Appliance, radio, and television	22	25,089	8,466	18.7	33.7
Furniture and home-furnishings	22	26,643	10,608	23.5	39.8
Department stores	3	91,364	18,881	41.7	20.6

Source: FTC Survey.

While extent of installment credit sales is the primary factor distinguishing low-income market retailers, there are also significant differences in the general business methods employed by this group. Prices and gross margins tend to be substantially higher for low-income market retailers. Bad-debt expenses are also considerably higher. Extensive use of credit together with higher prices and gross margins form a distinctive pattern for low-income market retailers. However, before discussing the findings concerning these differences, it is useful to place low-income market retailers in proper perspective with respect to the total market for appliances and home furnishings in the District of Columbia.

A PERSPECTIVE ON THE IMPORTANCE OF LOW-INCOME MARKET RETAILERS

The eighteen low-income market retailers had net sales for 1966 of $7.9 million (Table 2). This amounts to only 5.2 per cent of sales of all retailers surveyed. Nevertheless, it is a substantial amount when compared to total expenditures by low-income consumers on furniture and appliances. Low-income consumers within the District of Columbia accounted for only a fraction of total expenditures on furniture and appliances. The low-income market for such goods is considerably smaller than the total consumer market. No statistics are available on total expenditures for furniture and appliances by low-income consumers, but it is possible to make reasonable estimates. We estimate that District of Columbia households with an annual income under $5,000 in 1966 had total income of about $260 million.[4] Additionally, we estimate that in 1966 these households spent about $18 million on furniture and appliances.[5]

Low-income market retailers surveyed had total sales in 1966 of $7.9 million, about 44 per cent of our estimated total expenditures by low-income households for furniture and appliances.[6] This suggests that the low-income market retailers surveyed are definitely an important factor in the low-income marketplace, even though they did not account for a major portion of total retail sales of furniture and appliances in the District.

GENERAL MARKET RETAILERS

Forty-seven of the stores surveyed were classified as general market retailers, appealing either to a broad consumer market or primarily to middle and high-income groups. General market retailers were further classified into the following subcategories: furniture stores, appliance stores, and department stores. This was necessary for comparative and analytical purposes because, unlike the relatively homogeneous low-income market retailers, there were some differences in pricing and credit policies of the various types of general market retailers.

Appliance, Radio, and Television

There are two types of merchandise that are customarily sold and serviced by appliance, radio, and television retailers—brown goods and white goods. Television sets, radios, and stereo-phonographs are electronic home entertainment merchandise, collectively referred to among retailers as "brown goods." Washing machines, dryers, refrigerators, and freezers are collectively called "white goods." Sewing machines and vacuum cleaners are other household appliances customarily sold by brown and white goods retailers. The general market classification of appliance, radio, and television retailers included twenty-two companies operating stores primarily selling these types of merchandise. These retailers sometimes sell furniture and floor coverings, but only as secondary merchandise lines. Discount stores and full-service retailers are included in this retailer classification.

Furniture and Home Furnishings

Those retailers that specialize in the selling of furniture and home furnishings to a *broad* consumer market—a total of twenty-two— have been grouped together for analysis. Retailers selling furniture primarily to low-income consumers are included in the low-income market retailer classification. Among furniture and home furnishings retailers are those that carry a wide line of furniture, as well as a secondary line of appliances, and those that specialize in particular home furnishings items, such as rugs and carpeting.

Department Stores

The category of department stores, of which three included in this study sold goods on installment credit, includes large stores selling apparel in several merchandise departments, but also having departments engaged in selling furniture, home furnishings, appliances, radios, and television sets. Such stores are an important outlet for furniture and appliances. To qualify as a department store, a retail establishment must employ twenty-five people or more. Some smaller stores, classified in this study as low-income market retailers, also carry apparel and soft lines of home furnishings, as well as appliances and furniture.

LIMITATIONS OF THE SURVEY

This survey was limited to stores actually located within the District of Columbia. The District itself is part of a larger metropolitan area encompassing suburbs in Maryland and Virginia. In 1960 the population of the entire metropolitan area was 2 million, while the population of the District alone was 764,000. In terms of total retail sales, the 1963 *Census of Business* indicated that the District accounted for about 42 per cent of metropolitan area retail sales. The proportion probably is somewhat lower for furniture and appliance sales alone.

At first glance, it might seem that the survey is limited because data on suburban area retailing are not included. This is not likely to be a serious problem, however, when comparing practices of retailers selling primarily to low-income consumers with those selling to a more general market. Census data indicate that most of the low-income consumers live within the District itself rather than in the suburbs. Median 1959 family incomes for components of the Washington Standard Metropolitan Statistical Area are shown below:

Area	Median income	Area	Median income
Washington D.C.	$5,993	Fairfax Co., Va.	$8,607
Montgomery Co., Md.	9,317	Alexandria, Va.	7,207
Prince Georges Co., Md.	7,471	Falls Church, Va.	8,721
Arlington Co., Va.	8,670	Entire SMSA	7,577

Source: 1960 *Census of Population,* Series PHC(1), pt. 11, p. 15.

All of the suburban areas have a significantly higher median income than the District itself. While it would be useful to have data on suburban stores selling primarily to higher income consumers, it is doubtful that such data would alter the basic findings of the survey. One reason is that many of the large volume suburban stores are branches of retailers located in the District and probably follow similar policies. Also, inclusion of suburban discount retailers of furniture and appliances would tend to sharpen the contrasts in prices and margins found in this survey rather than to weaken them.

This survey was restricted to retailers of furniture and appliances. A more extensive survey would probably indicate the existence of a low-income market for other goods and services also. There is ample reason, based on information received from consumers by the Federal Trade Commission, to believe that many of the practices found in this survey are also prevalent in the sale of clothing, variety goods, jewelry, and services such as reupholstering and auto repairs. It was not possible to cover all forms of retailing in a single survey, however, and the focus was placed on furniture and appliances because this is a large segment of retailing and is reasonably homogeneous in terms of product lines sold.

The survey did not include any retailer with estimated 1966 sales of less than $100,000. Very small retailers were excluded for two reasons. First, such retailers do not usually keep detailed records and many would have probably found it impossible to complete the survey questionnaire. For example, many small retailers of furniture sell both new and used merchandise. In most cases such retailers could not meaningfully separate sales of the two types of furniture. Second, while there are a large number of small furniture and appliance stores, their total sales volume is not great. The 1963 *Census of Business* indicated a total of 264 establishments in SIC 571 (furniture and home furnishings), SIC 572 (household appliances), and SIC 573 (radio, TV, and music stores). Of these 264 establishments, 124 had three employees or less. This would be roughly equivalent to less than $100,000 per year in sales. While almost half the establishments fell in this small size category, their combined sales were only 7 per cent of the total. In SIC 531 (department stores) the Census indicates no establishments with sales of less than $100,000 per year.

Even restricting the survey to stores with over $100,000 in sales did not eliminate all sample problems. A substantial number of retailers had moved, gone out of business, or were unable to complete the survey questionnaire. Usually these were the smaller stores. The final group included eighteen low-income market retailers and forty-seven general market retailers. We believe the eighteen low-income market retailers surveyed provide an adequate sample to make meaningful generalizations about this type of retailer in the District of Columbia. Those retailers that conceivably could have been considered low-income market retailers but were *not* included in the final group represented a much smaller combined sales volume than the eighteen that *were* included. Moreover, Table 1 clearly indicates that the bulk of total sales in the categories surveyed was included.

III

In addition to obtaining information on the use of installment credit, the Commission survey requested financial statement data as well as wholesale and retail prices on popular appliance and furniture items. This information was classified by type of retailer and indicated that operating results for low-income market retailers differed significantly from general market retailers in a number of important respects.

GROSS MARGINS

Gross margins represent the difference between the wholesale cost of goods and total revenue derived from their sale at retail as a per cent of selling price. Gross margin is the amount remaining to the retailer to cover operating expenses, including salaries, commissions, rent, equipment, other overhead expenses, and net profit.

Though gross margins for different types of retailers in the survey sample varied, the most significant variation was found when margins of low-income market retailers were compared with those of general market retailers (Table 3). The eighteen low-income market retailers had an average gross margin of 60.8 per cent. The average for general market retailers was 37 per cent, ranging from a low of 30 per cent for appliance, radio, and TV stores to a high of 41 per cent for furniture and home-furnishings stores.[7]

Obviously, the higher the gross margin on a particular product, the higher will be its retail price. On the average, goods purchased for $100 at wholesale sold for $255 in low-income market stores, whereas the retail price was $159 in general market stores (see Fig. 1).[8] Thus, low-income market retailers marked up their cost 2½ times to determine their selling price. This was the average for the eighteen low-income market retailers in the sample. The retailer with the largest volume of sales in this group had a gross margin of 67.9 per cent of selling price, which means that he marked up his merchandise on the average to more than three times its cost.

TABLE 3.   Net sales and gross margins of District of Columbia retailers, 1966

Type of retailer	Number of com- panies	NET SALES Value ($000)	NET SALES Per cent of total	GROSS MARGIN[1] Value ($000)	GROSS MARGIN[1] As per cent of sales
Low-income market retailers	18	$7,874	5.2	$4,790	60.8
General market retailers	47	143,096	94.8	52,988	37.0
Appliance, radio and television	22	25,098	16.6	7,586	30.2
Furniture and home-furnishings	22	26,643	17.7	10,979	41.2
Department Stores	3	91,364	60.5	34,423	37.7
Total, retailers using installment contracts	65	150,970	100.0	57,778	38.3
Retailers not using installment contracts	31	74,842		26,902	35.9
Total, all retailers surveyed	96	225,812		84,680	37.5

[1] Gross margins reported by different types of retailers may not be strictly comparable. One low-income market retailer included finance charges and one general market appliance retailer included service charges in their net sales. Adjustments were made in these instances, but other retailers in the sample may have included such charges in their net sales and not reported their inclusion. To the extent that finance, service and other charges might have been included in net sales and no corresponding adjustment made in cost of goods sold, gross margins for these retailers would be slightly overstated. However, every effort was made to calculate gross margins in this study net of finance and other charges.

General market retailers that used no installment contracts were also contacted in the survey and their gross margins, as indicated in Table 3, did not differ significantly from the average for general market retailers as a whole. One appliance, radio, and TV dealer, who sold on a strictly cash basis, reported a gross margin of 7.2 per cent. This meant that any appliance selling at wholesale for $100 was resold at retail for only $107. This case is very exceptional, of course.

A number of substantial general market furniture stores reported that they relied on revolving credit accounts and used no installment

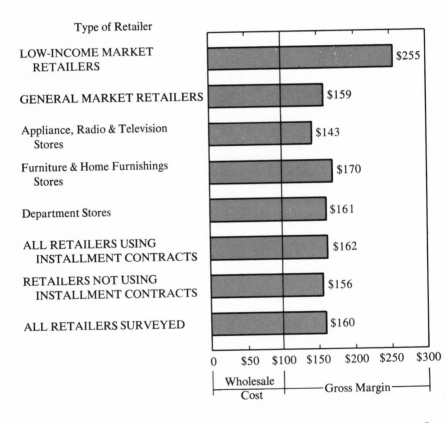

FIGURE 1. Average Selling Price, Assuming $100 Wholesale Cost, by Type of Retailer. (Source: FTC Survey.)

contracts. The gross margins of these retailers were somewhat higher than those that used installment contracts, averaging 46.6 per cent of sales. Likewise, there were three department store companies that reported no installment contract sales, employing instead revolving charge account plans. Their average gross margin of 34.9 per cent of sales was somewhat lower than the average gross margin of 37.7 per cent shown in Table 3 for those department stores using installment contracts.[9]

GROSS MARGINS ON SPECIFIC MERCHANDISE

Retailers surveyed were asked to select two "best-selling" items in each appliance and furniture line of merchandise and report their wholesale costs and selling prices. The difference between these figures (selling price minus cost of goods) represented the gross margin, which was expressed as a per cent of selling price. Table 4 gives the average gross margins on each merchandise item for each

TABLE 4.   Average gross margins of District of Columbia retailers on best-selling items of appliances and furniture, 1966

Average per cent gross margin of:

Merchandise items	LOW-INCOME MARKET RETAILERS	GENERAL MARKET RETAILERS		
		Appliance stores[1]	Furniture stores[1]	Department stores[1]
Television sets	46.4	23.7	28.4	25.2
Carpets	50.0	——	37.5	33.2
Refrigerators	50.6	24.5	24.9	34.6
Washing machines	51.0	25.0	32.3	35.3
Stereo-phonographs	52.7	33.0	36.5	34.7
Freezers	53.7	24.8	——	33.7
Dryers	53.9	25.7	28.4	37.7
Furniture	56.2	——	47.5	50.4
Vacuum cleaners	57.9	26.3	30.2	36.4
Radios	60.0	23.4	38.0	27.9
Sewing machines	66.3	49.0	——	42.7

[1] Appliance and furniture stores have been classified on the basis of their principal merchandise lines. Furniture stores carry appliances as a substantial secondary merchandise line, and for this reason average gross margins of appliances sold by furniture stores are included in this table.

Source: FTC Survey.

type of retailer surveyed. In some instances the gross margins given were for items especially reduced in price for volume sales. Consequently, the averages of these gross margins are somewhat lower than the average gross margins shown for each type of retailer in Table 3.

For every merchandise item specified, low-income market retailers had the highest average gross margins reported—ranging from 66.3 per cent on sewing machines, to 51 per cent on washing machines, and down to 46.4 per cent on television sets. General market appliance retailers had the lowest gross margins for 9 of the 11 merchandise items.

Certain merchandise items showed some consistency as to the market level of gross margins. Television sets were sold by all three types of general market retailers at gross margins below 29 per cent, and this item sold at the lowest (46.4 per cent) average gross margin reported by low-income market retailers. Furniture had relatively high gross margins for all types of retailers. There were some items, however, on which there was no consistency between types of retailers. For instance, radios were the second highest gross margin item (60 per cent) for low-income market retailers and the lowest gross margin item (23.4 per cent) for general market appliance retailers. Thus, a consumer who would have paid $250 for a radio from a low-income market retailer could have purchased a radio of comparable wholesale value at a general market appliance store for $130.

Table 5 converts these gross margins to a comparative price basis. Since the cost of the merchandise has been arbitrarily held constant, the "retail prices" shown in Table 5 directly reflect absolute differences in average gross margins by the type of store and make it possible to compare relative prices on each best-selling item when purchased from low-income market retailers or general market appliance, furniture or department store retailers. As shown in Table 5 and Figure 2, a television set that cost retailers $100 could have been bought for $131 in a general market appliance store, but would have been priced at retail to the low-income consumer at $187 by the average low-income market retailer. A washing machine with the same wholesale cost sold on the average in general market appliance stores for $133, in furniture stores for $148, in department stores for $155, and in low-income market stores for $204. The other merchandise items in Table 5 and

TABLE 5.   Average "retail prices" of District of Columbia retailers on best-selling items of appliances and furniture in 1966, assuming wholesale cost of $100 for each item[1]

Average "retail price" assuming $100 wholesale cost of:

Merchandise item	LOW-INCOME MARKET RETAILERS	GENERAL MARKET RETAILERS		
		Appliance stores[2]	Furniture stores[2]	Department stores
Television set	$187	$131	$140	$134
Carpet	200	——	160	150
Refrigerator	202	132	133	153
Washing machine	204	133	148	155
Stereo-phonograph	211	149	157	153
Freezer	216	133	——	151
Dryer	217	135	138	160
Furniture	228	——	190	202
Vacuum Cleaner	237	136	143	157
Radio	250	130	161	139
Sewing machine	297	196	——	174

[1] These are cash prices and do not reflect separately imposed finance charges.

[2] Appliance and furniture stores have been classified on the basis of their principal merchandise lines. Furniture stores carry appliances as a substantial secondary merchandise line, and for this reason average "retail prices" of appliances sold by furniture stores are included in this table.

Source: Calculated from average gross margins in Table 4, FTC Survey.

Figure 2 provide similar comparisons. In each instance the "retail price" projected for the low-income market retailers is the highest because reported average gross margins were highest, but the amount of the differential varies by merchandise items.

DIRECT PRICE COMPARISONS[10]

Hypothetical price comparisons are useful for purposes of generalization, but we need not depend on just such comparisons. The striking differences between the low-income market and the general market perhaps may best be illustrated by a comparison of prices for similar (in some cases identical) products. Table 6 matches similar makes and models of appliances sold by low-income market retailers as well as general market retailers. Not all of the products shown are identical models, but the similarity in wholesale costs suggests that the comparisons are valid. It should be pointed out that in a great many cases low-income market retailers simply did not carry the same lines of products as general market retailers. As a result, in most instances price comparisons could not be made.

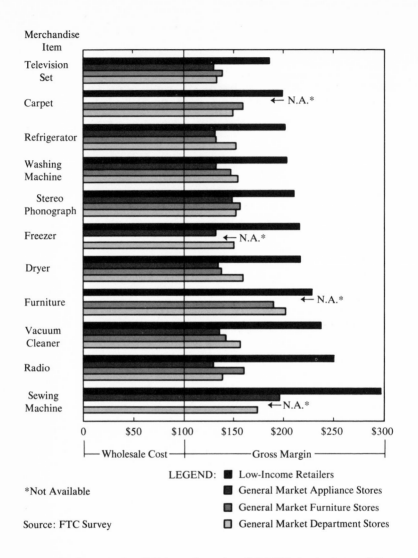

FIGURE 2. Average Retail Prices, Assuming $100 Wholesale Cost, of Comparable Merchandise Items Purchased From Low-Income Market and General Market Retailers.

While Table 6 illustrates extreme differences, it should be remembered that the retailers themselves reported prices for their two *best-selling* models in each product category. These comparisons were not made by researchers poking around in dusty corners of stores looking for grossly overpriced or mismarked items rarely sold. They are based on the retailers' own reported prices.

TABLE 6. Comparison of reported wholesale and retail prices for best-selling products, low-income market and general market retailers

	WHOLESALE COST		RETAIL PRICE[1]	
Products	Low-income market retailer	General market retailer	Low-income market retailer	General market retailer
Television sets:				
Motorola portable	$109.00	$109.50	$219.95	129.95
Philco portable	108.75	106.32	199.95	129.95
Olympic portable	[2]90.00	85.00	249.95	129.95
Admiral portable	94.00	91.77	249.95	129.99
Radio: Emerson	16.50	16.74	39.95	25.00
Stereo: Zenith	32.99	32.99	99.95	36.99
Automatic washers:				
Norge	144.95	140.00	299.95	155.00
General Electric	183.50	160.40	339.95	219.95
Dryers:				
Norge	80.00	87.00	249.95	102.45
General Electric	206.90	205.00	369.95	237.76
Admiral	112.00	115.97	299.95	149.95
Vacuum Cleaners:				
Hoover upright	39.95	39.95	79.95	59.95
Hoover canister	26.25	24.55	49.95	28.79

[1] Retail prices are cash and do not include separately imposed finance charges.
[2] Reported as approximately wholesale cost.
Source: FTC Survey.

The general conclusion that emerges from data contained in Table 6 is that the low-income market is a very expensive place to buy durable goods. On television sets (most of which are the popular 19-inch black and white portables) the general market retailer price is about $130. In the low-income market a customer can pay up to $250 for similar sets. Other comparisons include a dryer selling for $149.95 from a general market retailer and for $299.95 from a low-income market retailer; and a vacuum cleaner selling for $59.95 in the general market and $79.95 in the low-income market.

These comparisons indicate that the poor often do pay more when they buy durable goods from retailers catering to the low-income market. Why would anyone pay such high prices? The most probable reason is that the poor often cannot pay cash for such items and are attracted by the more liberal credit policies. General market retailers offering low prices have tighter credit policies. Low-income market retailers, on the other hand, feature "easy credit," but the customer pays a great deal for this privilege in the form of grossly higher prices. Table 6 does not take into consideration the finance charges.[11] As shown in Chapter III [full report], finance charges of low-income market retailers are generally somewhat higher than those of general market retailers.

Low-income market retailers often can recover the wholesale costs of merchandise when less than half the payments have been made. For example, suppose a customer buys the Motorola television listed in Table 6 from a low-income market retailer. He pays $219.95 plus finance charges. Assume the customer pays one tenth or $22 down. This leaves a balance of $197.95. At a 13.5 per cent add-on rate,[12] his finance charges would be $26.72 for one year. The total amount owed would be $197.95 + $26.72 or $224.67. If the customer makes twelve monthly payments, the amount of each payment would be $18.72.

In this circumstance, were the customer to default after making only six of his scheduled twelve payments, the low-income market retailer would already have recovered more than his wholesale cost. The six payments plus the original amount down equals $134.32—compared to the wholesale cost of $109 for the TV. Even if the low-income market retailer were to make no additional charges for financing, six months of payments would be more than sufficient to cover the original wholesale cost.[13]

A general market retailer would be in a much different position if a customer defaulted after making only half his payments. Assume that he sold the same TV set for $129.95, also with one tenth, or $13 down. Using the 12 per cent add-on rate,[14] the balance including finance charges would be $130.98. Monthly payments would be $10.92 for twelve months. If the customer defaulted after six payments, the general market retailer would have received only $78.52—compared to the wholesale cost of $109.50. Thus, he (or the finance company that held the contract) would suffer a substantial loss.

OPERATING EXPENSES AND
NET PROFITS

Not all of the low-income market retailers covered in this survey maintained and submitted financial statements adequate for detailed analysis of expenses and net profit. Likewise, most of the small-volume general market retailers did not submit detailed financial statements. Of the eighteen low-income market retailers, however, ten submitted statements permitting some analysis of specific expense items. These ten low-income market retailers were matched with ten general market retailers of comparable size and mix of merchandise who submitted statements permitting a comparative analysis of expenses and profits.

A comparison of expenses and profits as a per cent of sales for the matched samples of ten low-income market retailers and ten general market retailers of furniture and appliances is shown in Table 7. The ten low-income market retailers paid only 37.8 per cent of their sales

TABLE 7. Comparison of expenses and profits as per cent of sales for 10 low-income market retailers and 10 general market retailers of furniture and appliances in the District of Columbia, 1966

Revenue component	10 low-income market retailers	10 general market retailers	DIFFERENCE IN MARGINS AND RATIOS	
			Percentage points	Per cent of total
1966 net sales	$5,146,395	$5,405,221	—	—
	Per cent	Per cent		
Operating ratios as per cent of sales	100.0	100.0	—	—
Cost of goods sold	37.8	64.5	—	—
Gross profit margin	62.2	35.5	+26.7	100.0
Salary and commission expense[1]	28.2	17.8	+10.4	38.9
Advertising expense	2.1	3.9	−1.8	−6.7
Bad-debt losses[2]	6.7	.3	+6.4	24.0
Other expenses[3]	21.3	11.2	+10.1	37.8
Total expenses	58.3	33.2	+25.1	94.0
Net profit return on sales	3.9	2.3	+1.6	6.0

[1] Includes officer's salaries.
[2] Includes amounts held back by finance companies to cover bad-debt losses.
[3] Other expenses, including taxes, after deduction of other income.

Source: FTC Survey.

revenue for the merchandise they sold, while the cost of goods sold by the general market retailers was 64.5 per cent of their sales revenue. As previously noted, low-income market retailers sell comparable merchandise at much higher retail prices, which accounts for this wide difference in cost of merchandise as a percentage of sales. The remaining gross margin for the ten low-income market retailers was 62.2 per cent and for the ten general market retailers, 35.5 per cent of sales. The gross margin to cover expenses and net profit was 26.7 percentage points higher for the low-income market retailers.

Practically all of the substantially higher gross margin of the ten low-income market retailers was offset by higher expenses and did not result in markedly higher net profit as a percentage of sales. As shown in the right-hand columns of Table 7, of the total difference in gross margin of 26.7 percentage points, 94 per cent of the difference (25.1 percentage points) was accounted for by higher expenses and 6 per cent of the difference (1.6 percentage points) was accounted for by higher net profits on sales of low-income market retailers.

More than one third (38.9 per cent) of the higher gross margin of the ten low-income market retailers was spent on salary and commission expense. This expense item included all employees' compensation and officers' salaries and was 28.2 per cent of sales for low-income market retailers, compared to 17.8 per cent of sales for general market retailers. A major reason for low-income market retailers' higher personnel expense is believed to be their use of outside salesmen who canvass house-to-house or follow-up requests for home demonstrations and often make collections of installment payments at the home of the customer. Several of the ten low-income market retailers pay their outside salesmen-collectors commissions on both sales and collections. Other reasons for higher personnel costs of low-income market retailers could be that they have more sales personnel and pay higher rates of compensation compared to small-volume general market retailers; and since they finance all or a larger proportion of their own installment contracts, they require more employees to keep records of small payments on installment credit accounts.

The proportion of sales revenue spent on advertising was higher for the ten general market retailers than for the ten low-income market retailers. This is consistent with the lack of extensive citywide advertising among the low-income market retailers in the total sample. The difference in advertising ratios was 1.8 percentage points. The ten general market retailers spent 3.9 per cent of their sales revenue on advertising, while the advertising by the ten low-income market retailers amounted to 2.1 per cent of their sales revenue.

Higher bad-debt losses of low-income market retailers accounted for about one fourth (24 per cent) of the total difference in gross margins. It was evident from analysis of financial statements, finance charges, and retail prices of low-income market retailers that they often charge higher prices anticipating that part of the increased revenue will cover higher collection expenses of their method of doing business. For the group of ten low-income market retailers, bad-debt loss was 6.7 per cent of sales, while comparable size general market retailers had bad-debt losses of less than 1 per cent of sales.

Other expenses accounted for more than one third (37.8 per cent) of the higher gross margin of low-income market retailers. The remaining items of expense amounted to 21.3 per cent of sales for the ten low-income market retailers and to 11.2 per cent of sales for the ten general market retailers. Items of occupancy, delivery, and administrative expense were included among the other expenses, but a comparative analysis of these items could not be made because of inconsistency in expense account classifications and accounting methods. Nevertheless, there were certain items of expense that appeared more often and in larger proportionate amounts on the low-income market retailers' statements, which account for part of their higher ratio of other expenses to sales. Since most of the low-income market retailers financed their own installment sales, the expense of processing this credit and interest on borrowed funds appeared as substantial items on their statements. Legal and professional fees were larger items of expense among low-income market retailers, reflecting cost of suits filed for the collection of delinquent accounts. Insurance costs were generally higher as a percentage of sales for these retailers.

Net profit as a percentage of sales for the ten low-income market retailers was 3.9 per cent, as compared to 2.3 per cent for the ten general market retailers. This difference of 1.6 percentage points in higher net profit for the low-income market market retailers amounted to less than one tenth (6 per cent) of the total difference in gross margins. The business methods employed by low-income market retailers involved substantially higher costs which offset the higher prices charged, leaving no markedly higher net profit as a percentage of sales.[15]

Net profit after taxes as a per cent of owner equity was also determined for these two groups of retailers. This average net profit was 12.7 per cent for the ten low-income market retailers and 8.1 per cent for 9 out of the 10 general market retailers.[16] The variation in rates of return on owner's equity within each group of retailers was so great as not to warrant a conclusion that rates for one group were different from those of the other.

OVERALL NET PROFIT COMPARISONS

The previous section compared profits for a selected sample of ten low-income market and ten general market retailers. Less extensive data on income and profits were obtained from other retailers. Almost half the retailers surveyed submitted profit and loss statements and balance sheets. The companies included corporations, partnerships, and proprietorships. There was a considerable amount of variation in the accounting methods used and in individual firm returns. Nevertheless, it is possible to make some overall comparisons of net profits for each group of retailers. Low-income market retailers reported the highest net profit after taxes on net sales, 4.7 per cent (Table 8). Among the general market retailers, department stores were highest with 4.6 per cent. Furniture and home-

TABLE 8.   Net profit after taxes as a per cent of sales and rates of return after taxes for District of Columbia retailers surveyed, 1966

Type of retailers	Net profit after taxes as a per cent of sales	Per cent of rate return after taxes on stockholder's equity
Low-income market retailers	4.7	10.1
General market retailers:		
Appliance, radio, and television stores	2.1	20.3
Furniture and home-furnishings stores	3.9	17.6
Department stores	4.6	13.0

Source: FTC Survey.

furnishings stores earned a net profit after taxes of 3.9 per cent; and appliance, radio, and television retailers were last in order of profitability with 2.1 per cent profit after taxes on sales.

Low-income market retailers reported an average rate of return after taxes on net worth of 10.1 per cent. Rates of return on net worth varied considerably among general market retailers. Appliance, radio, and television retailers reported the highest rate of return after taxes, 20.3 per cent of net worth. Next in order were furniture and home-furnishings retailers with 17.6 per cent, and department stores with 13 per cent return on net worth.

Data on profits reported above are limited and to some extent inconclusive. It does not appear, however, that low-income market retailers made profits which were substantially higher on the average than general market retailers. The high prices charged by low-income market retailers must have been accompanied in many instances by substantially higher costs arising from their method of doing business. Some of these costs probably arose from greater losses on credit sales. To some extent, costs may have been higher because of smaller volume and generally more costly and less efficient store operation.

Poverty, Minorities, and Consumer Exploitation

Frederick D. Sturdivant
and
Walter T. Wilhelm

A number of reports, ranging from informal studies by journalists to carefully researched investigations, have provided evidence that residents of ghettos pay more for their consumer goods than do other Americans.[1] For example, David Caplovitz' study of 464 families living in three New York settlement houses revealed a consistent pattern of high prices, poor quality, high interest charges, and unethical merchandising techniques. He concluded that "The problems of low-income consumers stem from the same set of forces

Reprinted from "Poverty, Minorities, and Consumer Exploitation," *Social Science Quarterly* (December, 1968), pp. 643–650, by permission of the Southwestern Social Science Association.

See pages 286–287 for all footnotes to this chapter.

that have created that special system of sales-and-credit—the quasi-traditional economy—catering to their wants."[2] In California, The Governor's Commission on the Los Angeles Riots tended to reinforce this view. Following three months of investigation into the causes of the Watts riots, the Commission reported, "our conclusion, based upon an analysis of the testimony before us and on the reports of our consultants, is *that consumer problems in the curfew area are not due to systematic racial discrimination but rather result from the traditional interplay of economic forces in the marketplace, aggravated by poverty conditions.*"[3] (Emphasis added.) These studies suggest, therefore, that the market system works to the disadvantage of the poor because they are poor—not because of race or ethnicity. Any correlation between minority group status and exploitation is, according to these studies, attributable to the high incidence of poverty among minorities rather than some insidious form of discrimination.

The studies reported to date, however, have not provided adequate proof to support this conclusion. The California Commission, for example, reached its conclusion without conducting a series of comparative shopping analyses between ghetto and non-ghetto stores and utilizing shoppers of various racial and ethnic backgrounds. Instead, staff consultants and their research assistants "spot checked" prices in various locations throughout central Los Angeles.[4] Caplovitz did analyze certain of his data utilizing the variable of minority group status. His findings in this area, however, were unclear. On the one hand he noted, "The amount paid for appliances differs greatly among the racial [*sic*] groups. Whites pay the least, Puerto Ricans the most, with Negroes in between."[5] However, Caplovitz then noted that nonwhites tended to pay lower prices when the purchase is for cash. In fact, his data suggested that nonwhites paid less than whites when buying on credit in large stores outside the ghetto. This conflicting evidence was derived from the shopping experiences of the 464 cooperating families. The variables of method of payment, minority group status, and type of store were considered. However, *brand and model variations were not taken into account.* Thus, one does not know whether whites generally selected more expensive models and brands or if this shopping behavior was characteristic of either the Negroes or Puerto Ricans studied. Unless the variable of product brand and model is held constant, meaningful price comparisons cannot be made unless one subscribes to the rather risky assumption that brand or product quality selection is randomly distributed among the various ethnic and racial groups. In essence, the statement that exploitation in the marketplace is a function of economic status rather than minority group status is still untested.

RESEARCH DESIGN AND METHODOLOGY

The study was conducted in Los Angeles and involved the use of three couples and three shopping areas. The three couples represented the major populations of the city—Negro, Mexican-American, and Anglo-White. The shopping districts were the predominately Negro south central section of Los Angeles (which includes Watts), the Mexican-American section of east Los Angeles, and Culver City, a middle-class, Anglo-White community.

The criteria used in selecting the couples included not only minority group status, but also comparable "credit profiles." The similarity of their profiles was designed to neutralize any price or credit differentials based on alleged risk. The characteristics of the shoppers' credit profile are noted in Figure 1.

The stores selected for comparative shopping in the Negro and Mexican-American sections were determined, in part, on the basis of detailed studies of consumer shopping patterns in those areas. Appliance and furniture stores in the two areas were arrayed on the basis of shopping frequency patterns determined from nearly 2,000 consumer interviews conducted in an earlier study of Watts and East Los Angeles.[6] Stores were then either included in the sample or eliminated from the list depending on the presence or absence of the same brands and models available in the control area. Culver City was selected as the non-poverty shopping area because the composition of its retailing community and price structure typified shopping conditions for suburban Los Angeles area communities.

The attrition rate for stores to be included in the study was rather high because of the difficulty of finding the same brands and models in the disadvantaged areas versus Culver City. Comparative pricing analyses involving poverty areas and more prosperous sections in a city are very difficult because of variations in merchandise. When national brands are carried by a ghetto appliance dealer, he generally stocks only the lower end of the line. Retailers in higher income

Family Status	Married, 1-2 children
Age of head of household:	25-30
Employment:	Employed full time for 1-2 years on present job
Gross Income:	$2,850 to $3,250
Savings:	$0 to $100
Total Assets:	$300 to $450
Indebtedness:	$200 to $500
as % of gross income:	6.6% to 16%
as % of assets:	67% to 111%

FIGURE 1.   Shoppers' Credit Profile.

areas usually concentrate on the middle and upper price ranges of the product line. Furthermore, off-brand merchandise tends to make up a substantial part of the ghetto dealer's stock. Since these lines generally are not carried in other areas, direct price comparisons are impossible. Among the stores frequented by the residents of the two poverty areas, therefore, only six carried brands and models capable of direct price comparisons with stores in the outside community. The stores selected in the outside area were comparable to the ghetto stores in terms of size and estimated sales volume.[7]

The shopping procedure involved the selection of a 19-inch, black and white, portable TV set by each couple in each of the nine stores. Each couple (the order was determined randomly) selected a predetermined TV set and did everything necessary to obtain price data, except sign the contract. The shopping trips to each store were separated by a minimum of three days to avoid any suspicion by the sales clerks or management. The shopping was conducted during the last two weeks of July and the first week of August, 1967. A final briefing was given the similarly attired couples before they entered each store to make certain they selected the correct model. A typical dialogue in the store might be described as follows:

SALESMAN: May I help you?

SHOPPERS: Yes, we would like to see your portable TV's.

SALESMAN: They are right over here. Did you have anything special in mind? Color?

SHOPPERS: No, we want a black and white set.
(The shoppers look at several sets and then ask about the preselected set.)

SHOPPERS: This is a nice set. It is the type we had in mind.

SALESMAN: It is a very nice set. We could deliver it today.
(Salesmen often attempted to get the shoppers interested in a more expensive model.)

SHOPPERS: How much does it cost?

SALESMAN: (quotes the price)

SHOPPERS: How much would it run us a month?
The salesman figures out the credit terms. The couple specify that they want the smallest down payment and the lowest possible payments. Upon being told the monthly payment figure, the wife says they should think it over and asks the salesman to write down the credit terms. [Only one store refused this request saying that such information was "confidential and not allowed out of the store."]

In sum, the method included the selection of six of the most frequently used furniture and appliance stores in the two major poverty areas of Los Angeles for comparison with three stores selected on the basis of brand and model availability from an average suburban community. Fundamental to the method was the use of three disadvantaged couples, representing the three major population groups in the area, with basically the same credit characteristics. The three couples dressed in basically the same mode, shopped in the same stores, and priced exactly the same products. Thus, the only relevant variable not held constant was minority group status.

FINDINGS

In the process of testing for discrimination in the marketplace, data were collected which again confirm the presence of higher prices in ghetto stores. Ignoring the question of minority group status for the moment, Table 1 indicates that the average price asked the three couples for a given product was always higher in the disadvantaged area stores than in the control area (Culver City). The total cost or the credit price (shown in parentheses), averaged higher in the poverty areas as well.

TABLE 1. Average Retail and Credit Price for Portable TV Sets, by Area and by Brand

PRODUCT	AVERAGE PRICE[1]		
	Watts Area	East L.A. Area	Control Area
ZENITH X1910	$170 ($194)	—	$130 ($190)
OLYMPIC 9P46	$270 ($448)		$230 ($277)
RCA AHO668	$148 ($174)	—	$115 ($154)
ZENITH X2014	—	$208 ($251)	$140 ($190)

[1] Prices are averages computed from the shopping experiences of the three couples in each of the stores selected. Retail prices refer to the price asked for the product before adding on credit charges. Credit prices, *shown in parentheses*, are the total of retail prices, sales tax, and interest charges.

While there were notable differences in prices between areas, there was an observable consistency in retail prices within the stores.[8] Among the prices recorded in Table 2, 19 of the 24 retail prices asked for the four models of TV sets were the same, regardless of minority group status. The prices asked the couples in the three Watts area stores were identical. In the control area, Store No. 1 increased the price by $10 for both the Negro and Mexican-American couples. In this case, the Negro couple shopped the store first and was asked $119 for RCA Model AH0668. Four days later, the Anglo couple was offered the same set for $109. After a wait of another three days, the Mexican-American couple shopped the store and was asked $119 for the set. The other six shopping trips in the control area produced identical prices for all three couples. The Mexican-American area showed the greatest variation in prices. In part, this practice may be attributable to cultural patterns in the Mexican-American community where higgling and haggling is more common. There was no pattern of discrimination. In Store No. 1 the

TABLE 2. Retail[2] and Credit[3] Prices Portable TV Sets by Area, Store, Brand, and Race

Area & Store	ZENITH–X1910			OLYMPIC–9P46			RCA–AH0668			ZENITH–X2014		
	Negro	M-A	Anglo	Negro	M-A	Anglo	Negro	M-A	Anglo	Negro	M-A	Anglo
East L.A.												
Store 1												
Store 2[1]												
Store 3				$200 ($265)	$240 ($281)	$230 ($284)				$210 ($245)	$210 ($250)	$204 ($258)
Watts												
Store 1	$170 ($194)	$170 ($194)	$170 ($194)									
Store 2							$148 ($178)	$148 ($169)	$148 ($174)			
Store 3				$270 ($412)	$270 ($507)	$270 ($418)						
Culver City												
Store 1							$119 ($172)	$119 ($169)	$109 ($122)			
Store 2										$140 ($183)	$140 ($183)	$140 ($203)
Store 3	$130 ($145)	$130 ($152)	$130 ($140)									

[1]The model preselected for this store was sold before the experiment was completed.
[2]Retail prices refer to the price asked for the product before adding on interest charges.
[3]Credit prices, *shown in parentheses,* are the total of retail prices plus interest.

114

Mexican-American couple was asked the highest price while in Store No. 3 the Mexican-American and Negro couples were charged a slightly higher price than the Anglo couple.

When credit prices are considered, however, it becomes clear that credit and carrying charges are the devices most commonly used to exercise exploitation. In the East Los Angeles stores, for example, the Anglo-White couple was not quoted the highest retail prices, but they were charged the highest credit price in both stores. In all nine cases in the control area there were differences in credit charges even though the retail price differed in only Store No. 1. The most blatant case of discrimination occurred in Culver City Store No. 1. While the legal limit on interest is 10 per cent on a twelve-month install-ment contract in California, the Mexican and Negro couples were asked to pay 42 and 44 per cent respectively.[9] The Anglo couple was asked the legal rate. In Store No. 3 in Culver City, the two minority group couples were also charged a higher (and illegal) rate of interest. In Store No. 2 all three couples were charged an illegal rate with the Anglo couple being charged the highest amount.

In the predominately Negro area stores, where all three couples had been asked identical retail prices in the three stores, only one store charged the same legal rate of interest on its eighteen-month installment contracts. There were minor variations in the charges assigned by Store No. 2, with the Negro couple charged the highest amount and the Mexican shoppers the lowest. At Store No. 3 the retail price was quoted at $270 before tax. Adding tax at 5 per cent, the total retail price before financing should have been $283.50. Deducting the required minimum down payment of $15.80, the total to be financed was $267.70. At the legal rate of 15 per cent for an eighteen-month contract interest charges would have amounted to $40.16 for a total price of $322.66. However, the total price to the Anglo and Negro couples was approximately $420, or an interest rate of nearly 50 per cent. The total cost to the Mexican couple was $506.62 with charges of 82 per cent.[10]

SUMMARY AND CONCLUSIONS

In spite of the difficulties associated with finding identical pro-ducts in ghetto and non-ghetto stores, this study has attempted to determine the basis of price discrimination experienced by disadvantaged shoppers in the marketplace. The research question was, "Is exploitation in the marketplace a function of low income or minority group status?" By selecting three pairs of disadvantaged shoppers whose only significant difference was their race and ethnicity and having these couples shop in the same stores for identical merchandise, the research design attempted to answer this question.

The findings demonstrate that installment purchases, which especially characterize the purchasing behavior of the disadvantaged, produce major variations in the prices paid by the poor. Although no perfect pattern of discrimination based on minority group status emerged from the study, it should be noted that it was common for the couples to be charged higher credit costs when shopping outside of their own areas. In East Los Angeles, the Anglo couple received the highest charges. In the Watts area, the store charging the highest and most varied prices asked a substantially higher price of the Mexican couple. In two of the non-ghetto stores the minority shoppers were charged higher and illegal amounts.

The findings indicate that merchants find credit charges an excellent vehicle for exercising economic and racial or ethnic discrimination, but Table 2 demonstrates that however substantial and illegal many of these charges may be, they are not as significant as price variations between disadvantaged and prosperous areas. While the minority couples were subjected to discriminatory pricing in two of the three control area stores, in no case did they pay more than they would have paid in ghetto stores for the same merchandise. In most instances the prices were substantially less. It might be concluded that disadvantaged minority shoppers pay more, but especially in the ghetto.

The presence of high business costs, parasitic retailers, and the dominance of inefficient "mom-and-pop" firms in the ghetto underline the importance of comparative shopping by the disadvantaged. At the same time, the willingness of certain "outside" retailers to take advantage of the poor, especially members of minority groups, suggests that the disadvantaged are still subject to economic exploitation even when shopping beyond the boundaries of the ghetto.

Notwithstanding the difficulties of designing a test of minority groups and economic exploitation (a parallel study of automobile prices had to be abandoned in this project), additional studies should be undertaken. Experiments involving this phenomenon in other major American cities would provide a more complete understanding of these practices. Doubtless, this situation is not unique to Los Angeles, and the extent to which it is reflective of a national pattern of discrimination against the minorities and the poor it is deserving of further analysis and correction.

Prices in Poor Neighborhoods

Phyllis Groom

Recent endeavors to protect consumers against misrepresentation and lack of information have led to charges that the poor pay more for what they buy than those who are better off.[1] As part of the investigation of this question, the Bureau of Labor Statistics was asked to find out whether merchants charged higher prices in low-income neighborhoods than in better-off areas.[2] The full reports of three surveys it made will be published; this article presents some of the findings, along with work of the Bureau and others that bear on the question. In general:

1. For equivalent rents, poor families get poorer housing than families with higher incomes.

2. Food prices are associated with the kind of store rather than with the geographic area. In buying food, the poor pay more if they

Reprinted from "Prices in Poor Neighborhoods," *Monthly Labor Review* (October, 1966), pp. 1085–1090, of the Office of Publications, Bureau of Labor Statistics.

See pages 287–288 for all footnotes to this chapter.

shop in the small independent stores rather than in the large independents and the chain stores, whose prices are lower. In poor neighborhoods, small sizes are more popular than the relatively cheaper large sizes.

3. For clothes, appliances, and other items, the survey results are inconclusive. What is confirmed is that the poor do not buy the same items as the better off.

These conclusions are based on data from a 1960–61 survey of housing units, the pricing in the spring of 1966 of eighteen food items in chain stores and large and small independent stores, and of sixteen other items in department stores, appliance stores, clothing stores, and drug stores. In the six cities surveyed,[3] the sample for food consisted of fifteen stores in the low-income area and fifteen in the higher income area. Eight stores in each area were surveyed for the other items.

The low income and higher income areas were classified by 1960 social and economic census data, the most recent available. The stores surveyed for low-income buying were in the lowest quartile area of the city according to income, education, and rate of unemployment and, where possible, in areas representing the lowest part of that quartile. To represent higher income buying, stores were selected from stores regularly priced for the Consumer Price Index in the rest of the city.

As a yardstick for measuring the data in the following discussion, shelter and food each take about 30 per cent of the income of non-farm families with "low consumption patterns."[4] Among these families, the uneducated, the unemployed or underemployed, and the Negro or other minorities predominate. Those with incomes of less than $2,000 after taxes have an average age of sixty-three. In the $2,000 to $3,000 a year income class, families are twice as likely as the lowest income families to include children under eighteen years of age.[5]

POOR FAMILIES HAVE POORER HOUSING

Generally, the space provided and the condition of owned dwellings is better than those of rented dwellings, but fewer than 40 per cent of urban families with incomes under $3,000 own their own homes.[6] Sixty per cent of the families with higher incomes are homeowners. In 1960, a fourth of the urban families with incomes under $3,000 lived in housing that was dilapidated or lacked plumbing (i.e., hot and cold running water, private toilet, or inside bathroom facilities). Only 6 per cent of the owners and 13 per cent of the renters with income over $3,000 occupied such housing. This is the overall picture, one which is brought into focus even more vividly by the BLS analysis.

It shows that poor families[7] get less for their rent dollar than higher income families, considering condition of the housing, heating and plumbing facilities, number of rooms, and the quality of the neighborhood.[8] (Some poor families do acquire standard housing. What it costs them in terms of undernourished children, pooled living arrangements for the elderly, and unmet health needs has been put most cogently in Alvin L. Schorr's *Slums and Social Insecurity.*[9])

Nearly 80 per cent of the $40 to $60 a month apartments occupied by the lowest income families in Houston were deteriorating or dilapidated according to criteria established by the Bureau of the Census. On the other hand, only 21 per cent of the apartments in the same rent range that were occupied by families with incomes of $3,000 to $6,000 were dilapidated or deteriorating. While this is the most extreme example, in all cities studied, the higher the family income, generally, the less likely that the dwelling (at any given rent level) was rundown. The chances of a low-income family occupying a sound structure at a low rent level were much better in New York. Studies of the prevalence of subsidized housing and policies of enforcement of antidiscrimination laws and housing codes in the six cities should contribute some insight to these statistics. New York City, which has a form of rent control, has relatively more public housing than other major cities.

Most dwellings had some sort of heating system, although in all cities except Chicago some units in the lowest rent range, occupied by those whose incomes were less than $3,000, had no heat. Generally, the higher the income, the more likely the family was to have central heating. But in New York, 5 per cent of the $40 to $60 apartments occupied by families with incomes of $3,000 to $6,000 had no heat, while all of those occupied by families with less income had heat.

Although most rented dwellings had one or more private bathrooms, a large percentage of those of lower income people than those of higher income families lacked complete toilet facilities. In the $80 to $100 rent class in New York, where all units had hot and cold running water, nearly 12 per cent of the families with incomes lower than $3,000 did not have complete bathroom facilities, compared with less than 7 per cent in the $3,000 to $6,000 income range.

Half of the apartments of Atlanta residents with less than $3,000 income whose housing cost less than $40 a month did not have hot water. On the other hand, only 20 per cent of the homes of families receiving between $3,000 and $6,000 renting in this range did not have hot water. The variation was greater in Atlanta than in most of the cities, but except in New York (where everyone had hot and cold water) the poor lack hot and cold water more often than the others in the low-rent ranges.

Less than 40 per cent of the $40 to $60 rental housing occupied by families with less than $3,000 income was in areas labeled ordinary residential or better by the BLS agents, as contrasted with over 70 per cent of those with incomes between $3,000 and $6,000. The differences are not as extreme in other cities, but at a given rent level, as one's income goes up, one's chances of living in undesirable or slum neighborhoods goes down, and the probability of living in ordinary, good, or exclusive areas rises. Again, in New York the income level does not appear to be as important a criterion as it is in other cities.

As might be expected from the other data, the number of rooms occupied at a given rent level tends to increase as family income goes up. There are some variations, however, which may reflect a tendency for smaller families to choose better quality housing rather than more rooms.

FOOD

The BLS survey found no significant differences between average food store prices in poor neighborhoods and those in better-off areas, when the same types of stores (chains, large independents, small independents) and the same quantities and qualities of food were compared. This is a rather empty conclusion, since BLS price agents found very few chains in very low-income areas.

Prices

Median food prices in the chain stores were the same; average prices in the small independent stores were little different in the two income areas, and the same held true for the large independents. However, the survey showed that in both income areas the small independent store prices averaged higher than those of the large independent or the chain store.

Although the cost of the market basket, wherever priced, was little different in stores of the same type, there was usually a rather wide dispersion in price of any given item. Analysis showed that the extremes in both the high- and the low-price ranges were scattered among the eighteen commodities surveyed. To illustrate: While the price of coffee may have varied widely from low-income area stores to high-income stores it was not consistently high nor consistently low in either area and in one area it might be coffee that was high and in the next it might be sugar.

Quantities Bought

Five of the eighteen food commodities studied—flour, milk, sugar, bread, and cola drinks—were commonly found to sell in smaller amounts in poor neighborhoods than in higher income areas. The brands bought were likely to be different, too. Stores in low-income areas frequently reported two pounds of flour as the volume seller, but a few in Atlanta reported ten pounds as the most popular quantity. The most commonly purchased amount bought in better-off neighborhoods was five pounds.

Quality and Service

Price collectors found that meat and produce were not as fresh in poor areas and that the stores were less clean and orderly. The survey supported the common allegation that the condition of fresh produce in stores in poor areas is inferior to that in other areas. There was no way to tell whether this was due to the shipment of poor quality goods to these stores, to slower turnover, less care by store management, or rougher handling of merchandise by customers.

All stores marked prices on most commodities, although in a

relatively few stores, prices were not marked for certain categories of goods. Generally, unmarked items were those that were either highly perishable or subject to frequent price change. Nonmarking was so infrequently reported in both income areas no valid comparisons could be attached to this characteristic, although there did appear to be a tendency for fresh fruits and vegetables to be marked less frequently in outlets in low-income areas and prices of fresh milk and eggs to be unmarked more frequently in higher income areas.

The Food Bill

If the price relationships among the three types of stores are representative of the relationships for the full range of food purchases of poor families, it is likely that the poor do pay more because of the differences in the kinds of stores where they shop and the quantities they buy. To draw any more precise inferences it would be necessary to have information on the volume and distribution by food sales, income area, and family expenditures by type of store and geographic area within the city.[10]

SHOPPING FOR CLOTHES AND APPLIANCES

From what is left of their income after food and shelter are paid for, the poor buy clothes, furniture, appliances, medical care, and other necessary goods and services. Here the BLS survey ran into difficulties. The price agents tried to get eight quotations on each of the eight items studied in the two kinds of neighborhoods, but in many cases, the volume selling variety in the poor neighborhood was not available in the better area. In one city's poor area, "only the low-end quality was available in nearly all stores." In another, "most of the independent stores carried jobber's lots." Thus, we reach the not astonishing conclusion that the poor, at least when shopping in the neighborhood, buy different kinds of articles than the more well-to-do.

Again, other methodological problems of the study reveal the actual purchase-sales practices. "The appliances priced in low-income stores in one city were 1965 models and could not be matched with models in the higher income area." In several cities, low-income area stores seemed to stock primarily used and reconditioned washing machines and TV sets.

No data were available to distribute the pricing across the various types of stores in proportion to their sales of each item. Nor was there a sufficient number of each kind in each area to match samples. While this shows up as a methodological problem in the BLS surveys, what it boils down to are illustrations that the same kinds of stores may not be available in both areas. For example, few department stores were found in poor neighborhoods.

To the extent that prices of identical items could be compared, the findings were as follows:

Drugs

Prescription drugs show widespread price differences by area and by stores within an area. For example, in Washington, prices ranged from \$1.30 to \$2.45 in poor areas for the same brand and quantity of sulfisoxazole tablets and from \$0.75 to \$2.15 in the higher income areas. Price differences among stores within an income area also were apparent in other cities. The average relationships reflect considerably lower prices in the low-income areas in three cities but higher prices in similar areas of the other three.

Instructed to obtain two prices for the prescription drug in each outlet in each of the two income areas—one by brand name and one by generic name, price agents in all six cities reported "none sold by generic name" for stores in both income areas.

For the over-the-counter drug priced in the survey, average price ratios fell within a more limited range than for the prescription drug. Again the overall picture was mixed, i.e., lower prices were charged for the volume selling quality of the aspirin-salicylate compound in the low-income area in four of the six cities, but higher prices for cough syrup in the low-income areas in five of the six. Individual store price differences again were apparent.

Clothing

The difference in the prices charged by stores in the two income areas was negligible when the same quality, brand, and style of clothing were compared. Analysis of the data indicated that the inability in many cases to price the same quality/brand/style in both income areas was not solely the result of a wide variance in the merchandise price lines available in the two areas; rather it appeared to reflect the complexity of the market, i.e., the large number of brands and style lines within brands currently on the market. In only three instances was the same brand/style reported as the high volume selling quality by more than one store within a city. Similarly, in only three cases was the same brand reported in more than one city.

Household Supplies

Little price difference existed when prices from the same types of stores were compared.

Services

Data indicate that prices for two of the three service items (men's haircut and dry cleaning) are lower in the low-income areas. Prices of shoe repairs revealed no discernible patterns. Since it has not yet been possible to define quality features of such services, no comparisons of quality were attempted.

Appliances

Prices for both appliances priced—television sets and washing machines—were higher in poor neighborhoods in four cities but lower in two. Had the differences been more one-sided, our knowledge of what poor families pay would still be a patchwork, with a number of pieces missing. For one thing, the cost of appliances is affected greatly by whether the purchase is a cash or a credit transaction. While people in the middle-income groups are the ones most likely to be installment debtors, in 1963, 22 per cent of the households with incomes under $2,000 owed installment debt.[11]

CREDIT

The Bureau surveys indicated that in poor neighborhoods, 35 per cent of the food stores made credit sales and in higher income areas, 30 per cent. The relative volume of credit sales was similar in both kinds of neighborhoods.

In most cities, fewer stores priced for nonfood items in the low-income areas offered credit than similar stores in the higher income area. The per cent of clothing stores offering credit was as follows:

	Higher income area	Low income area
Atlanta	100.0	46.2
Chicago	57.1	46.2
Houston	87.5	54.5
Los Angeles	71.4	81.8
New York	81.8	68.2
Washington	88.2	63.0

The volume of sales financed by credit varied by store type. To be more specific, 74 per cent of the appliance stores located in the low-income areas reported that 50 per cent or more of the volume was accounted for by credit sales, whereas only 44 per cent of such stores in the higher income areas indicated a similar credit volume. For clothing stores, there is less difference—11 per cent of the stores in the low-income area and 17 per cent in the higher income area indicated that credit sales accounted for 50 per cent or more of total volume.

When credit was offered, most stores in both income areas required monthly payments. Repayment arrangements varied among stores but there were no reports of any appreciable differences as to frequency of payments, charges, etc. In most of the cities, agents commented on a "credit service operation" which serviced stores in both income areas. Reference was also made to stores turning the financing of purchases especially of "big ticket" items, over to banks and finance companies. The most common repayment arrangements reported were regular accounts with full payment at the end of the month or accounts requiring partial payment each month, with a service or interest charge on the balance.

The Cost of Credit

Unpaid balance charges were usually stated as 1 per cent to $1\frac{1}{2}$ per cent per month or from $8\frac{1}{2}$ per cent to 15 per cent per year in the BLS survey. The information gathered by the pricing agents thus seems to indicate that the servicing of credit is commonly handled on a citywide basis and therefore one might infer that it operates even-handedly for all. On the other hand, there are studies that suggest otherwise. A small study of installment credit plans by two Department of Agriculture economists[12] found a range of annual interest rates from 7 to 36 per cent. "There were differences related to the purpose for which the credit was used, the size of the loan, and the length of the repayment period, as well as between lending agencies." All of these have implications for the low-income buyer. A study of consumer durable purchases by Caplovitz[13] presents evidence from New York City that poor families pay more for credit. Those who are sporadically or marginally employed find it difficult to arrange credit from what Caplovitz calls the "bureaucratic" sources, such as the department store. They deal most commonly with the neighborhood merchant or the door-to-door salesman.[14] In one particularly revealing comparison on the purchase of television sets, Caplovitz found that ". . . although the higher and lower income families do not differ much in using credit to buy television sets (70 per cent of those with an income over $3,500 and 74 per cent of those with an income under that amount used credit)— they do seem to differ in what they pay for credit. The higher income families tend to pay somewhat less for credit, if we may judge from the results summarized in the following tabulation:

The joint association of income and method of payment with cost of television set (per cent paying "high price")[1]

Method of payment	Under $3,500	Over $3,500
Cash	17	14
Credit	56	47

[1] $400 or more.

"Among the cash payers, there is a difference of only 3 percentage points between the two income strata; among the credit users, the difference amounts to 9 percentage points. These differences are small, but they may reflect the dissimilarity between credit positions of the poorer families and of those better off. This may result in part from merchants putting higher markups on the goods they sell on credit to poorer families in order to compensate for their greater risk, and in part from the dependence of poor families on the more costly, because longer, payment plans."

The Caplovitz study goes on to say: "Although the use of credit has little to do with income it is closely related to where families shop. Of those who paid cash for their television sets, 70 per cent reported that they bought them outside the neighborhood, compared with the 50 per cent of those who used credit."

Although there are studies of the extent of credit buying and of the availability of credit, many questions remain to be answered. For example, the claims that higher prices are charged for items bought on credit than for those bought for cash have not yet been proved, nor is it known to what extent poor families might be affected by such practices.

Little systematic work has been done on how much of the cost of an item is attributable to its being bought on time—either by raising the selling price or by finance charges, and how these vary, particularly on goods bought in the neighborhood stores or from the door-to-door salesman. The results of a study recently begun at the Survey Research Center of the University of Michigan's Institute for Social Research should add to our knowledge of credit patterns at various income levels. Variables to be considered in this examination of the consumer use of credit include income level, stage in life cycle, amounts of savings and of debt, past debt behavior, and general economic trends.

CONCLUSIONS

The BLS survey of rents shows that the poor do not get an even break in housing. What part is due to racial discrimination and what part to variations in enforcement of housing codes, and to what extent these are exacerbated by the overall scarcity of adequate housing, is a matter for further analysis.

The food survey, which was published earlier, has created widespread comment about the need for supermarkets, with their cost advantages of centralized purchasing and distribution, in poor neighborhoods.

Few price comparisons can be made from the survey of purchases of nonfood items, but it is clear that buying habits in low-income areas differ from those in other areas.

White Withdrawal: Ghetto Merchants Shy Away from Civic Ties in Areas They Serve

Albert E. Varon, a white man who sells produce to the Negroes of Watts, is walling out danger with concrete and steel. In Chicago's West Side Negro ghetto, other white merchants are withdrawing behind walls of apathy.

Such reactions are dismaying to many whites and Negroes who had hoped for something far different in the wake of ghetto rioting in the nation's major cities. It was expected that white merchants, many of whom watched their stores go up in flames or suffer heavy damage, would react initially with fear and shock. But it also was hoped that this reaction would wear off, and that the merchants would help to make further riots less likely by taking a more active role in the affairs of the black communities they serve.

However, interviews with Negroes and whites in Los Angeles, New York, Chicago and Cleveland indicate that white merchants

Reprinted from "White Withdrawl: Ghetto Merchants Shy Away from Civic Ties in Areas They Serve," *The Wall Street Journal* (August 16, 1966), p. 1, by permission of *The Wall Street Journal*.

in these ghettos are making no special efforts to involve themselves. Indeed, many are becoming even more withdrawn. If anything, Negro complaints about price gouging and economic domination by whites are louder than ever—and with some reason, as a little comparison shopping shows. Attitudes of white merchants generally reflect resignation, fear, or indifference.

ANYTHING SHORT OF 90 mm

A good many, like Mr. Varon, are taking more physical precautions. Though his old store was burned to the ground in the bloody Los Angeles riots a year ago, he insists his customers bear him no ill will ("They call me Pop") and claims that his store burned only because fire spread from an adjoining building. But he obviously is not taking any chances; his new store, now under construction, is being built to withstand anything short of a "90 mm cannon."

This citadel of commerce is being constructed of twenty-two panels of concrete reinforced with $\frac{5}{8}$-inch steel rods, each panel weighing 18 tons. The roof will be high enough so that the wick of a Molotov cocktail thrown from the street would be snuffed out before reaching the top of the building, he hopes. Just in case it isn't, though, the roof will be covered by a layer of asbestos and surfaced with gravel. An alarm system and a night guard will complete Mr. Varon's precautions.

In Chicago, the walls apparently are psychological. After last month's riots on the heavily Negro West Side, the area's Midwest Community Council sent letters to 200 local merchants asking them to attend a meeting with Negro community leaders. Six showed up. Adrian Robeson, executive director of the council, says: "The white storekeepers in this area are living on borrowed time."

PULLING INTO THE BACKGROUND

In New York's Harlem, a Negro patrolman assigned to community relations says that fear plays a large part in white merchants' reluctance to participate in local activities. "They won't come to community meetings because they don't want to get involved in controversy," he explains.

John Robinson, Negro manager of a shoe store in central Harlem, says that white shopkeepers appear to be hiring more Negro help, but comments: "They don't want their white faces to be obvious. They're pulling further into the background rather than joining the group." Community leaders in Cleveland's Hough district note much the same reaction there.

There is deep resentment in Watts. Frederick D. Sturdivant, assistant professor of marketing at the University of Southern California, conducted a consumer survey there recently and concludes: "It would be safe to say most of the merchants in Watts failed to adapt since the riots." The most frequently heard complaint by Negroes was that the white storekeeper "treats us like animals."

Negroes in many other ghettos display antagonism against white merchants, and slights to their pride play a part in this.

Before the recent riots in Cleveland's Hough neighborhood, for example, a whiteowned supermarket was burned out. Larry Evert, white executive secretary of Cleveland's Business Men's Interracial Committee, believes the market was a target because the owner had hired a security officer to catch shoplifters. Residents confirm this. "The people resented that rent-a-cop," says one. "He reminded them that the store owner didn't trust his own customers."

AFTER HOURS SUBURBIA

There also is a deep undercurrent of resentment over the "strictly business" pattern of white proprietorship. Most merchants spend only their work day in the ghetto, giving little or none of their time to civic and social activities there. Then they return to their homes in white neighborhoods or suburbs.

William McCurin, director of the Greater Lawndale Conservation Committee, a community group in one Chicago neighborhood, says most Negroes there firmly hold the image of "Brinks trucks pulling up at the doors of all these merchants and carting the money out to the suburbs."

Some merchants say they just don't have time to participate. "I'm too busy doing business," says James Ciccia, owner of the Madison–Sacramento Drug Co. in Chicago's West Side. Mr. Ciccia recently hired a Negro pharmacist after his store was picketed by a neighborhood group. The picketing occurred after he had wounded a Negro robber in his store.

Other businessmen complain that the community and business groups in the ghettos are ineffectual, or that they don't seem to want white members anyway. Carl Pechuls, owner of a combination jewelry store and pawnshop in Watts, attended an organizational meeting of a largely Negro businessmen's association there but didn't join. "They were all sitting on their hands, not doing anything, and they wanted me to run around contacting absentee owners for them. I told them to drop dead," he says.

Theodore Casey, who owns a big independent supermarket in the riot area near Watts, hasn't become a joiner of late. "They (the Negro community) don't want to have anything to do with me, so I won't have anything to do with them," he says. Another merchant serving Watts residents sees no reason to be accommodating. "I wasn't doing anything against these people before—why should I change now?" he declares.

The insularity of white ghetto merchants rankles Negroes a good deal, but they are even more incensed about what they claim is inferior merchandise sold at high prices that they insist are inflicted upon them by these merchants. One of the bitterest complaints among Hough residents is that white businessmen raise their prices on "Mother's Day"—the tenth of each month, when mothers receive aid-to-dependent-children welfare checks.

It's clear that ghetto Negroes in a number of cities have to pay more for some items than whites. Mark Levins, white owner of a Chicago camera and sporting goods shop, says: "Sure, some merchants are exploiting the Negroes. They have a legitimate complaint about that. We sell a wrist watch for $19 that's being sold just down the street for $99 on a credit plan. Because a lot of Negroes here aren't educated doesn't mean I should take advantage of them."

"NOT INTERESTED IN PRICE"

Carl Murphy, a Negro who owns Carl's TV Service in Chicago, charges that white competitors have sold stereo TV combinations usually retailing at $319 for $500. "Sometimes they sell used sets for new," he alleges. "Many of the people in this area have come from the South recently and they're not interested in price; just so it's no money down."

Higher food prices are a major gripe of ghetto Negroes. A comparison between prices of a dozen items at two outlets of one store chain, one in Harlem and one in a white neighborhood of Manhattan, shows that Harlem shoppers must pay more for half of them. The marked-up items include one brand each of coffee, eggs, milk, spaghetti, aluminium foil, and breakfast cereal. Five items carried the same price tags in both stores and only one—a brand of beer—was cheaper in Harlem. In Watts, Professor Sturdivant of USC found that one supermarket chain with an outlet in the riot area charged 3 per cent more per average item than another store near posh Beverly Hills.

In Cleveland, comparison shopping between two Pick-N-Pay markets owned by Cook Coffee Co. showed that prices in one Hough store were higher on one brand each of mayonnaise (pint jar), bleach, and canned corn than they were in a market in suburban Shaker Heights. But the suburbanites paid a little more for jumbo-sized eggs and a brand of pork and beans. A spokesman for Pick-N-Pay says the differences were due to "simple mechanical errors" in pricing.

ON-THE-SPOT PRICE CUT

Prices apparently can change fast at other stores in the ghetto. As one Cleveland merchant was being interviewed about alleged price gouging, a little Negro girl asked for a box of cereal. He handed it to her as the interviewer stood by, then hurriedly withdrew it to change the marked price from 51 cents to 47 cents.

Mrs. Daisy Craggett, a Negro member of the local Council on Economic Opportunity, is critical not only of higher prices but of what she regards as low-quality merchandise in Cleveland's Negro neighborhoods. She says she found one market selling "green chickens" and planned to picket the store but never got the chance. The merchant was burned out in the riots.

Some merchants—but very few—are candid about charging more in the ghetto. Mr. Cassey, the supermarket owner in Watts, holds up a 5-lb. bag of sugar marked at 59 cents and says: "See that? You could get that for 51 or 52 cents outside this area." He says he has to charge that much because "my customers are stealing me blind."

Many other ghetto merchants report sky-high rates of pilferage and also groan over rising insurance costs. Mr. Pechuls, the Watts jeweler-pawnbroker, paid only $144 a year for fire insurance before the riots; now he must pay $621 for the same coverage from a "risk pool" of insurance companies. His store wasn't touched, perhaps because he stood in front of it with a shotgun and revolver.

"TREMENDOUS PRICE"

In Cleveland, one tenement owner in a Negro neighborhood reports his fire insurance premium quadrupled last November. Merchants in Hough are paying "a tremendous price" for insurance now, according to Armand Robinson, director of the Cleveland Small Business and Opportunity Corp.

An economist who has conducted studies in Watts believes that retailers and their customers there are caught in a cost-price whirl. "A revolution in retailing there is necessary," he says, "to rid the section of the dilemma of the small businessman who has to charge more because of high insurance rates and crime rates, and the customer who can least afford it having to pay more." He suggests a Federal subsidy to big chains so that they could offer more reasonably priced goods in ghetto outlets, and some protection against loss should they be burned out in rioting.

While they wait for help from this unlikely quarter, many ghetto merchants are taking particular care not to offend their black customers. "You have to be extra nice so they won't have an excuse to pick you out and make trouble," says a Harlem druggist. "If a guy comes in here with 40 cents instead of 43 and wants cigarettes, I give them to him. I figure that'll stabilize him."

Others, of course, have decided to pull out of the ghetto altogether and still more would leave if they could. "I'm locked in with a five-year lease, all this inventory, and not a buyer in sight," mourns one Watts businessman.

Most of those who remain seem to believe it's enough to donate money to community or civil rights causes (quite a few white ghetto businessmen interviewed give regular donations to the National Association for the Advancement of Colored People). Almost all are pessimistic about their prospects, however, and a substantial number firmly believe that riots will recur in their areas.

OPTIMISM AT GIANT TIGER

Here and there, though, some merchants are taking a brighter view, and a few are taking part in community activities. Louis Weisberg, president of Giant Tiger Stores, Inc., in Cleveland, says one of the discount store chain's ghetto stores shortly will be remodeled at a cost of $300,000. Giant Tiger also will begin interviewing Hough residents for some 75 to 100 jobs in stores in Negro and white neighborhoods alike. Giant Tiger just completed a new store in the ghetto.

Sol Moreno, co-owner of Gus & Sol's men's clothing store in Watts, has joined the newly-formed Watts Business and Professional Men's Association. He says he didn't do it just to win community approval, but to be of real help. "Even a small collective voice gets more done than one man alone can do," he says.

Gus & Sol's also is proud of having outfitted—free of charge and from head to toe—the teenage representative of a local antipoverty organization for a trip the youth was making to Washington. Mr. Moreno says he bought his interest in the store from a former owner who "had a nervous breakdown following the riots."

Negro and Jew

Paul Jacobs

The six Negro women and I sat, talking, in an apartment in the Nickerson Garden public housing project in the heart of Watts. Outside, the kids were screaming at play and the bells of an ice cream truck kept playing the same tune, maddeningly, over and over again. The women were all friendly, for I had been brought there by someone they trusted.

They were talking about the "Jewboys," about how they get cheated, especially by one man, whom they always call "Leon the Jewboy." They explained that on the first and fifteenth of each month, "Leon the Jewboy" drives a truck into the housing project, takes out a rack filled with clothes and rolls it from door to door trying to sell them merchandise on credit. "Jewboys" weren't the same as white people to them, and when I asked them how they tell the difference, one woman patiently explained it to me, as if I was a slow-witted but nice child:

Reprinted from "Negro and Jew," Shlomo Katz (ed.), *Negro and Jew: An Encounter in America* (New York: The MacMillan Company, 1967), pp. 74–80, by permission of Paul Jacobs.

"The white man don't have time to be knockin' on no door, and that Jew, that's his stick—(as I heard her use the word "stick," I realized that here is cross-culturalization at its best or worst—a Yiddish word being used in an anti-Jewish context)—he's been doin' it for years, that's why he controls most of the money. Now I know a Jew isn't a white man and besides he talks Jew—"

Another woman interrupted, "He'll tell you, you don't have to pay me but a dollar or whatever you got, you just give it to me and I'll come back—"

"Uh-huh," said the first woman, "the white folks don't do *that*."

"You can pay him two dollars a month and he'll come back for the next twenty years," chimed in still another, as they all broke out laughing.

They vied with each other in telling me stories of how they'd been cheated, and there was even an element of bitter admiration in their description of how the "Jewboys" take advantage of their foolishness and ignorance. I asked if they ever saw any Jews in the project except the salesmen. There was a pause while they thought, and then someone said, rather incredulously, "For what? For what would they come down here? They come down here they're gonna make them some money, you know. The 'Jewboy' always done that. I remember my father used to tell about when he'd go into a store to buy a suit, and he'd put the suit on and the Jew catched it in the back and holds it and says it fits real good. And when you get home two folks can wear that coat."

They burst out laughing again, and continued regaling me and each other with stories of how they've been "taken by the Jew." They never say "Jewish," either, but always refer to "the Jew" or the "Jewboy." I asked whether any of the white storekeepers in the area cheat, too.

"They all cheat," is the answer I got. "They have to cheat 'cause we don't have nowhere else to go. If I know you don't have no-where else to go, I'll charge you what I want because you ain't got no other way to go and no transportation to go and get it. So you want it, you need it, so I'll make you pay for it. You know you're gonna buy it."

These were poor Negroes speaking, all of them either welfare recipients or women working at very low-paid jobs, and I have heard such discussions fairly often during the past year. In the area of

Los Angeles where they live, no adequate transportation system exists, so there is no place for them to do their shopping except at the fringes of the housing project. And before August, 1965, when the burning and rioting took place, most of the furniture and clothing, and a good many of the liquor and grocery stores in the area were Jewish-owned, and many of the owners did act in the way described by the women. Specifically, in addition to charging high prices for often inferior merchandise or standard brands, some shopkeepers also made the women purchase an item like a broom or a mop before they would cash their welfare checks. The liquor store owners, too, often insist that a bottle of expensive liquor be purchased before they will cash the checks.

It is difficult to estimate just how widespread among Negroes is the view of the Jew as the cheating merchant. The poor Negro's perception of a Jewish world is a very limited one; he knows little or nothing of Jewish culture, religion, or of the Jewish intellectual. No Jewish organizations function among the poor Negroes of Los Angeles. And since even middle-class or wealthy Negroes are hardly ever more than a generation removed from being either poor themselves or the children of poor Negroes, the Jew as seen by the poor remains a distinct impression, even among those who have escaped poverty.

It is difficult too, to find Negro families with more than one generation's background of education. The percentage of Negro college graduates whose parents were also college graduates is still small; the percentage of Negro high school graduates whose parents also graduated is much smaller than that of the white population, too.

When I talk with poor Negroes, it never occurs to them that I am Jewish, and when I tell them that I am, they refuse to believe it. Since they have little or no connection with the civil rights movement, they know nothing of the Jewish role in it, and the names of Mickey Schwerner or Andrew Goodman are only vaguely familiar to them. When I identify them and explain that they were two Jewish boys killed by white men in the South, they find it hard to accept.

However, the notion of the money-grubbing cheating Jew is by no means restricted to poor Negroes. A friend of mine, well educated, who works for a state agency, has written a personnel questionnaire satirizing those given by large corporations to Negro applicants for employment. Among the questions he invented was, "A new Jewish clothing store opens in the area and claims to give easy credit. It turns out that the easy credit is 65 per cent interest per month. How long will he stay in business?" His selection of answers includes: "(a) Until he gets rich. (b) Until he dies. (c) Until he retires. (d) Until the next riot."

But educated Negroes whose contact with the white society is through involvement with civil rights or improvement organizations obviously tend to reflect the attitudes most acceptable in such groups: very little anti-Jewish sentiment is expressed, and most members of this group seem to understand the important role played by some Jews in the civil rights movement. But other middle-class Negroes, aspiring to take part in the free enterprise system by becoming merchants themselves, see the Jew as a competitor who will try to undersell the Negro merchant in order to maintain a hold over the Negro market.

So the view of "Goldberg" riding around in his "Jew canoe," as a Cadillac is called by some Negroes in Los Angeles, milking the community of its money, does have some credence among Negroes, especially since that view is encouraged by a few of the fanatical Black Nationalist leaders. But among educated and even intellectual Negroes, this view of "Goldberg" is modified by reality. They know better, but their knowledge brings with it no impelling reason to proselytize about the evils of anti-Semitism among the poorer and less educated Negroes. The more cynical among them will joke about the Jewish girls who come to the ghetto; they're glad, they say, to help those girls rid themselves of their guilt.

And, despite the differentiation the women in the housing project make between Jews and white people, there is an obvious overlap in attitude toward both groups. The generalized hostility toward the whole white world takes in the Jews, too, and the specific hostility toward the Jewish merchants contributes to the generalized hate of the white world.

It is very difficult to assess how much hostility is directed toward the Jew, as being separate from the whites: my own estimate, based on only the evidence I have seen, is that the Jews are *not* the primary target of the Negroes' frustration. Instead the order of hate runs, I think, roughly about as follows: white people, police, merchants, and the Jews, as a separate group, last.

Yet the separation made between Jews and white people is disturbing. One reason usually attributed for Negro anti-Semitism is that since the Jews are the whites with whom the Negroes have the most contact, they are therefore venting their animosity toward whites on the handiest target which happens to be Jews. In this explanation, the fact that Jews owned 80 per cent of the burned and looted furniture stores; 60 per cent of the food markets and 54 per cent of the liquor stores may be taken to reflect only that a high percentage of the retail trade among Negroes was conducted by Jews, some of them cheating and unscrupulous people.

But I suspect that the distinction made between Jews and whites may have an additional basis: Negroes deal with a white world of a welfare system, the police department, the schools, the probation officers, the county hospital, the unemployment insurance office, a work situation. Perhaps the notion of the Jew as being different from the white is absorbed from daily contact with this world, and reflects the view held by the society-at-large toward the Jew. Is it possible that the place of the Jew in America is mirrored more accurately in what the Negro perceives as the "white" notion of the Jew?

Yet I want to emphasize that I have never heard of anti-Jewish sentiment expressed by Negroes about any other question than the economic one. The picture of the Jew as the Communist or beatnik seems not to exist among the Negroes; neither is the Jew regarded as an object of religious suspicion or hate, as was true in Europe. The Black Muslims, too, do not overtly preach anti-Semitism, and I have never become aware of any special degree of covert anti-Semitism among them.

What does all this add up to? Unfortunately, not a very encouraging picture, although I do not believe Negro anti-Semitism is a very serious problem at present. In the California Negro ghettos with which I am now more familiar than the eastern ones, some Negroes do identify the Jew as the exploiting, cheating merchant who derives his income from ghetto dwellers, and takes it all out with him to his fancy home someplace else. Among this group there is very little perception of the Jew in any other role than that of the businessman. At the same time, a kind of bitter admiration exists, directed toward the way in which the Jews allegedly stick together, take care of their own and wield effective political power. No significant forces exist within the ghettos combatting that view of the Jew, and I see little possibility of any developing. None of the Jewish organizations concerned with anti-Semitism have any impact in the ghettos.

In the Negro neighborhoods of Los Angeles I know best, "pushing peanuts up Goldberg's nose"—the term for teasing the Jewish storeowner—was a favorite occupation of unemployed teenagers before the fires were set and the stores emptied. But most of the burned-out Jewish stores are still empty, and now the poor Negroes are being exploited by the Chinese. If that process continues, perhaps some day I will hear the kids on the street shouting a phrase that means they're going down the corner to taunt the Chinese storekeeper.

But now I get a terrible feeling of depression of *déja vu* as I listen and argue. I have been here before, and heard these same comments all my life. I remember in the 'thirties hearing a North Dakota farmer, the militant head of a farmers' organization fighting mortgage foreclosures, inveigh against the "Jew bankers who were screwing the farmers." When I was a union organizer, I heard workers shout at people going through a picket line, "Don't go to work in a Jewshop!" And I have heard union officials, too, talk about the "Jewshop owners" and their smart "Jewboy lawyers."

I have heard the answers given by the Jewish storeowners and employers before, too. "The schwartzers steal me blind so I'm gonna charge them more." "The colored people don't make their payments, so we have to have a high rate of interest in order to make up for our losses." "In a way, I'm doing the niggers a favor selling to them. No one else will go down there and if I didn't they wouldn't have anything." And the final answer: "Business is business."

If I seem depressed in what I write, and offer little hope for change, this reflects accurately how I feel. As long as some Jewish businessmen exploit poor Negroes, they will help reinforce some Negroes' distorted and generalized view of the Jew, which is just as inaccurate as the distorted and generalized view of the Negro held by some Jews. But why should a Jewish businessman behave differently than a Christian one or one who worships Buddha? We Jews keep insisting we're no different from anyone else, don't we?

Better Deal for
Ghetto Shoppers

Frederick D. Sturdivant

However remote and unreal the newspaper photos of large numbers of looters carrying furniture, groceries, appliances, and other merchandise through the streets of many of this nation's major cities may seem, their message for U.S. business is profound. "Such poverty as we have today in all our great cities degrades the poor," warned George Bernard Shaw in 1928, "and infects with its degradation the whole neighborhood in which they live. And whatever can degrade a neighborhood can degrade a country and a continent and finally the whole civilized world . . ."[1]

Over the past two years an epidemic of this contagious disease

Reprinted from "Better Deal for Ghetto Shoppers," *Harvard Business Review* (March–April 1968), pp. 130–139, by permission of *Harvard Business Review* © 1968 by the President and Fellows of Harvard College; all rights reserved.

Author's note: The research for this study was partially supported by a National Defense Education Act grant and funds provided by the University of Southern California Research Institute for Business and Economics.

See page 289 for all footnotes to this chapter.

has struck with great violence in Los Angeles, New York, Rochester, Chicago, San Francisco, Newark, Detroit, and other large U.S. cities. There is the threat of more riots to come. A major share of the responsibility for halting the epidemic and preventing further assaults on the structure of society rests with the business community.

No informed citizen questions the presence of large numbers of people living in poverty in the United States. Indeed, most Americans have tired of the debate which attempts to quantify and measure a state of existence that is too qualitative and miserable to be measured precisely. Many companies have participated in private and governmental programs by hiring and training individuals from disadvantaged areas.[2] In fact, efforts to deal with the dilemma of the underskilled and unemployed have represented the major thrust of the business community's commitment to the War on Poverty. In some areas of high unemployment such programs have led to significant improvements in local conditions.

While few would question the importance of training and employing the disadvantaged, a fundamental point is generally ignored. *The most direct contact between the poor and the business community is at retail level.* The greatest opportunity to assist and to revolutionize the daily lives of the poor rests in the retailing communities serving poverty areas.

While it is a great step forward to create jobs for the unemployed or to train men for better-paying jobs, such improvements can be nullified when the worker and members of his family enter the marketplace as consumers. Very little may be gained if they are confronted with a shopping situation that generally offers them higher prices, inferior merchandise, high-pressure selling, hidden and inflated interest charges, and a degrading shopping environment. Such conditions are closely related to the frustrations that have produced the spectacle of looted and burned stores throughout the nation.

A TALE OF TWO GHETTOS

The first of the terribly destructive and bloody Negro riots took place in the south central section of Los Angeles in August 1965. In the aftermath of the nearly week-long Watts riots, which seemed to set the pattern for subsequent revolts around the country, it was apparent that retail establishments had been the primary target of the rioters. Of the more than 600 buildings damaged by looting and fire, over 95 per cent were retail stores. According to the report of the Governor's Commission on the Los Angeles Riots, "The rioters concentrated primarily on food markets, liquor stores, furniture stores, department stores, and pawnshops."[3]

Manufacturing firms and other kinds of business facilities in the area, which in many cases contained valuable merchandise and fixtures, were virtually untouched, as were public buildings such as schools, libraries, and churches. Not one of the twenty-six Operation Head Start facilities in the Watts area was touched.

Even a cursory survey of the damage would indicate that a "vengeance pattern" might have been followed. The various news media covering the riots reported many interviews which revealed a deep-seated resentment toward retailers because of alleged exploitation. The possibility that the rioters were striking back at unethical merchants was reinforced by the fact that one store would be looted and burned while a competing unit across the street survived without so much as a cracked window.

In the fall of 1965, facts and questions like these prompted a two-year study of consumer-business relations in two disadvantaged sections of Los Angeles:

1. As the center of the Los Angeles riots, Watts was an excellent place to begin the study. Consumers and merchants were very willing to discuss their experiences and to explore the causes of the riots. Civil rights groups and merchants' organizations were eager to cooperate with an "objective" research effort which would vindicate their respective points of view. In effect, there were a number of advantages in studying the conditions in Watts while the rubble still littered the streets and participants in the destruction were seeking to be heard.

2. But Watts by itself was not sufficient for an objective investigation. The basic retail structure of the area had been virtually destroyed, and it was impossible to contact many of the merchants who had been burned out by the rioters. In addition, feelings were so intense on both sides that the danger of distortion was greatly magnified. Since the population of the area was heavily Negro, the investigation might have become a study of exploitation of this minority rather than an analysis of the relations between business and

the poor in general. Therefore, a second study area was selected—a disadvantaged section of the Mexican-American community in east Los Angeles.

In each area, more than 25 per cent of the population fell below the government's $3,000 poverty line. In addition, each area had high unemployment (7.7 per cent for Mexican-Americans and 10.1 per cent for Negroes), a high incidence of broken homes (17.2 per cent for Mexican-Americans and 25.5 per cent for Negroes), and the many other household and community characteristics which are associated with ghettos.[4]

Over a period of two years, more than 2,000 interviews were held with consumers and merchants in these two poverty areas, numerous shopping forays were conducted, and price-quality comparisons were made with stores serving the more prosperous sections of Los Angeles and surrounding communities. Although there were a number of interesting differences between the findings in the two areas (the differences were based for the most part on cultural factors), the evidence points to two basic flaws in local retailing which were present in each of the areas:

1. The prevalence of small, inefficient, uneconomical units.

2. A tendency on the part of many stores to prey on an under-educated and relatively immobile population with high-pressure, unethical methods.

These findings, I believe, apply rather generally to the retail segments serving disadvantaged areas in U.S. cities. Let us look at each of them in more detail.

INEFFICIENT "MOMS AND POPS"

One of the cruelest ironies of our economic system is that the disadvantaged are generally served by the least efficient segments of the business community. The spacious, well-stocked, and efficiently managed stores characteristic of America's highly advanced distribution system are rarely present in the ghetto. The marvels of mass merchandising and its benefits for consumers normally are not shared with the low-income families. Instead, their shopping districts are dotted with small, inefficient "mom and pop" establishments more closely related to stores in underdeveloped countries than to the sophisticated network of retail institutions dominant in most of the U.S. economy.

With the exception of one outdated supermarket, no national or regional retailing firms were represented on the main street of Watts before the 1965 riots. Following the riots, when 103rd Street was dubbed "Charcoal Alley," not even that lone supermarket remained. On Brooklyn Avenue, the heart of the poorest section in east Los Angeles, one found such establishments as Factory Outlet Shoes, Nat's Clothing, Cruz Used Furniture, Villa Real Drugs, and Chelos Market, ranging in size from 315 square feet to 600 square feet. Of the 175 stores in the shopping district (this figure excluded service stations), only five were members of chain organizations, and two of these firms traced their origins back to a time when the neighborhood was a middle-class district.

Lacking economies of scale and the advantages of trained management, the "moms and pops" muddle through from day to day and, in the process, contribute to the oppressive atmosphere of such neighborhoods. Their customers generally pay higher prices, receive lower-quality merchandise, and shop in shabby, deteriorating facilities.

Inflated Prices and . . .

The most controversial of these conditions is pricing. The phrase, "the poor pay more," was popularized by Columbia University sociologist David Caplovitz' widely read book with that title.[5] Unfortunately, in addition to being an eye-catching title, it describes reality. While the small, owner-operated stores do not have a monopoly on high prices in the ghetto, they contribute significantly to the inflated price levels. Consumers in Watts, for example, can expect to pay from 7 per cent to 21 per cent more for a market basket of thirty items if they shop for groceries in one of the small local stores than would a family shopping in a supermarket in affluent Beverly Hills. Similar or even greater price differentials prevail in most merchandising categories.

Comparative pricing analyses of the disadvantaged area and the more prosperous sections in a city are very difficult to make because of quality differences. When national brands are carried by a ghetto appliance dealer, for example, he generally stocks only the lower end of the line. Retailers in higher income areas usually concentrate on the middle and upper price ranges of the product line. Furthermore, off-brand merchandise tends to make up a substantial part of the ghetto dealer's line. Since these lines are not carried in other areas, direct price comparisons are impossible. In food stores, the problem is particularly acute with respect to meat and produce items. Commercial grades of meat are generally carried by ghetto stores, and visual comparisons reveal major qualitative differences in the produce carried, but precise measurements of these quality distinctions are impossible.

Depressed Looks

The physical setting also does little to enhance ghetto shopping. Resentment over the appearance of stores is deeply felt in Watts. I have encountered many reactions like these:

"The manager of that grocery store must think we are a bunch of animals," charged one middle-aged Negro woman with whom I talked. She continued, "The floors are filthy, there are flies all over the place, they handle our food with dirty hands and never say thank you or nothing that's nice."

Commenting on the shabby appearance of the stores on 103rd Street, one young Negro activist said, "The merchants don't give a damn about Watts. They take our money back to Beverly Hills and never spend a cent fixing up their stores."

While such charges are influenced by emotion, the reasons for the bitterness become understandable when one takes a walk down "Charcoal Alley" with its many vacant lots, one dozen or so vacant stores, two thrift shops, six liquor stores, one dime store, one drugstore, one pawnshop, one record shop, one appliance-dry goods store, and a few bars. Although the number and variety of stores along Brooklyn Avenue in east Los Angeles is greater, 53 per cent of the stores are more than twenty years old and have had no apparent improvements made since their construction. Of these stores, 6 per cent are in obvious need of extensive repair and remodeling.

PARASITIC MERCHANTS

While the deteriorated condition of shopping facilities obviously does little to attract shoppers from outside the area, the ghettos do act as magnets for high-pressure and unethical merchandisers who become parasites on the neighborhoods. Take New York, for example. Because of the predominance of parasitic merchants in the ghettos of Manhattan, Caplovitz describes business communities there as "deviant" market systems "in which unethical and illegal practices abound."[6]

The parasitic merchant usually deals in hard goods and emphasizes "easy credit." He stocks his store with off-brand merchandise,

TABLE 1.   Ghetto shoppers pay more for appliances

Product	Prices		
	Watts area	East L.A. area	Control area
1. Zenith portable TV (X1910)	$170	—	$130
2. Olympic portable TV (9P46)	$270	$230	—
3. RCA portable TV (AH0668)	$148	—	$115
4. Zenith portable TV (X2014)	—	$208	$140
5. Emerson portable TV (19P32)	$210	$200	$170
6. Olympic color console TV (CC337A)	—	$700	$630
7. Zenith clock radio (X164)	—	$42	$19
8. Eureka vacuum (745a)	—	$35	$30
9. Fun Fare by Brown (36" free standing gas range)	—	$200	$110

Note: Prices for items 1–4 are averages computed from the shopping experiences of three couples (Mexican-American, Negro, and Anglo-White) in three stores in each of the three areas. The three couples had nearly identical "credit profiles" based on typical disadvantaged family characteristics. The stores located in the Mexican-American and Watts areas were selected on the basis of shopping patterns derived from extensive interviews in the areas.

Items 5-9 are the only prices obtainable on a 24-item shopping list. One low-income Anglo-White couple shopped 24 randomly selected stores in the disadvantaged areas.

All prices are rounded.

uses bait-switch advertising, offers low down payments and small installments, employs salesmen who are proficient at closing often and fast, and marks up his merchandise generously enough to assure himself of a very good return for his effort. Again, direct price comparisons are difficult because of brand differences, but Table 1 reflects the higher prices paid by ghetto shoppers compared with store prices in a middle to lower-middle class suburb of Los Angeles.

Data gathered on markups further confirm the presence of exploitation. The major furniture store serving the Watts area and its unaffiliated counterpart in east Los Angeles both carried Olympic television model 9P46. This model wholesales for $104. The retail price in the Watts area store was $270, a markup of 160 per cent, and $229.95 in east Los Angeles, a markup of 121 per cent. The latter store also carried a Zenith model number X1917 priced at $269.95, or 114 per cent above the wholesale price of $126.

Are such substantial markups justified because of the higher risks associated with doing business in a ghetto? It would seem that such risks are more than offset by the interest charges on the installment contract. The rates are highly volatile, but never low. A Mexican-American couple and a Negro couple with virtually the same "credit profile" shopped a number of furniture and appliance stores in the two disadvantaged areas as well as stores in the middle-class control area. An "easy payment" establishment serving south central Los Angeles applied the same high-pressure tactics to both couples, who shopped for the same television set. The retailer charged the Negro couple 49 per cent interest on an 18-month contract, while the Mexican-American couple really received "easy terms"—82 per cent interest for eighteen months!

Charges of this magnitude go well beyond any question of ethics; they are clearly illegal. In California the Unruh Retail Installment Sales Act sets the maximum rate a dealer may charge on time contracts. For most installment contracts under $1,000, the maximum service charge rate is five-sixths of 1 per cent of the original unpaid balance multiplied by the number of months in the contract. Accordingly, the legal rate for the television set selected by the two couples was 15 per cent.

While it is true that most ghetto merchants do not exceed the legal limits, their customers still pay higher credit charges because of the inflated selling prices on which the interest is computed.

How They Get Away With It

Parasitic merchants are attracted to disadvantaged areas of the cities by the presence of ill-informed and generally immobile consumers. Operating from ghetto stores or as door-to-door credit salesmen, these merchants deal with consumers who have little understanding of contracts or even of the concept of interest. Given their low-income status, one dollar down and one dollar a week sounds to the buyer like a pretty good deal. The merchants are not at all reluctant to pile their good deals on their customers with the prospect of repossessions and garnishments.

Comparative shopping outside his own neighborhood would, of course, provide a ghetto resident with a vivid demonstration of the disadvantages of trading with the local merchants. Unfortunately, the idea of comparing prices and credit terms is little understood in the ghetto. And for those residents who can appreciate the advantages of comparative shopping, transportation is often a barrier. In Watts, less than half of the households studied had automobiles. The public transportation facilities, which are inadequate at best throughout the city of Los Angeles, are archaic. Infrequently scheduled, time-consuming, and expensive bus services are of little value to the area's shoppers.

In east Los Angeles, the Mexican-Americans have greater mobility; 73 per cent of the households studied had an automobile, and bus services were better than in Watts. The Mexican-Americans also have relative proximity to modern shopping facilities. However, there are strong cultural ties that encourage residents to forgo shopping advantages offered in other areas. They choose, in effect, to be reinforced continually in the existing cultural setting by frequenting stores in the disadvantaged area where Spanish is spoken. Whether for reasons of transportation problems or self-imposed cultural isolation, the local merchant enjoys a largely captive market.

SHUNNING DEPRESSED AREAS

Not all merchants in disadvantaged areas are there for the purpose of exacting all they can from a neighborhood of undereducated and poor consumers. As noted before, many of the small shops offer their customers higher prices and lower quality because of inefficiency, not by design. The great villain, say the retailers, is the cost of doing business in disadvantaged areas. For example, it is said that small merchants normally cannot afford insurance protection. Of the merchants interviewed in Watts, fewer than 10 per cent had insurance before the riots. Retailers in slum areas have always paid higher insurance rates. According to California's insurance commissioner, rate increases of 300 per cent following the riots were not uncommon. In this respect, the riots throughout the country have only magnified the problem of good retail service, not relieved it.

Since so few small merchants attempt to insure their businesses, the major effect of the abnormally high rates is to deter larger organizations from investing in ghetto areas. An executive responsible for corporate planning for a retail chain would be hard pressed to justify building a unit in Watts or east Los Angeles when so many opportunities and excellent sites are available in fast growing and "safe" Orange County (in the Los Angeles area). A parallel could be drawn with building in the South Side of Chicago as opposed to the prosperous and rapidly expanding suburbs on the North Shore, or in virtually any central city slum area contrasted with the same city's suburbs. Large retailers not only are frightened away by insurance costs, but also point to personnel problems, vandalism, and alleged higher incidences of shoplifting in disadvantaged districts.

This is not to suggest that there are not profits to be made in such areas. Trade sources, especially in the supermarket industry, have pointed to unique opportunities in low-income neighborhoods.[7] The managements of supermarket chains such as Hillman's in Chicago and ABC Markets in Los Angeles admit that, while there are unique merchandising problems associated with doing business in depressed areas, their profit return has been quite satisfactory. It might also be noted that companies that do a conscientious job of serving the needs of low-income consumers are highly regarded. For instance, interviewees in Watts were virtually unanimous in their praise for ABC Markets. Perhaps the most dramatic affirmation of the chain's position in the community came during the riots: not one of the company's three units in the area was disturbed during the week-long riots.

My interviews with executives of Sears, Roebuck and Co. and J.C. Penney indicate that these companies have been highly successful in adapting to changing conditions in transitional areas. Those of their stores located in declining neighborhoods have altered their merchandising programs and the composition of their work forces to adjust to the changing nature of the market area. The result has been profits for both firms.

Yet, in most cases, such opportunities have not been sought out by large retailers, but stumbled on; they have been happily dis-covered by older stores trying to readapt themselves in areas where the racial and economic makeup is changing. New stores are built only in trading areas where the more traditional competitive challenges are to be found. As one executive said, "Our target is the mass market, and we generally ignore the upper 10 per cent and the lower 15 per cent to 20 per cent of the market." The upper 10 per cent, of course, can be assured that Saks Fifth Avenue, Brooks Brothers, and a host of other such firms stand ready to meet their needs. The poor, however, are left with "moms and pops" and the easy-credit merchants.

A WORKABLE SOLUTION

Most critics of business-consumer relations in disadvantaged areas have called for legislation designed to protect consumers and for consumer education programs. Indeed, laws designed to protect consumers from hidden and inflated interest charges and other forms of unethical merchandising should be passed and vigorously enforced. Consumer economics should be a part of elementary and secondary school curricula, and adult education programs should be available in disadvantaged areas. However, these approaches are hardly revolutionary, and they hold little promise of producing dramatic changes in the economic condition of the disadvantaged.

A crucial point seems to have been largely ignored by the critics and in the various bills introduced in the state legislatures and in Congress. This is the difficulty of improvement so long as the retail-ing segments of depressed areas are dominated by uneconomically small stores—by what I call an "atomistic" structure. Indeed, many legislators seem eager to perpetuate the system by calling for expanded activities by the Small Business Administration in offering assistance to more small firms that do business in the ghettos. Another common suggestion is for the federal government to offer low-cost insurance protection to these firms. This proposal, too, may do more to aggravate than relieve. If the plight of the ghetto consumer is to be dramatically relieved, this will not come about through measures designed to multiply the number of inefficient retailers serving these people.

Real progress will come only if we can find some way to extend into the ghettos the highly advanced, competitive retailing system that has so successfully served other sectors of the economy. To make this advance possible, we must remove the economic barriers that restrict entry by progressive retailers, for stores are managed by businessmen, not social workers.

How can these barriers be removed?

INVESTMENT GUARANTEE PLAN

Since shortly after the close of World War II, the federal government has had a program designed to eliminate certain barriers to investment by U.S. corporations in underdeveloped countries. In effect, the government has said that it is in the best interests of the United States if our business assists in the economic development of certain foreign countries. In a number of Latin American countries, for instance, the program has protected U.S. capital against loss through riots or expropriation. The investment guarantee program does not assure U.S. firms of a profit; that challenge rests with management. But companies are protected against the abnormal risks associated with building facilities in underdeveloped countries. If a guarantee program can stimulate investment in Columbia, why not in Watts or Harlem?

I propose a program, to be administered by the Department of Commerce, under which potential retail investors would be offered investment guarantees for building (or buying) a store in areas designated as "disadvantaged." A contract between the retail firm and the Commerce Department would guarantee the company full reimbursement for physical losses resulting from looting, burning, or other damages caused by civil disorders as well as from the usual hazards of natural disasters. In addition, the contract would call for compensation for operating losses sustained during periods of civil unrest in the area. To illustrate:

A Montgomery Ward store established in the heart of Watts would, under this program, be insured for the book value of the establishment against damages caused by natural or human events. If the firm emerged from a period of rioting without suffering any physical damages, but was forced to cease operations during the period of the riots, Montgomery Ward would be compensated for operating losses resulting from the forced closure.

COSTS AND RESTRICTIONS. The costs to a company for an investment guarantee would be minimal in terms of both financial outlay and loss of managerial autonomy. An annual fee of 0.5 per cent of the amount of insured assets would be charged. There is no actuarial basis for this rate; rather, the fees are charged to cover the costs of administering the program and building a reserve against possible claims.

There would be no restriction on either the size of the investment or the term of the guarantee contract. The contract would be terminated by the government only if the firm violated the terms of the agreement or if the economic character of the area improved to the point that it was no longer classified as disadvantaged.

In addition to paying annual premiums, the participating companies would be required to conform to state and local laws designed to protect consumers (or minimum federal standards where local legislation is not in effect). A participating retailer found guilty of violating state law regarding, let us say, installment charges would have his contract terminated.

In effect, the ethical merchandiser would find no restrictions on his usual managerial freedom. So long as he abided by the law, his investment would be protected, and he would have complete freedom in selecting his merchandise, setting prices, advertising, and other areas of managerial strategy.

Enlarged Investment Credit

The guarantee program would offer the manager maximum discretion, but it would not assure him of a profit. The guarantee phase of the program merely attempts to place the ghetto on a par with nonghetto areas with respect to investment risk. The final barrier, the high costs associated with doing business in such areas, would have to be offset by offering businesses enlarged investment credits. Credits of perhaps 10 per cent (as compared to the usual

7 per cent under other programs) could be offered as an inducement to outside retailers. Firms participating in the guarantee program would be eligible for such investment credits on all facilities constructed in disadvantaged areas.

The more generous investment credits would serve as a source of encouragement not only for building new facilities, but also for expanding and modernizing older stores that had been allowed to decline. For example, the Sears Roebuck and Penney stores located (as earlier mentioned) in transitional and declining areas would be likely targets for physical improvements.

Key to Transformation

Perhaps the most important characteristic of the investment guarantee and credit program is the nature of the relationsip that would exist between the government and the business community. The government is cast in the role of the stimulator or enabler without becoming involved in the management of the private company. The program is also flexible in that incentives could be increased or lowered as conditions warrant. If the investment credits should fail to provide a sufficient stimulus, additional incentives in the form of lower corporate income tax rates could be added. On the other hand, as an area becomes increasingly attractive as a retail location, the incentives could be reduced or eliminated.

If implemented with vigor and imagination, this program could lead to a dramatic transformation of the retail segment serving ghetto areas. While size restrictions would not be imposed, the provisions of the program would be most attractive to larger retail organizations. Thus, the "atomistic" structure of the retail community would undergo major change as the marginal retailers face competition with efficient mass distributors. The parasitic merchants would also face a bleak future. The study in Los Angeles revealed no instance in which a major retail firm was guilty of discriminatory pricing or inflated credit charges. In addition, the agency administering the investment program could make periodic studies of the practices of participating firms, and use these investigations to prod companies, if necessary, to assure their customer of equitable treatment.

CONCLUSION

No one program will solve a problem as basic and complex as that of the big-city ghetto. A variety of projects and measures is needed. While the program I propose has great potential, its promise is more likely to be realized if it is supported by other kinds of action to strengthen local businesses. For instance:

Various "activist" groups have been bringing pressure on unethical retailers. In Watts, some limited efforts have been made to boycott retailers who do not conform to a code of conduct that has been promulgated. In Washington, D.C., a militant civil rights organization, ACT, has launched a national campaign to encourage bankruptcy filings by the poor in order to deal a severe blow to parasitic retailers.

In Roxbury, Massachusetts (a part of Boston), Negroes are organizing buying cooperatives. Such cooperatives have limited potential, but many people believe they can compensate for at least some of the problems of smallness and inefficiency which plague "mom and pop" stores in the area.

Some corporate executives are trying to help Negro businessmen develop managerial knowhow. Business school students have recently got into this act, too. A group of second-year students at the Harvard Business School, with the financial backing of The Ford Foundation, is providing free advice and instruction to Negroes running retail stores and other firms in Boston. The instruction covers such basic matters as purchasing, bookkeeping, credit policy, tax reporting, and pricing.

Some large stores are reportedly considering giving franchises to retailers in ghetto areas. Assuming the franchises are accompanied by management assistance, financial help, and other advantages of a tie-in with a large company, this step could help to strengthen a number of local retailers.

Some of the large-scale renewal projects undertaken by business have, as a secondary benefit, introduced residents of run-down areas to progressive retailing. In the 1950's, a 100-acre slum section of south Chicago was razed and turned into a 2,009-apartment community with a shopping center. In the shopping center were branches of various well-known organizations—Goldblatt's Department Store, Jewel Tea Supermarket, Walgreen Drug Stores, and others. Similarly, if a group of Tampa business leaders succeed in current plans to rebuild part of Tampa's downtown business district, such leading stores as Macy's, Jordan Marsh, Bon Marche, and Sears, Roebuck plan to open branches in the new buildings. In both cases, residents of the poor areas adjoining the shopping sections would be able to take advantage of progressive retailing. Projects like the foregoing would be welcome allies of the program proposed in this article. For this program, despite its many great advantages, will not be easy to carry out. The major retailers attracted to disadvantaged areas will face many challenges. Studies will have to be undertaken to help them adapt successfully to local conditions. Creative and imaginative managers will be needed at the store level.

The new program should be good for retailers from the standpoint of profits. In addition, retail leaders should derive a great deal of satisfaction from demonstrating that U.S. enterprise is capable of contributing significantly to the solution of the major domestic crisis of the twentieth century. An efficient and competitive retail community in a ghetto would certainly discourage ineffective and unethical store managers in the area. And while the new program would not solve all of the problems of the nation's cities, it could do a great deal to reduce the injustices suffered by the poor and to eliminate the bitterness that feeds the spreading civil disorders.

TWO

CORRECTIVE ACTION AND REACTION

This section includes a number of papers offering possible solutions to the plight of the disadvantaged consumer and the problems faced by retailers attempting to serve the market in ghetto areas. Although several articles restate the basic problems and conflicts, the papers generally focus on proposed solutions and reactions to those proposals.

The article by Hencke expresses concern with the activities of certain employees of the federal government who under the provisions of the Economic Opportunity Act of 1964, have been engaging in consumer education activities. Hencke charges that these education programs are often antibusiness in nature and that they cause hostility toward merchants and in turn antagonize the business community.

The Governor's Commission on the Los Angeles Riots notes that consumer complaints were frequently heard during their investigation of the causes of the Watts riots. The Commission suggests a four point program aimed at solving the major problems of the ghetto consumers. The report concludes that these problems are not due to systematic racial discrimination, but rather to the traditional economic forces that are at work in poverty areas. Consumer education and protection are the basic approaches recommended.

The *Food Topics* article focuses on the important subject of food distribution in low-income urban areas. It is generally recognized that the lack of efficient, high-volume chain supermarkets in ghettos is a cause of higher food prices to those least able to pay. The article discusses the need for involvement by supermarket chains in such areas. It also presents information on the obstacles and problems that restrict entry into low-income neighborhoods. Successful supermarket operations, however, such as ABC Markets in south-central Los Angeles, are discussed. The article concludes that if the private sector does not assume its responsibility in low-income districts, the government will become more directly involved in grocery retailing.

Shortly before his death, Senator Robert Kennedy's program for business development in ghetto areas was entered in the *Congressional Record*. Although he viewed education and housing as important factors in the urban problem, the late senator felt new jobs and opportunities for private investment must be emphasized. His plan called for government to aid existing business through tax credits to encourage job-creating investment in poverty areas. In addition, Kennedy proposed a program of federal loans, interest subsidies, and repayment guarantees on private loans to increase manufacturing and retailing activities in ghettos. His plan places special emphasis on encouragement to minority entrepreneurs to establish businesses. This effort would be coupled with technical management assistance provided jointly by federal and local governments as well as the business community.

The *Merchandising Week* article by Hall and Williams reports on a survey of retailers in response to the program suggested by Senator Kennedy. Although many businessmen feel that entering ghettos with new retail outlets is feasible with government assistance, others indicate that such areas hold little or no promise regardless of help offered by the government. However, for retailers willing to open outlets in ghettos, government aid in some form appears to be essential.

Rosenthall reports on a national survey of what retailers experienced during the 1967 summer riots and their thoughts concerning the future of retailing in the ghetto. Many retailers view the riots as a vindicative war by the ghetto poor against the merchants. They express fear of the antibusiness attitude that is spreading in the ghettos and are pessimistic about the long-range problem. For many of the retailers who are concerned about the problem and are attempting to change conditions by hiring more local residents and changing their merchandise practices, there is a feeling of futility about their efforts. There is a general feeling of fear among retailers that even their best efforts will not prevent future riots. And yet, the low-income market remains a large and potentially attractive market.

Miss Jones emphasizes a different view of the poverty problem. Following the passage of the Economic Opportunity Act of 1964, the Federal Trade Commission organized a program aimed at correcting retail trade practices that victimize the poor and to help these citizens spend their limited funds more effectively. As a first operational step, concrete and detailed information was collected concerning the ways in which the poor are victimized. One of the important underlying problems pointed out was the lack of consumer know-how among the poor which places them at a disadvantage in any purchase transaction. The remedy suggested is to provide the poor with basic information about alternative sources of credit and goods. In addition, the FTC is engaged in an accelerated effort aimed at eliminating the deceptive trade practices that now victimize the poor.

The final article in this section suggests that the concept of black capitalism as a solution to economic problems in black communities should not become a matter of public policy if that policy encourages separatism. This article suggests that economic development of ghettos should be integrated in the sense that talent and resources from outside as well as within the ghetto should be utilized. Examples of successful, integrated development are cited.

Is War On Poverty Becoming War on Business?

Paul Hencke

In some American cities the war on poverty seems dangerously close to becoming a war on business.

Consider these recent examples of this new and militant trend:

- In the front window of a "consumer education" office on a boulevard near the Capitol in Washington, tax-paid poverty fighters have plastered a handbill depicting the profit-bloated, horned caricature of a business leader in the act of snatching bread from the outstretched fingers of children.

- In a similar center run by antipoverty workers at another Washington address, an ex-labor lobbyist—whose salary also comes largely out of tax funds—proudly shows off an exhibit of well known

Reprinted from "Is War On Poverty Becoming War on Business?" *Nation's Business* (March, 1966), pp. 41, 58–61, by permission of *Nation's Business* © 1966—the Chamber of Commerce of the United States. Reprinted from the March issue.

162

foods, soaps and cosmetic products. She uses the items to warn low income shoppers against what she calls "the deceptive packaging practices" of some firms.

- In Baltimore, poverty workers on the public payroll accompany housewives on shopping field trips, urging them to buy at large chain stores and pass up the small neighborhood markets they have traditionally patronized.

- In San Francisco, the director of a pilot project in consumer action freely concedes that "consumer advisers" in his federally subsidized, $256,000 program get many of the buying hints they pass along to shoppers from cooperatives, the columns of the labor press and from the pages of product-rating consumer magazines.

- Back in Washington, a high-spirited band of social workers, civil rights activists and others on the poverty program payroll turned out on a workday recently to help the Student Nonviolent Coordinating Committee (SNCC) stage a city-wide boycott of the D. C. Transit Co. in protest against a proposed five-cent fare increase. The boycott snarled traffic and cost the privately owned bus facility an estimated 150,000 fares.

Each of these incidents suggests that the escalating consumer education phase of the government's war on poverty is being fought with some questionable weapons and on fronts a good deal larger than those Congress had in mind when it passed the Economic Opportunity Act of 1964.

Businessmen are well aware of the plight of the poor; with other Americans, they applaud the accomplishments of those who are struggling to eliminate poverty. At the same time, businessmen can hardly accept unquestioningly some of the things that are occurring under the guise of a war on poverty.

The 1964 Antipoverty Act, for example, did not give poverty fighters the right or mission to subject businessmen to vitriolic public ridicule. And yet this is happening.

The Act did not empower poverty program operatives to propagate their own judgments as to what constitutes "deceptive" packaging. Yet this is happening—and at a time when Congress itself is still undecided about enacting so-called truth-in-packaging legislation.

The Act did not authorize persons whose salaries come from federal funds to direct customers into or away from specific places of business. Yet this is happening.

Nor did the Act call for massive mobilization of the poor for purposes such as boycotts, or buyers' strikes. Yet this is happening. The potential consequences of this development alone, when considered in the light of the racial tension in some cities, are sobering cause to question the course a government-initiated program can take, once begun.

It should be stressed that an anti-business posture is not the conscious intent of responsible anti-poverty warriors. From the press-wary front office at the Office of Economic Opportunity in Washington, down to the most naïve neighborhood antipoverty worker, the expressed goal is the same: To show the indigent and uninformed how they can stretch their buying dollar, and to help them avoid the few merchants who exploit the poor through high-pressure salesmanship, high-interest installment buying, trick contracts or other devices.

It is in the execution of this objective that the program has jumped the tracks.

A poverty-war adviser working in a consumer information center will step beyond simply giving poor people advice on how to draw up a family budget and tell them to avoid buying one brand because it costs more than another. Or the shopper will be urged to patronize chains, on the theory that the chains buy in large volume and are likely to charge less than a low-volume, independent retailer. This leads to naming chains and naming the smaller stores.

If a shopper is unable to read, or is slow-witted, the poverty program employee may go along to pick out items for her. In one instance, a young woman assigned as a consumer aide in Washington escorted an employed, middle-aged man into an appliance store. Once there, she talked him out of buying one kind of TV set he had decided on, and into buying another, lower priced model. This young woman told *Nation's Business* that whenever shoppers ask her advice on buying washing machines, she always tells them: "Whatever you do, don't get a ———. I have one of those myself, and it's lousy."

Large-scale federally supported consumer education programs now are operating in six cities—Washington, Baltimore, St. Louis,

San Francisco, Los Angeles and Providence, R. I.—and OEO officials say consumer-related services are available on a smaller scale in upwards of seventy-five other communities where they are currently spending $24 million. Federal poverty officials admit that they don't know the exact number.

In some of the larger consumer centers, a help-seeker can get anything from hints on how to use federal food stamps to advice on planned parenthood (together with free contraceptive supplies). Legal aid, credit unions and other related services are frequently tied in, and one consumer office in Washington even sports a coffeehouse next door. There the poor of the area assemble on weekends to hear poetry readings, a jazz combo and lectures on handwriting analysis.

Edna Johnson, director of Baltimore's consumer protection program, an activity subcontracted by the OEO through the Urban League, says the poor sometimes are more to blame than unscrupulous merchants for the buying fixes they get themselves into.

"Some of these people are trying to get something for nothing," she asserts. "They plunge into big debt apparently thinking they can get out of paying it. They know what they are doing, but they do it anyway. Why, I had a man call up the other day and ask me what he should do about $45 worth of parking and traffic violation tickets he had accumulated."

But Mrs. Johnson has equally critical words for merchants who prey on the gullible poor. She cites a recent case handled by her office in which an eighty-year-old Negro man purchased what he thought was a $40 mattress, only to discover later that he had signed an order for a $270 orthopedic model.

In some city neighborhoods, consumer advisers have set virtually no limits on the scope of their activities for and with the needy.

Washington is a conspicuous example of this open-ended operation. Poverty program personnel working under the United Planning Organization, the city's local agency for the federal program, canvass entire slum neighborhoods. They acquaint residents with the new services available to them and urge the poor to form their own units for concerted action against store owners and landlords against whom they may have a grievance, whether over store conditions, credit policies, inventories, rents or whatnot.

HOW TO RUN A BOYCOTT

The boycott of the D. C. Transit Co. discloses just how potent such organizing efforts can be.

While the boycott was sponsored by SNCC, publicly paid anti-poverty workers throughout the capital left their regular duties to join in. They participated in the pre-boycott planning, posted and distributed leaflets announcing the boycott (and bitterly attacking D. C. Transit owner O. Roy Chalk) and drove special "freedom cars" that carried hundreds of both low and middle income Negro and white residents to and from their jobs during the protest.

Various rider-strike command posts were set up around the city for the boycott. Tax-salaried antipoverty workers, as well as SNCC representatives and unpaid volunteers, planned their strategy in military fashion on large maps of Washington which had been hung, war-room style, on office walls.

At one point before drivers scrambled for their cars, an otherwise soft-spoken social worker who heads up UPO activities in Southeast Washington raised his voice to issue this order: "Don't forget, stop wherever you see people waiting for a bus and tell them, 'Don't ride D. C. Transit!' "

The man who issued the strident command—like most of those who were listening to him—is paid, at least in part, from UPO's federal input of $4.7 million.

On the morning of the boycott, traffic moved at a slow pace through streets and intersections patrolled by specially assigned police. Arteries leading into Washington over its Anacostia River bridges were thick with automobiles and almost empty buses. Some buses and trucks owned by churches and other groups were pressed into emergency service. Many workers were late in reaching their jobs and others stayed home. By the time the day was over, SNCC pronounced the boycott a "90 per cent success," and began at once to lay plans for similar demonstrations.

Less dramatic, but equally vigorous, efforts to organize people for protest action are being directed by E. Pauline Myers, who runs a federally funded UPO consumer center in one of Washington's poorest districts.

Miss Myers is a stout, outgoing woman whose background is not in home economics, as you might expect, but in what she likes to call "propaganda." As early as the 1930's she was a Washington lobbyist for the Brotherhood of Sleeping Car Porters and the National Fraternal Council of Negro Churches. Among other things, she lobbied for the first fair employment practices legislation. It is in her office that the truth-in-packaging exhibit is displayed. It was loaned to her by a Maryland co-op.

Her manner, like that of many in the antipoverty program, is engaging and warm. For the most part, living conditions in the area she serves are deplorable, with basements of some old buildings split up into two and even three apartments that rent separately for as much as $60 a month. Many residents collect welfare payments. The crime rate is high. The Black Muslim movement, in Miss Myers' words, is "growing at a disturbing rate," especially among men who have prison records.

Her voice seldom changes in its soft and even tone, but she drops an occasional phrase that sounds jarringly militant.

"We're about to have confrontations with some of the merchants," she said at one point, while being interviewed by a *Nation's Business* editor. "We've had complaints about unsanitary conditions in one of the big markets in particular, and we are going to get the manager and some of our neighborhood people together here for a confrontation."

CRACKDOWN ON SMALL MERCHANTS

The effectiveness so far of Washington's "confrontations" is not really clear. Some small merchants, when visited by delegations of neighborhood residents and antipoverty personnel, have promised to do what they can to improve the appearance of their stores and to eliminate conditions deemed unsanitary by the complaining parties. Major changes are difficult for most because they don't have the capital.

Some small merchants are understandably bitter about being pressured at all. In many instances they have been doing business in low income neighborhoods for many years, have granted long-term credit to their patrons and have made other personalized services available—such as storing in their freezers turkeys and cuts of meat too large to be safely kept in their customers' antiquated ice-boxes and refrigerators.

One store operator, who asked that he not be identified, complained to *Nation's Business*: "I don't understand. Suddenly I'm being told what to do and what not to do. They want me to stock more and to spruce up the place, but I haven't got the money for that. At the same time, the poverty people are telling my old-time customers to use the bigger stores.

"The two things don't jibe. Do they want me here, or not? If they keep on encouraging people to buy somewhere else, I am going out of business for damned sure."

James Love, a well-groomed young high school dropout who now works as a consumer aide in a neighborhood near the Capitol, enthusiastically told how he had organized people in a five block area to protest unsanitary conditions in a corner grocery.

"Some of my people said, 'Let's close him down,' " the youth recounted, "but I explained that we didn't want to run the man out of business—just get him to clean up his store, put in some new window glass and offer more variety in the things he has to sell. We went over there and met with the man and he has done a few things. He fixed one of the windows, anyway. Took down a wooden partition that was keeping out light and put in some real glass."

Out in San Francisco, where Art Danforth runs the federally subsidized Bay Area Neighborhood Development (BAND) consumer action program, the picture is somewhat different. Low income Negroes and whites, including many Spanish-speaking immigrants, live in the three areas BAND covers. Mr. Danforth has a number of field workers on his total staff of forty-eight full and part-time people, but they stick to "budget and fraud counseling" for the most part and have not yet moved into any militant large-scale organization.

However, Mr. Danforth feels that something along these lines will probably develop in time.

"When people have lived in frustration for years and years, as many of these poor people have, they finally want to do something," he says.

At centers in Hunter's Point-Bayview, North Oakland and the Mission District, BAND's consumer advisers offer people who phone in or drop in advice on what they conceive to be the best buys in "groceries, cars or whatever." Not all of the advisers are fully qualified to be doing this, Mr. Danforth admits, so they rely on the recommendations of product-rating consumer magazines and materials issued by cooperatives and the federal government. Some quote Sidney Margolius, whose consumer-oriented column has long been featured in the *AFL-CIO News* and other labor papers.

Mr. Danforth's last job, before he took over at BAND, was as educational director of the Consumers Cooperative Society of Palo Alto, Calif., and before that in community fund-raising. To get the necessary 10 per cent of local capital needed to match the 90 per cent available from the federal Office of Economic Opportunity, he turned to California Associated Cooperatives of Richmond, Calif. At one point he was accused of "trying to organize one huge cooperative among the poor of the Bay area," but he says this charge was baseless.

HELP FROM BUSINESS

Concerned business groups, including the National Dairy Council, a furniture house and a meat firm, recently have been giving BAND staffers coaching in how to explain to people what to look for, and what to avoid, when they buy products in those fields.

Business has moved to help the poverty fighters in other parts of the nation, too, but the effort to date has been limited. In Washington, for example, some firms have donated kitchen equipment for use in homemaking instruction, canned goods for distribution at "food banks," sewing machines, fabrics, utensils and other items.

But the incongruities crop up even here. In a large, privately owned apartment project, for example, the owners provided space free of charge for a complex of antipoverty services, including an office for neighborhood organizers, a food and clothing bank and rooms to house field placement personnel of the U.S. Employment Service. And yet, some of this same business-donated space was used during the Washington transit boycott for hanging SNCC handbills in which the president of the transit company was pictured as a snarling "buslord" who demanded 30 cent fares from passengers at gunpoint.

Some businessmen are surprised when they learn of the extent of the consumer services now being offered as a result of the Johnson Administration's war on poverty, and some admit to a feeling of "sheer fright" over the influences which people lacking a business grounding can bring to these activities.

Others react differently.

One group of businessmen recently spent a day with consumer education specialists in a major Eastern city, and found much they could do to help. These men came away concerned that some of what they had seen and heard did not make much sense in terms of hard-nosed economics ("They are teaching some people skills that aren't in demand," grumbled one member of the delegation) but impressed with the zeal of the antipoverty team. Before returning to their offices, they huddled to plan ways for putting together special training materials that could be productively used in the program they had inspected.

"You know," mused one gruff entrepreneur in the group, "this war on poverty isn't going to go away. The poor are on the move. I think we'd better get in there and make sure the job gets done right."

Violence in the City— An End or a Beginning?

The Governor's Commission on the Los Angeles Riots

THE DISADVANTAGED CONSUMER

The Commission heard recurrent testimony of alleged consumer exploitation in south central Los Angeles: of higher prices being charged for food there than in other parts of town, of spoiled meat or produce or old bread being sold at the same price as fresh, of high interest rates on furniture and clothing purchases, of shoddy materials at high prices. Complaints were also registered to the effect that there is a bias against the curfew area in the practices of insurance companies and institutional lenders. In a related vein, a number of witnesses advanced the view that there was a vengeance pattern to the destruction of stores in the curfew area, that it was a retribution

Reprinted from The Governor's Commission on the Los Angeles Riots, *Violence in the City—An End or a Beginning?* (December, 1965), pp. 62–65.

on merchants who were guilty of consumer exploitation, and particularly on Caucasians who were said to "take from the area but put nothing back into it."

Our study of the patterns of burning and looting does not indicate any significant correlation between alleged consumer exploitation and the destruction. On the contrary, a number of stores with a reputation for ethical practices and efficient and low-priced operation suffered major damage (". . . the beautiful blocklong market . . . which was 99 per cent Negro staffed, was the second to burn . . ." said one witness), while businesses which were widely unpopular came through the riot unmarked. (Another witness stated, "I hate to say this, but . . . the one they didn't burn—I don't know why they didn't burn that if they were going to burn something—we don't buy anything out of there.") There was some evidence that businesses which were apparently Negro-owned were spared—many by hastily-posted signs such as "Negro-owned," and "Blood brother"—but there is also evidence of the destruction of some Negro-owned businesses.

The consumer problem for many curfew area residents has the double bite of poverty and race. The practices that such residents criticize are a classic pattern in impoverished communities. But the factor of race—the merchants are for the most part white—sometimes leads the curfew area resident to conclude that oppressive or seemingly oppressive practices are directed against him to keep him in his place. Thus, regardless of actual exploitation, the area resident may believe he is exploited. However, our conclusion, based upon an analysis of the testimony before us and on the reports of our concultants, is that the consumer problems in the curfew area are not due to systematic racial discrimination but rather result from the traditional interplay of economic forces in the market place, aggravated by poverty conditions.

We have no doubt, however, that there are serious problems for the consumer in this disadvantaged area, just as there are wherever there is poverty. One is the costly and inadequate transportation from within the south central area to other parts of Los Angeles which tends to restrict residents of that area to the nearby stores, and which we discuss in more detail later in this section. Another problem is "easy credit" which can become harsh indeed if the disadvantaged person defaults on his installment obligations. The debtor may experience the loss of his property through repossession, or the loss of his job through repeated garnishments of his wages. While it is easy to say that the improvident debtor brought this state upon himself, we deplore the tactics of some merchants and lenders who help induce low-income persons to become heavily debt-burdened. Still another problem for the Negro consumer is the lack of an adequate remedy when he feels he has been unfairly treated. Public and private agencies exist to help the consumer in such a situation, but while manned by able and conscientious professionals, these agencies are generally understaffed, underfinanced, and over-burdened. Often the consumer does not even know of the agency's existence.

Having considered the consumer problem, we suggest that useful steps might be taken in the following areas:

1. The Civil Division of the Public Defender's Office might consider expanding its services in the curfew area by opening branch offices and publicizing their availability. The Neighborhood Legal Services Offices, soon to be opened under the antipoverty program, will provide an additional needed resource. These agencies should consider instituting preventive legal programs to inform the consumer concerning his legal rights.

2. The Better Business Bureau, a private agency which receives complaints regarding consumer practices and is active in consumer education, should open a branch office in south central Los Angeles and equip it with a competent staff. More immediately, courses in consumer education should be expanded in the adult education schools of the Los Angeles City School System and by the many volunteer and private groups working in the curfew area. Further, we encourage law enforcement departments, such as the Consumer Fraud Division of the Attorney General's Office, to investigate vigorously, and prosecutors to prosecute firmly, those who criminally victimize citizens in this area.

3. Based upon our informal survey of conditions of sanitation in food markets in the curfew area, we recommend that the County Health Department increase and improve its inspection program for the markets in all disadvantaged areas of the city.

4. We are persuaded that the businessmen in the curfew area should show a greater interest in the community where they work, or, if already taking an interest, should make more energetic efforts to acquaint the community with what they are doing. We feel it is imperative that positive initiatives be taken immediately by the entire business community. In particular, we believe that lending institutions should treat Negro borrowers and Negro clients on the basis of each individual's responsibility rather than establish policies for all members of a race or geographical area irrespective of individual differences.

Should Supermarkets
Take a
New Look at
Urban Areas?

The supermarket industry has been urged on many occasions, by the highest levels of the Administration in Washington, to do more in the area of opening modern supermarkets in low-income, urban areas.

The reasons are apparent. According to the Bureau of Labor Statistics' recent survey of food prices, comparing prices of food in suburban supermarkets with those of supermarkets in urban areas, prices were not appreciably different from one area to another. More important, prices in smaller, typical, corner grocery stores ranged anywhere from 8 to 15 per cent higher than prices in supermarkets, according to other surveys conducted by various newspapers, social services and agricultural agencies. But . . .

Reprinted from "Should Supermarkets Take a New Look at Urban Areas?" *Food Topics* (February, 1967), pp. 10–23, by permission of Conover-Mast Publications.

OPERATORS AREN'T VERY INTERESTED

Ask a large chain or successful independent supermarket operator: "Are you interested in opening new locations in the grey areas of the average metropolitan community, to say nothing of the slums?" His answer will probably be something like, "Not much."

On the other hand, there are many retailers of successful super-markets—at least one or two in each community—that will tell you that operating a supermarket in a low-income area is no different from running a store anywhere else. Why the great difference in attitude? It's hard to say, but like most things in retailing, there are at least two divergent points of view about everything. Depending upon the circumstances, both can usually be supported by empirical evidence, and both appear to be true.

One thing is clear. Supermarket operators will soon be facing new competition in the form of cooperative buying groups, stimulated by the Office of Economic Opportunity, and new opportunity for store locations through the "Model Cities" and "Model Neighborhoods" legislation.

The problem has two sides, then. One: urban locations, in general, and, two: urban locations in low-income areas.

At first, these problems appear to be separate and distinct. But as they are examined more closely, it is apparent that they are intimately connected. Much of the impetus to urban renewal today stems from a realistic attempt to deal with slums and grey areas on a neighborhood and community basis—as an entity.

LAW CALLS FOR COMPREHENSIVE PLAN

One of the stipulations of the Model Cities program standards is that a comprehensive plan should "provide adequate public and commercial facilities to serve the residents of the areas."

Another key section of the program of interest to supermarket operators specifically states: "The program calls for **private initiative and enterprise of all kinds—the initiative and enterprise of individual homeowners, contractors, and builders to improve housing and environmental conditions; the involvement of business leaders and financial interests in carrying out the program, and the creation of an environment in which private enterprise can prosper in meeting the needs of the residents."**

Announcement has recently been made that communities may now begin applying for planning funds. Some seventy to eighty cities will be selected on the basis of the excellence of their plans. Congress has authorized $11 million for planning purposes during the fiscal year of 1967, while $900 million has been authorized for 1968 and 1969 for the purpose of carrying out the plan. Roughly 350 cities have expressed strong interest in participating in the program.

As *model* or *demonstration* neighborhoods and cities begin moving into firm plans this year, the pressure for consumer co-op store locations in the projects will undoubtedly rise. Businessmen, merchants and supermarket operators need to know all they can about these proposed redeveloped areas. New thinking is needed about the kinds of services, locations and placement necessary to create interesting, diverse, active community life.

One city planner, who understood early the need for diversity and commercial involvement in community planning, is a man named Sho Maruyama, now program specialist with the Economic and Youth Opportunities Agency of Greater Los Angeles. Formerly, Mr. Maruyama had been associated with urban planning in Philadelphia. As a social and city planner, Mr. Maruyama is unique. He understands that business-oriented, profit-motivated supermarkets do more to improve the life and activity of a neighborhood than any other single commercial or service facility. His is the kind of thinking and planning that can help bridge the widening gap in the "private" and the "public" sectors of our lives.

This is the opportunity for supermarket operators, large and small, to become active in a local program of urban renewal that offers a real chance of business participation. Too often, supermarket operators have found in the past that they were unaware of urban renewal plans until too late. Now is the time for retailers to express a voice locally in the kind of program best suited for local and neighborhood situations.

THE DIFFICULTY OF COMMUNICATION

Why is this important? Businessmen find it difficult, if not impossible, to communicate with social and city planners. As a result, the planners often think of business and commercial participation in city planning as, at best, a necessary evil. It is imperative that communication between businessmen, especially merchants, and the directors of federal projects begins now. It will do little good to stand aside and say, "We can't get in."

At the same time, it will be necessary for supermarket operators who want to find new locations in the urban areas—and what retailers do not want new locations?—to learn something about how to merchandise to the rapidly changing ethnic mixtures of present urban areas.

With this in mind, *Food Topics* visited several urban areas in the cities of Boston, Chicago, St. Louis and Los Angeles. In each of these locations, we were able to find successful retailers of modern, clean, well-run supermarkets. Their individual attitudes, merchandising policies and operating practices are revealing to those who lack urban experience.

Parallel with this motive, we sought to prove that independent or chain supermarket operators can do a better job of running competitive supermarkets for any community—high- or low-income —than some of the alternative procedures that we more than suspect are in the cards for many communities in the not too distant future.

Urban planners and social planners, as we have said, with some notable exceptions, usually have difficulty in understanding the real benefits and long-range dependability of the "selfish" or "self-interest" business motive. This is why there is so much talk among OEO groups, and other consumer action groups today of the "Berkeley-type," consumer co-op supermarket. This can work in selected, highly active, usually college-oriented communities. In the low-income, grey areas and slum areas of the nation, it hasn't much chance of success.

CONSUMER ACTION AND THE POVERTY PROGRAM

However, today there is a difference. The difference lies in OEO approach. Already, in several communities across the nation, some 20,000 consumer "aides" on the OEO payroll are spreading the consumer co-op gospel. They're busy forming buying clubs and setting up depots for buying and bagging groceries through 1,000 Community Action Centers. Some are in operation now, in the Bedford-Stuyvesant section of Brooklyn, N.Y., and the Harlem section of Manhattan. According to an article which appeared in *Barron's*, Oct. 17, 1966, the OEO has signed a contract with the Cooperative League of the USA to supply technical assistance. The League has completed a survey of eight states on the problems, needs and development patterns of existing co-ops.

"Bit by bit," the article states, "the OEO's super colossal co-op schemes are coming to light. But not by official intent: Busy as they are informing the poor, Mr. Shriver's forces have done as little as possible to spread the news among equally affected private merchants."

CHANGING CONSUMER GROUP ATMOSPHERE

On January 14, in New York City, some thirty organizations representing consumer and urban groups, social services, housing, and trade and retail unions met to discuss consumer problems. Called the Consumer Assembly, the group resolved to keep some kind of consumer council committee in action on a continuing basis. Addressed by Mayor John Lindsay, Congressmen Wright Patman and Benjamin Rosenthal, all phases of consumer interests were discussed. There were no representatives of merchants or business, although the air fairly crackled with antibusiness, antimerchant attacks.

Clearly, the atmosphere of consumer groups is changing. They are no longer composed merely of the better educated, middle- and upper-class campus types. There is now the element of political action, combined with a genuine interest in the problems of the poor, and a zealous attack on the "establishment."

But poverty, social welfare, urban renewal and consumer information are aspects of our society of interest to all well-meaning segments of American life—not the professional activists, alone. The businessman, the merchant, is an important, vital member of any society.

THE DILEMMA OF THE GHETTOS

Advice to businessmen, then, in entering this area, is to go carefully—with great patience. But "go" the businessman must. The consumer movement in the U.S. is growing in numbers, growing more militant, and growing more antibusiness. Even the well-meaning people, honestly concerned with the problems of the poor, are easily convinced that the businessman is not concerned with social welfare, but only with profits—unfair, illegitimate profits.

Of course, all businessmen have an obligation to the business or to the stockholder to invest in enterprises that present a good chance for a fair return.

Supermarket operators, then, should examine carefully the possibilities of opening new urban locations in changing communities on the fringes of grey and slum areas.

The three major problems to supermarket operators in low-income areas are these:

1. Finding, training and keeping adequate staff. The need for integrated staffs in heavily nonwhite communities is vital. The availability of employees and managers qualified to operate in these communities is even more limited than the general condition. The high degree of personal service, guards and part-timers, tends to drive up costs.

2. Low rate of return on investment. Many retailers (although there are exceptions to this statement in the following sections) find that the need to provide special merchandise lines, in addition to regular merchandise offered in suburban stores, drive up operating cost. The high degree of small purchases per capita of traffic increases costs. The tendency to do most shopping on Friday night and Saturday, after payday, adds to lopsided cost. High cost of store maintenance and pilferage are also listed by experienced retailers.

3. The difficulty of finding good locations of large enough size. This is another limiting and discouraging factor, especially when parking must be provided. Often, many parcels of land must be pieced together before clear title to a site is attained.

WHAT ROLE CAN GOVERNMENT PLAY?

Can federal and local governments help retailers in locating and operating supermarkets in urban areas?

Many retailers want no help from federal government, other than dealing with the problems of poverty and conditions of "anarchy" which they feel must be altered before they will consider low-income urban locations. Others feel that some government aid in the form of tax incentives, insurance guarantees, and land clearance could be helpful. It has also been mentioned that local government could assist in providing municipal or joint parking lots that would share facilities with others, such as public libraries, post offices, etc.

THE CHALLENGE TO THE FOOD INDUSTRY

This article, then, points up the need for the supermarket operator to become aware of the many government programs in operation that will affect his future.

The "War on Poverty," it would appear, is a war that provides effective means, ways, and money for dealing with inadequate segments in the distribution system of food. The poor often do pay more, through ignorance, inflexibility and lack of opportunity to take advantage of the more advanced forms of retail outlets. Two federal projects are offering a challenge to the ingenuity of the food industry to deal with all segments of the consumer public adequately. It is a truism of modern political life in America—either the so-called "private" sector finds a way of dealing with inequities in economic disadvantage, or the "public" sector will. But it should be remembered. *Where the public sector enters, it rarely, if ever, leaves.*

Chains and Independent supermarket operators in St. Louis are quite concerned about the problems of getting modern supermarkets into low-income areas.

They would like to see private enterprise solve the problem, but they are by no means in agreement about either the magnitude of the needs or the way to meet them. At least one is trying to find out.

General Grocers Co., a wholesaler, has enough questions about inner-city supermarket opportunities that "a top man" has been detached from regular assignments to prepare a five-week study.

"We want to know what the needs are in this kind of area," explains Eugene M. O'Neill, president of General Grocers. "From there, we'll make our own decisions about the opportunities."

FEDERAL HELP

Reactions to the idea of federal help in servicing low income neighborhoods in St. Louis ran the gamut from mild enthusiasm to skepticism to bristling opposition, with emphasis on the latter.

"It would be a detriment to the American way of life," snaps General Grocers' O'Neill. "If there's a need, I'm confident private enterprise can fill that need. Any other attempt would be harmful."

"I don't like it when the government passes legislation restricting our activity, and conversely we're not looking to the government for any handouts," sums up a top Kroger Company executive.

"If they'd do something for individual enterprises, that might be beneficial," allows Oliver Wetterau, President of Wetterau Foods Inc. "But what I hear about are efforts to encourage customers to become owners—putting it on a consumer-cooperative basis—and in my book that's a move to cut individual opportunity."

He thinks retailers would find the availability of low-interest loans the most effective form of federal help.

"I'd like to see some kind of tax incentive—something on the order of the old income tax investment credit," volunteered Donald Schnuck, executive vice president of Schnuck Markets. "That would go a long way toward giving store owners a reason for locating there."

However, when queried about his own operation, he judged that "we probably couldn't succeed" in low-income urban areas because of an image factor. "The only reason we haven't tried is because we beam our business at middle class and above," he explained.

LACK OF POTENTIAL

Executives were hesitant to discuss expansion plans—in low-income areas or anywhere else—but seemed at least partially decided on the opportunities afforded in low-income neighborhoods.

"Stores are expensive to operate in low-income areas because of low volume," says a top official of the Bettendorf-Rapp division of Allied Supermarkets Inc. "Most people in these neighborhoods make maybe $5,000 or less—how much can they spend on food?" He said Bettendorf-Rapp operates two markets in low-income areas.

Jack Conreaux, president of Associated Grocers, disagrees. "Low income has no relationship to the supermarket business. The first requirement of nature is to eat—no matter what your income," he said.

"We have a fine working relationship with many residents of

low-income neighborhoods," said Conreaux, whose AG co-operative services some 600 stores in this market, in "every kind of neighborhood. Many of them are good, solid people."

Sums up IGA supplier Wetterau: "Generally the opportunity is not as great there (low-income neighborhoods), because the growth of population is not as great."

On the possibility of locating in fast-growing redeveloped areas, he responds: "We have not been successful in getting in there. By the time it gets to be worthwhile in terms of having enough people around you, most of the leases are gone."

Says a top executive of National Food Stores, Inc.: "We operate and plan to operate very few stores in these (low-income) areas. The people seem to prefer the neighborhood type of store—I suppose because it's small, and close, and operated by some fellow who lives in the community."

MERCHANDISE

Companies who said they operated stores in low-income areas gave varying accounts of their operation. "We sell a lot more second-label types of food," says Robert Phillips, who directs real estate operations for Tom Boy Stores Inc.

For Tom Boy, the individual transactions, he remarked, are more likely to be consistently small, and the customers less likely to be interested in stamps or prize premiums. He admitted pilferage is "more of a problem" and said some store owners "are having trouble finding window insurance in run-down neighborhoods."

However, AG's Conreaux flatly denied "that we have any more trouble with stealing or vandalism" in low-income areas than in others. The "size of the store—not where it's located," he said, is the only determining factor in product lines. The Kroger executive thought residents of these areas "will buy more of the upgraded product—when they have the money—than people in middle-class sections."

With the exception of Tom Boy (who mentioned some lower prices), every store interviewed denied that price variations existed, citing uniform prices at chains and "retail price guides" at the co-ops and voluntaries. AG and Kroger both said product lines are determined only by the store's size and volume, and both denied there are any special problems in obtaining personnel or sustaining theft losses.

PROFIT RETURN

The Kroger official admitted that "as a group, the stores in low-income areas are somewhat below average" in profit returns. Countered AG's Conreaux: "We don't find there's much difference in profits when you use the same prices and have the same type of expenses." Wetterau and Tom Boy's Phillips both commented that the profit picture depends solely on the operator—how well he meets the needs of clientele and how shrewd he is in buying ahead at special prices to compensate for low per-customer transactions.

On the subject of rents, the Kroger executive allowed only that "a lot of times we're amazed at what those low-income area sites go for."

REMODELING

The factors taken into consideration on when to remodel are volume of business and profits in the past, nearly every owner stated. No one said that just because a neighborhood is getting rundown the opportunity for future business does not warrant remodeling. "We're remodeling our low-income area stores just as fast as anywhere else," says AG.

"The only thing I want to know is how much money it's been making. It's a business decision—not a social move," says the Kroger executive. "We treat any store in any neighborhood the same when it comes time to remodeling—we ask ourselves whether the volume is worth the outlay."

"First and most important factor," says AG's Conreaux, "is how much the owner can afford to spend. Can you tell the man who has enough to buy a Chevrolet to hold off until he's got enough for an Imperial?"

However, two store owners said their remodeling time-tables differ according to the neighborhood. "We generally take longer to remodel in low-income areas because there is a bigger investment per dollar earned there," says Tom Boy's Phillips. "This goes back again to the small transaction per-customer factor. The volume is lower, so in effect you're spending the same on each customer, but more on each transaction when you remodel a low-income area store."

Adds Wetterau: "We may delay remodeling longer there (in low-income area) than somewhere else because of the uncertainty of the neighborhood." Since remodeling expenditures should be recovered over a long period, he explained, he wants to make sure no radical or sudden changes are in store for a given area before making the investment.

Hillman's Fine Foods operates the only supermarkets within the confines of Chicago's loop. Its management has a definite policy of never lowering the store's image to conform to the earning power of the immediate neighborhood. As Gardner Stern, Jr., the executive vice-president points out, Hillman's has had integrated personnel at all levels of its operation for nearly two decades.

"I guess we've been color blind all these years," he points out.

Founded in 1896 as a department store, Hillman's management group entered the grocery field in 1929. It now has fourteen stores in Cook County, including ten in Chicago, and two more stores are currently being built in the western suburbs. In addition, it also has two Stop & Shop stores—gourmet-type outlets. All this adds up to an annual volume of over $50 million.

THERE BY DESIGN

Hillman's is also unique in that two of its supermarkets are located in depressed areas, one by virtue of a changing neighborhood and the other on purpose.

The former is located at 63rd and Halsted Streets, one of Chicago's busiest shopping areas. For many years, it was a middle-class, white neighborhood. Hillman's operates a high-volume supermarket at that corner—or underneath it. It was, and still is, located in the lower levels of the Sears, Roebuck & Company store there. About ten years ago, the store underwent virtually a complete remodeling, despite the changing neighborhood. Local independent merchants were utterly confused by Hillman's decision.

"We really weren't trying to confuse anybody," Stern says. "The alterations were in the plans and we merely proceeded on schedule.

The fact that the neighborhood was undergoing a radical change obviously had no bearing on the situation."

Today, that same store, which was always one of the best, volume-wise, ranks even higher on the corporate books—even though the neighborhood is now made up of about 75 to 85 per cent Negroes in the low-income brackets.

A PUZZLE

"When we attempt to analyze this, we find that we can't. We don't buy differently. Our local management is virtually the same. And the pricing is the same as in any of our other stores," Stern muses. "Sure, we stock a few items which are in demand in that neighborhood—just as we do in any neighborhood where tastes differ. But it must be emphasized that the items are in *addition* to our regular stock, not in place of.

"Perhaps the answer lies in the fact that the Negro clientele doesn't want things to be different. They want the store to be basically the same as would be found in white neighborhoods. You might say that they want democracy on the store shelves, and justifiably so."

PILFERAGE IS AVERAGE

Hillman's 63rd Street store is not located in an urban renewal area, and there is very little demolition going on. The neighborhood is densely packed and has a low-income rating. Despite this, there is not a noticeable difference in pilferage as compared to other stores in high-income neighborhoods.

"Apparently, mutual respect pays off," Stern feels.

Hillman's purposeful venture into a depressed area was at the Lake Meadows Shopping Center, an urban renewal area. This started out as a private enterprise. However, the general surroundings are now a combination of both private and government activities. It is located at 35th and South Parkway. Hillman's, together with Jewel, are the only supermarkets in the center, which is complete with about two dozen specialty stores. Hillman's supermarket has a frontage of 120 feet, with 12,000 square feet of selling area.

Again, stock is the same as in any other Hillman's store, plus the usual ethnic item demands. Stern feels that, from the beginning, Hillman's should have had an integrated store (employee-wise), instead of all-Negro personnel. Since the store opened ten years ago, the employee mix has been modified. Now it includes a substantial number of whites and orientals.

"The Negro customer, more integration-conscious than most people, was looking for an integrated working force."

The store manager is white, but this, again, was not a measured move. Two previous managers were Negro, one of whom had a master's degree in business administration from the University of Chicago. He eventually decided to go into business for himself.

Personnel turnover is no different at Lake Meadows or 63rd Street than at any other of the Hillman's stores, Stern adds.

MOVE IN!

"It's good business to build in depressed areas," he feels. "The tendency has been to leave a changed or changing neighborhood underserviced. As a result, the local merchants take full price advantage of the noncompetitive situation.

"The bigger chains would be wise to step in and offer their usual good services, quality merchandise, and low prices in competition with the local merchants. Above all, they should not tailor the store downwards for the neighborhood in terms of construction, merchandise or service. It isn't appreciated and it's a definite slap in the face to the prospective customer."

A large Boston chain, one which operates well over one hundred stores in four New England states with several of them in low-income areas, says this about low-income areas:

"Operating a store in such an area does not *necessarily* mean a lower return. Conversely, higher income areas do not mean, *per se*, higher profits. The point is, *where* you're operating isn't the primary factor. It's *how* you operate that counts."

To get down to actual cases, however, one of the best examples of what it takes to operate in a low-income neighborhood is Blair's Foodland Inc., a fifty-year-old Boston independent.

Blair's currently operates three supermarkets—all three in the lowest income, highest density area of the city of Boston. It's now negotiating to open a fourth.

SATISFIED WITH SITES

This firm is completely happy with where its markets are located. Philosophy is simple: "People are people."

Harold A. Burg, treasurer of Blair's, was quick to point out that the community at large is all too prone to get the wrong idea about the trading areas in which Blair's operates. They are largely Negro.

"Our experience has been that these people are fine persons to deal with—I couldn't ask for any finer." He went on to note that Blair's has never had any extraordinary problems with pilferage.

Blair's oldest store—half a century old in 1968, to be precise—is located in the heart of Boston's Roxbury district. Store No. 2, which opened just four years ago, is in adjacent Dorchester, a section of Boston also predominantly Negro.

But store No. 3, which opened for business just last October, is Blair's pride and joy. Strikingly modern, spacious and beautifully lighted, this supermarket is located in the Washington Park urban renewal area. Once, this section in Roxbury consisted largely of blighted and rotting tenements. Today, Washington Park is a showplace. Visitors who want to see what Boston is doing in urban renewal of residential areas are taken there.

Blair's demonstrated its faith in the concept of urban renewal by building a $2 million shopping center in the heart of the project. Blair's itself occupies 22,000 sq. ft. of the center. The remainder is leased to tenants. The largest of the ten tenants is the Zayre Dept. Store chain, which occupies 55,000 sq. ft.

Burg pointed out that without the urban renewal program, Blair's could never have gone into the Washington Park area on the scale it did. It could never, for instance, have razed the derelict buildings and cleared the land.

But, he was quick to add, apart from the *indirect* assistance from the federal government represented in the razing of beyond-repair buildings and the resale of the land at a reasonable price, the only other assistance was substantial aid from the Boston Redevelopment Authority.

WRONG NOTIONS

William E. Battles, grocery supervisor for Blair's, pointed out that as far as *operation* in a low-income neighborhood is concerned, there are many misconceptions among retailers.

"For instance, they're often surprised," he says, "to discover that we carry top lines here. We have, as an example, 144 S. S. Pierce items, a big seller with us."

Battles also noted that Blair's carries strictly national brands—a policy which extends to its perishable bakery goods.

"This may be a low-income area," put in Burg, "but that doesn't mean our customers want low-quality products. Quite the reverse is true. We stock top merchandise all the way—and that most certainly includes our meats."

Local tastes and demands are catered to, of course. Battles pointed out that he carries products from areas of the South if he gets enough requests for them. And, because there is a large number of Puerto Rican residents newly arrived in the neighborhood, he caters to their tastes, too.

"Pork and poultry are very big here. And we sell a lot of such items as pigs' ears and heads, hocks, chitlins—that sort of thing."

In a way, Battles' statement was borne out by another chain operator, with stores in both low- and non-low-income areas. He points out:

"A low-income area often can afford you a better merchandise 'mix'—that is, it enables you to sell the whole animal rather than just the parts favored by higher-income clientele. And you can plan your meat features around this idea—the higher-priced grades at the end of the week, near pay-day, cheaper items on other days."

OUT OF STAMPS

What about stamps and games in a low-income neighborhood?

That turned out to be the most timely question of all for Blair's which has just dropped its S & H trading stamps.

"We are discounting prices across the board," Burg said, "and will be relying on volume rather than percentage. We are going to compete price-wise."

He concluded that the recent flurry of price boycotts across the U.S. "helped us to make up our minds about dropping stamps." However, Blair's feels that, simply from a good-business point of view, the time was ripe for such a move.

"We took on stamps because our customers expected them," he

said, "and we're dropping them because our customers want lower prices."

Thus, the change in policy really has nothing to do with the fact that Blair's operates in low income neighborhoods, according to Burg. Rather, it is simply a response to what their customers, like shoppers everywhere, seem to want.

Currently, Blair's is negotiating to open a fourth market. This one would be located in a new shopping center in the Columbia Point public housing project—also a low-income neighborhood.

PROBLEMS AREN'T BIG

In summing up, Burg feels that there are really no enormous problems to operating in low-income areas. Some chains are convinced that supermarkets in such areas are unprofitable. Blair's, however, points to its own profitable operation to contradict this.

Blair's doesn't feel it has to use any special merchandising programs to suit the needs of low-income customers, other than catering to the tastes of those who have recently arrived from other areas of the country.

The fact that shopping is generally done on Fridays and Saturdays —or on the first and fifteenth of the month, when welfare checks come in—is no great handicap, Blair's feels. They simply add extra part-time help on these days.

As for the quality of help, Blair's follows a policy of hiring from the neighborhood—the firm has had no more trouble than anyone else in finding reliable help. The store made it a point to confer with local civil rights groups—such organizations as CORE, NAACP, the Urban League—to get their assistance in locating good help and also to get their advice on operation in general. Because of this policy, a misunderstanding that arose a few months ago over hiring policies was quickly cleared up by "talking out" the problem. A picketing threat never materialized.

On the other hand, the larger chains who operate in the Boston area, those who have had experience in low-income areas, remain reluctant. They point to a lower return in these areas, while the cost of doing business is just as high as in other neighborhoods.

Paul Kodimer knows the Watts section of Los Angeles about as well as any white man can. He should—he operates supermarkets right smack in the middle of Watts, Los Angeles' Negro ghetto.

Kodimer is in favor of government action, where it counts, but would like to see a community center in Watts that offered something tangible—more tangible than trees and bushes and malls. He'd like to see a supermarket in the middle of the center with good secondary tenants and service agencies. "Why not joint parking for these services and other tenants," he asks? But right now he's busy running supermarkets where most other retailers won't.

Kodimer has been operating ABC stores in Negro trading areas for twenty-eight years. He has three stores now and is building a fourth. He intends to keep expanding his operations *strictly* in Negro communities.

It makes sense for him, because he's been successful. Currently, his three ABC units do $15 million a year in an average selling area (per store) of 15,000 square feet! Gross profit on dry groceries stays within the range reported by Super Market Institute in its recent western regional survey: 21.8 per cent out-of-warehouse or 22.8 per cent for the overall store.

There are certain basics that guide operations for the ABC stores:

- The stores are modern, well-decorated, landscaped and kept spotlessly clean.
- Negroes comprise the majority of store help—65 per cent of the 275 employees.
- The chain is an active partner in community affairs, particularly through financial help. Contributions are made to all community churches.
- Shoppers feel at home in ABC stores. They find exactly the kind of merchandise they want most—at the right price. It took Kodimer years of study to get this balance—it's the most vital element in his success.

"Price appeal is the first consideration in any low-income area, anywhere," Kodimer says. "You must find and offer bargains—but the merchandise must lend itself to end stacks so you can increase your gross potential." These ends zero in on ethnic tastes. They have strong price appeal and profit return is figured to the fraction. The ends must return a minimum profit of $65 a week or the product never gets stacked again.

CUSTOMER PROFILE

Kodimer has studied his customers, so he rarely misses. "The housewife in this community still cooks. She will buy frozen vegetables and pies, usually in large family sizes, but not convenience items. She wants the basics: flour, sugar, vinegar, salt and pepper, produce, canned and powdered milk, paste goods, uncooked cereals and shortening." Kodimer finds his customers greatly concerned about cleanliness. "Compared to other areas, she spends more for household cleaners and cleansers, waxes and polishes, bleaches and detergents, deodorizers and insecticides, and toilet soaps and personal deodorants."

Kodimer feels it's useless to try to merchandise beef to his customers. "Her family wants pork and poultry. A good price on frying chickens or on ham, bacon, pork loins or smoked shoulders will draw her like a magnet. And she always chooses whole poultry, rather than parts."

In produce, Kodimer says "she buys lots of potatoes, and lots of collards, mustard greens and turnips. She has more children than her white counterpart—this reflects in her buying."

Kodimer's customers respond to couponing, redeem them immediately. They are drawn by a mailer featuring a photo of an ABC housewife-shopper. And, their loyalty to national brands is extremely weak. It is easily replaceable with good quality controlled or owned labels—which outsell national brands at ABC.

IT WORKS

"There's no use pretending that we've been able to solve all interracial problems in our ABC stores," Kodimer confides. "But I think we have built a great deal of good-will. And we're delighted with our customers."

It must work the other way, too. Not only is ABC successful, but it bears no mark from the Watts' trial-by-fire.

A Business Development Program for Our Poverty Areas

Robert F. Kennedy

No single problem underlies the poverty of our urban centers and rural backwaters. Poverty means inadequate educational systems which result in high-school drop-out rates often reaching nearly 70 per cent. Poverty means inadequate health conditions which doom thousands of children before they even reach school age. Poverty means broken families and high crime rates. It means inadequate housing and inadequate social services. And it means going to school on an empty stomach and going to bed hungry.

But above all else, poverty means a lack of jobs. For a young man, it means being cut off from the ability to sustain himself and his family—from contributing to his community and his Nation.

Reprinted from "A Business Development Program for Our Poverty Areas," *Congressional Record* (May 29, 1968).

It means living without the dignity and pride that comes from working at a meaningful job paying a meaningful wage.

During the last six years, we have tried to solve this terrible problem. Almost every Congress has enacted another bill designed to put people to work: the Area Redevelopment Act, the Manpower Development and Training Act, the Investment Credit Act, the Economic Development Act, and the Economic Opportunity Act. But despite all these efforts and despite the uninterrupted rise in prosperity experienced by the rest of the Nation:

More than 11 million working age Americans are either unemployed or have jobs which pay less than a living wage;

More than 4 million of our citizens cannot find jobs at all today, 750,000 of whom have given up looking;

For 2 million of these unemployed no jobs exist no matter what their qualifications and new jobs must be created for them;

In our urban slums unemployment is two and three times higher than in surrounding communities and the subemployment rate is as high as 45 per cent;

In rural areas, where 14 million of our 29.7 million poor live, 800,000 Americans cannot find jobs.

But these dismal figures measure only the shortage of jobs. They fail to reveal that to millions of Americans who sit in idleness and despair, participation in the *economic* life of their country, their state and their community is denied. It is not simply jobs that our unemployed lack. They also lack what the Kerner Commission called "a stake in the economic community"—the opportunity to own or manage a business. And this is especially true for minority groups:

Negroes own only 50,000, in terms of population, one tenth their proportion-share of businesses across the country.

In cities like Newark, with a majority of its population Negro, only 10 per cent of the businesses are owned or managed by Negroes.

In Washington, D.C., where the population is 63 per cent Negro, only 13 per cent of the businesses are owned by Negroes.

One large corporation has reported that not one of its 7,000 subcontractors is Negro-owned or managed.

Most Negro business, except for a few moderate sized banks, insurance companies and publishing houses are marginal enterprises —small retail groceries, lunch counters, and small contractors which provide little income to their owners and have no opportunity to expand.

Similar problems exist for low- and moderate-income white residents of poverty areas.

Clearly then, our main focus must be on providing employment opportunities which will enable the residents of poverty areas to participate in the economic life of their community—a task which we have not yet begun nationwide, but which has already been demonstrated in one community.

In 1966 I helped organize in New York City's Bedford-Stuyvesant area, a new joint venture between residents, and the business community, with the support and assistance of local and state public officials from both parties. We have demonstrated there that meaningful social and economic change can be made in the country's most populous black community. *Newsweek* magazine has called the Bedford-Stuyvesant project "the most sweeping and comprehensive rehabilitation effort ever brought to bear on a single American community."

Some of the accomplishments in Bedford-Stuyvesant to date illustrate the major changes that are taking place:

Community residents have worked out their own programs for jobs, housing rehabilitation, and educational advancement with financial help furnished by government and by some of America's largest corporations.

Two community corporations, the Restoration Corporation and the Development and Services Corporation, one controlled by residents and the other by some of the leading businessmen in the nation, are working together on all phases of the project. They are developing, for example, local Negro-owned businesses and they have succeded with assistance from the Federal Special Impact program in getting local franchises for community residents from national firms.

A $100 million commitment has been made by more than eighty banks and insurance companies to provide long-term mortgage money which, will reduce residents' monthly payments by as much as one third.

A major corporation has announced plans to build a plant in the area to create 300 new jobs.

Labor unions have cooperated in training young men to work on housing rehabilitation projects.

A new community college will be established.

The community has its own television program—in effect, a community newspaper—twice a week.

All these efforts, and others in Bedford-Stuyvesant have demonstrated that our slum areas can be rebuilt through local ownership, self-determination and cooperation.

But new programs are needed—programs which will create new jobs, which will enable the hard core unemployed to fill existing job vacancies, and which will open new opportunities in private enterprise.

We must make it possible for urban ghetto residents to move out of the ghetto if they so choose. Jobs must be made available throughout our metropolitan areas and transportation assistance must be given to enable ghetto residents to travel to those jobs.

We must have an immediate emergency employment program, a program that I have cosponsored in the Senate providing jobs in public service with built-in training so that those on the job can move up career ladders. Public service employment is growing at nearly four or five times the rate of private employment. Major contributions can be made by community residents to meet the need for constructing and maintaining new community facilities and for improving our schools, libraries, hospitals and police forces.

We must also promote on-the-job training in existing private industry. This is now being undertaken with increased emphasis on the hard core. But direct subsidies of employer training costs, while helpful, are of limited value since alone, on-the-job training will not create new jobs. Unless private businesses can also expand existing establishments or build new facilities, the hard core and the unskilled person will simply replace another more qualified worker who might have filled a vacant job.

We must, if we are to solve the employment problems of the poor, provide new jobs in our poverty areas. We must create an economic climate in which businesses, especially those owned and managed by members of minority groups and residents of poverty areas, will be willing to establish new facilities and expand existing facilities in the centers of our cities and in the midst of our rural poverty areas.

But the role of private enterprise can only complement other community efforts. There must be new community-based institutions such as Community Development Corporations, controlled by local residents, through which their wishes will be made known. This is central to the success already demonstrated in Bedford-Stuyvesant. It is essential that indigenous resident participation be coupled with economic development programs.

We must make these efforts for these reasons:

First, we must begin to stem the tide of migration from our farms and rural villages. Without a viable economic base for rural America, a base which can support the men, women and children of these areas at more than a bare subsistence level, millions of poor people will continue to pour into our cities, straining their resources to the breaking point.

Second, we know that at the present time, large numbers of the urban poor cannot be induced to take jobs far away from the areas in which they live. As the Secretary of Labor told the Senate Executive Reorganization Subcommittee, "most of the unemployed in the slums" are so "conditioned by a century of insecurity" that even distances of "more than six or eight blocks away from where they live" create a severe problem. Most new job openings are, of course, much more than a few blocks outside poverty areas.

Third, most cities lack the mass transportation facilities to take them to and from their place of work at a price they can afford to pay. The Department of Labor has found that "present transportation systems are both inadequate and too expensive to bring the slum residents to these jobs."

Fourth, location of new industrial facilities in or near poverty areas will have an important "multiplier" effect on the creation of jobs. New auxiliary businesses will be spun off in the same area to service the needs of the primary facility. New retail and service facilities—restaurants and food stores, barbershops, dry cleaners, and clothing stores—will be required to satisfy the demands of the workers at the primary establishment. Most of these derivative jobs and entrepreneurial opportunities will be open to poverty area residents.

Fifth, location of investment and jobs in or near poverty areas is important for its own sake. Partly, it is important to end these areas' isolation—to bring not just individual residents, but the entire community, back into contact with the mainstream of American life.

It is important that children and young people see change and development take place through the work of their own fathers and brothers—providing concrete hope through living example. And, it is vital that poverty areas, like other communities, be able to develop a sense of joint community achievement and purpose.

But merely to reach the conclusion that it is necessary for new businesses to establish facilities in and near urban and rural poverty areas will not suffice. For the simple fact is that businesses are not presently making any efforts to establish such facilities in these areas.

Private corporations are, of course, responsible to their stockholders. Large-scale investment in poverty areas will certainly be more costly and difficult than investment elsewhere. Land, transportation, procurement of supplies, training of workers, extra supervision—all these are so costly in poverty areas as to make investment there, under present conditions, uneconomical. If private enterprise is to play its full part in relation to poverty areas, therefore, it must have the support of government to help make up for increased costs.

I have already proposed the first step in this effort. Last July I introduced legislation to provide this support to certain businesses locating facilities in the poorest urban and rural areas. That bill is designed to provide such businesses with tax credits and excess deductions which they can offset against income derived directly from the new facility or against income derived from another source.

In brief, this tax incentive program would work as follows:

First, it would apply only to companies constructing new facilities or expanding existing ones in poverty areas.

Second, full consultation with the residents of the poverty area affected would have to take place before any industrial facility was constructed.

Third, any qualifying business would have to meet certain hiring requirements both as to number and percentage of low-income, unemployed persons.

Fourth, job training would be undertaken to prepare men for specific roles in clearly designated and available jobs.

Fifth, any qualifying business would receive the following tax incentives during the ten years immediately following the time that it began operations.

- A 10 per cent credit on machinery and equipment in lieu of the normal maximum 7 per cent credit.
- A 7 per cent credit on expenditures for constructing an industrial facility or for leasing space for a qualifying business.
- A credit carryback of three taxable years and a carryover of ten taxable years.
- A useful life, for purposes of depreciation, of $66\frac{2}{3}$ per cent of the normal useful life.
- A special deduction of an additional 25 per cent of the salaries paid to all workers hired to meet the requirements of this act.

That the use of tax incentives to encourage industrial development in this nation's poverty areas is both a necessary and appropriate step has received growing recognition. In its recent report, the President's Advisory Committee on Rural Poverty concluded that for firms locating in poverty areas, tax incentives in the form of "liberalized investment . . . credits, accelerated depreciation . . . and broader carry-forward, carry-backward provisions be given." This conclusion was strongly seconded by the National Advisory Commission on Civil Disorders. In a special report to the commission by a businessmen's group headed by Charles Thornton, chairman of Litton Industries, tax incentives in the form of credits, accelerated depreciation and excess salary deductions were recommended.

Thus, the two most extensive studies done on the problems of inducing private enterprise to come into this nation's poverty areas have concluded with one basic recommendation. They have found that tax incentives must be utilized if new facilities are to be built in these areas.

Clearly, the time has come for the Administration to support and the Congress to act on these recommendations.

But while enactment of a system of tax incentives would constitute a major achievement in bringing jobs to those who most need them, it is only a first step.

Businesses can only utilize tax incentives after they have opened new plants. They cannot use them to raise capital.

For all but our largest public companies, the task of obtaining capital to open a new facility—especially one that is in a poverty area is an insurmountable obstacle. The present tight money market and increased fears of loss due to riots, crime and vandalism have made financing particularly difficult for businesses seeking to begin operations in economically distressed areas.

Present federal economic development programs have proved inadequate. The Economic Development Administration has moved too slowly and cautiously. In 1967, its disbursements totaled only $34 million—a fraction of the money which should have been made available for the financing of new businesses. Although Congress gave EDA authority in 1967 to operate in urban poverty areas, it had previously been confined almost entirely to rural areas—this authority has still not even begun to be implemented. Even when EDA does begin to make urban loans, its interest rate and loan period authority is still too restricted to provide any substantial stimulus to business to open new facilities in urban or rural poverty areas. The tools available to the Small Business Administration are similarly inadequate.

A new capital creation program is clearly needed. We must provide a mechanism which will break the cycle that turns capital away from businesses seeking to establish facilities in poverty areas. In short, we must provide a flow of short-term and long-term loans to those businesses which will open and expand badly needed industrial and commercial facilities and help turn these economic wastelands into areas of hope and opportunity.

With these needs in mind, I propose two new programs which will directly attack the problem of increasing the flow of capital into poverty areas. Both are designed to create new jobs for the unemployed and underemployed.

The first proposal would make long- and short-term credit available to any industrial or commercial enterprise, including those owned by members of minority groups and poverty area residents, opening a new business or expanding an existing facility having nine or more employees, two thirds of whom are poverty area residents. Loans would be made available from private lenders and the federal government, with federal interest subsidies and repayment guarantees up to 50 per cent of the total loan. Short-term loans would be subsidized up to 3 per cent below the market rate for short-term credit; long-term loans at a rate of 1 per cent below federal borrowing costs.

The second proposal, supplementing the first, is designed to promote the ownership of retail, commercial and industrial enterprise by members of disadvantaged minority groups and residents of poverty areas. Any new or expanding business, at least 30 per cent of which is owned by such persons and which employs six or more persons, two thirds of whom are poverty area residents, would be eligible for special loan and technical assistance and would have first priority for direct federal loans. Federal loan guarantees would cover 90 per cent instead of 50 per cent of the total loan.

Loan assistance to minority- and resident-owned business would be coupled with a technical assistance program which would help open up new business opportunities, seek out capital and provide counseling and management training to eligible borrowers and other poverty areas businessmen.

Long-term credit will be provided through a New Fund administered by the Secretary of Commerce and coordinated with the Administrator of the Small Business Administration and the Secretary of Labor. The proposed New Fund will have a first year appropriation of $400 million which will be increased by $150 million each year thereafter, reaching a maximum authorization of $1 billion.

Short-term credit will be provided from Treasury Tax and Loan Accounts—tax and bond purchase payments made to the federal government which are then deposited in commercial banks throughout the country.

The principal features of these two programs are explained briefly in the following.

CAPITAL LOANS FOR POVERTY AREA BUSINESSES

Eligible Areas

The areas at which this proposal is directed are: the 193 poverty areas which are located in our major metropolitan centers; this nation's worst rural poverty areas; and, Indian reservations.

Eligible Businesses

Virtually any type of industrial or commercial enterprise that can be conducted in or near an urban or rural poverty area, will be eligible for assistance under this bill. Thus, manufacturing enterprises as well as service establishments dealing with other business enterprises will be permitted to obtain financing. Safeguards will be provided to assure that loans are not available merely for the purpose of moving an enterprise from one area to another.

Employment Criteria

The facility must employ at least nine persons. Of these, at least two thirds must be poverty area residents and one third must have been low-income persons at the time they were hired.

A New Fund

A New Fund, to be directed by the Secretary of Commerce in collaboration with the Director of the Small Business Administration and the Secretary of Labor will coordinate all long term lending policies. Short-term lending policies will be directed by the New Fund in conjunction with the Secretary of the Treasury.

The proposed New Fund will start with an initial appropriation of $400 million the first year—an appropriation which will increase by $150 million per year so that at the end of five years the fund will have reached its maximum authorization of $1 billion.

Direct and Guaranteed Loans

The primary purpose of the New Fund will be to guarantee and, in some cases, to make long-term loans to poverty area businesses.

In providing financing, the specified preference will be for the New Fund to guarantee private loans rather than to provide direct loans. In short, the New Fund will operate as a lender of last resort—making direct loans only when there exists a reasonable assurance of repayment and when comparable financing cannot be obtained by the borrower from private sources, even with the type of guarantees which could be made by the Fund. As a general rule, all private loans will be subject to a guarantee against loss up to 50 per cent of the amount of the loan, except that when the borrower is one of our major public companies, only a 10 per cent guarantee will be provided.

Interest Subsidies and Loan Periods

In order to raise the rates of return which can be derived from poverty area investment—thereby compensating for the unusual risks and difficulties involved in opening a business facility in these areas—direct and guaranteed loans will bear a subsidized interest rate. Long-term loans made directly or guaranteed by the New Fund will carry an effective interest rate 1 per cent below federal borrowing costs. The only limitations on these subsidies will be that the federal payment cannot exceed 5 per cent on any private loan, and, if the business is receiving tax incentives it can also receive subsidies. In order to take account of the economic realities of opening poverty area businesses, the New Fund will be authorized to guarantee and provide direct loans for terms up to thirty-five years. It will also provide loans for up to 80 per cent of project cost. Both in terms of the repayment period and interest charges, these provisions offer great advantages over current federal loan programs.

Approval of Guaranteed Loans

In order to avoid red tape and the bureaucratic delays that have invariably occurred in guaranteed loan programs, this proposal rejects the idea of specific government approval for each loan. Rather, the New Fund will be permitted to enter into two-year agreements with private lending institutions under which these institutions will be authorized to make guaranteed loans and investments up to a specified quota. Periodic assessments of the performance by lenders will be made and unused quotas will then be reallocated.

Short-term Capital

In regard to the development of short-term working capital for poverty area businesses, we must establish a further mechanism beyond that of government loans and guarantees.

For years it has been the policy of the federal government in its capacity as a purchaser of goods to promote the development of distressed areas and to assist small businesses. In my judgment, the federal government should now adopt a similar economic development policy by utilizing deposits of public funds as a mechanism for encouraging private banks to provide short-term bank credit for poverty area businesses.

Most funds which flow to the federal government in the form of taxes and bond purchase payments remain in the commercial banks through which they are paid in the form of deposits of the federal government. These deposits—which in recent years have normally amounted to about $4 billion—are called Treasury Tax and Loan Accounts and any bank may become eligible to hold such an account. The monies deposited of course earn income for the bank when they are invested, but, as in the case of any demand deposit, the bank pays no interest or other fees to the depositor.

In my judgment, the Secretary of the Treasury would be authorized to establish certain minimum requirements for loans to poverty area businesses, which must be met by special depositaries located in or near these poverty areas. The requirements would be tied to the average balance in the bank's Tax and Loan Account, so that the performance level that a bank would be expected to meet would relate to the benefit which the federal government gives the bank in the form of interest free deposits. The requirements might start as low as 3 per cent of the bank's Tax and Loan Account during the first year and rise in subsequent years to as much as 15 per cent.

This proposal would not simply constitute an additional burden for each depository bank. Any bank which met its percentage requirement would be eligible to receive further deposits of the federal government equal to a significant percentage of its qualified loans. These deposits—which would be in the range of 20 to 50 per cent of the funds put into qualified loans would not be kept in the bank's regular Tax and Loan Account where they would be subject to withdrawal. In an effort to give a greater incentive to the bank, these new compensating deposits would be maintained in separate accounts which would be kept open by the federal government for at least a calendar quarter.

The funds to meet these additional balances for the banks which do meet their percentage requirement, would be derived in the first instance from withdrawals from the banks which do not meet their percentage requirement. If most banks meet them so that there is insufficient money available for noncomplying banks to provide extra deposits to complying banks, the New Fund would deposit some of its reserve underlying the loan guarantee in complying banks.

Short-term loans made by these depository banks would be subject to the same guarantees by the New Fund that will apply to long term loans. Moreover, an interest rate subsidy up to a maximum of 3 per cent will be paid by the federal government. This subsidy will be utilized to reduce the short term costs of capital to qualified poverty area businesses.

SPECIAL LOAN AND TECHNICAL ASSISTANCE TO MEMBERS OF DISADVANTAGED MINORITY GROUPS AND POVERTY AREA RESIDENTS

While the above program providing credit to business operating in or near poverty areas will, of course, apply to businesses owned by members of disadvantaged minority groups and by low- and moderate-income residents of poverty areas, its primary benefit will be in inducing outside, established business to enter poverty areas. Special assistance should, in addition, be made available to members of disadvantaged minority groups—Negroes, Spanish, and Mexican-Americans, Puerto Ricans and Indians—and to poverty area residents. These are the people who have the greatest stake in the future of their own communities. They must be assisted to enter the mainstream of American economic life.

Special Loan Assistance

I therefore propose that for enterprises, at least 30 per cent of which are owned by members of minority groups and low and moderate income residents of poverty areas, the provisions of the above-described capital loan program be modified so that:

1. If there is a shortage of federal funds for direct loans or for loan guarantees, priority will be given to such businesses.
2. Retail businesses, as well as commercial and industrial enterprises, will receive both short and long term loans.
3. Federal guarantees will be for up to 90 per cent of the total project cost, instead of 50 per cent.

4. Eligible businesses need employ only six employees, instead of nine.
5. Loans will be for up to 90 per cent of the total project cost, instead of 50 per cent.
6. The federal government provide guarantees of up to 50 per cent of equity investments of institutions such as small business development corporations in order to create new sources of equity capital. No existing federal program provides guarantees for equity investments which are generally subject to rigid repayment requirements.
7. Community groups within poverty areas will be authorized to obtain loans for purchasing and building facilities for lease back to any businesses qualifying for long or short term loans.

Technical Assistance

Capital, while vital, is not enough to establish viable businesses owned and managed by members of disadvantaged minority groups and low- and moderate-income residents of poverty areas. These groups have been so long excluded from business activities that they also need technical management assistance.

Present federal technical assistance efforts are underfinanced and suffer from serious deficiencies.

First, there has been significant lack of coordination. Some cities have several programs, others have none. Programs rarely work closely with each other, either nationally or locally. As a result, tools which are available to one group are often not used by others. Neither successes nor failures are known so that newer efforts frequently do not learn from earlier experience.

Second, most of the businesses created or helped by existing programs are marginal and many are sole proprietorships. It is important to help existing small establishments even if they are not competitive. But it is a mistake to make such enterprises the major focus of a government effort. Instead, if indigenous persons are to play a significant role in American economic life, they must own and operate automobile dealerships, shopping centers, small and medium sized manufacturing companies, and the like, and mechanisms must be established which will start a continuing process to create and maintain significant numbers of larger enterprises.

Third, existing programs have generally lacked expertise. They have rarely had the full-time participation of trained staffs with business experience. Minority and poverty area citizens must know when and how to get assistance, both from the government and private industry. They must be able to understand and put together complicated financial arrangements, and be able to communicate with other businessmen.

I therefore propose that a minimum of ten million dollars a year be appropriated to provide federal grants for local technical assistance programs. These programs should enlist the combined efforts of business leaders, local government, and other important elements in the community, with substantial participation and control by the leaders of minority groups and poverty area residents they are to serve.

At the same time, these programs must have on their staffs full-time business experts. As our large corporations become increasingly interested in meeting the problems of poverty, they may be willing to lend some of their best talent. All programs should include at least these elements:

They must reach out to members of minority groups and residents of poverty areas to motivate them to enter business or to expand and improve existing businesses.

They must help open up new business opportunities—for example, by creating a committee of large corporations committed to providing sub-contracts; by helping businessmen obtain contracts from the federal and local governments; by obtaining franchises to be operated by minority and poverty area businessmen; by starting shopping centers in urban renewal and model cities areas; and by persuading urban renewal and other government agencies to contract with poverty area contractors to build and rehabilitate housing.

They must provide sources of capital—for example, by starting Small Business Investment Companies to provide equity and working capital, perhaps by seeking funds in the community; by starting Local Development Companies to provide the physical facilities and land needed by new businesses; by persuading private financial institutions to ease credit criteria for business or to provide loan pools; by assisting minority or poverty area businessmen to obtain loans from private financial institutions, SBA, or EDA and through the new program which I have proposed today.

They must provide continuing training, counseling, and assistance—for example by persuading established corporations to offer internships in their own marketing, accounting, cost control or other departments prior to receiving subcontracts from assisted companies; by persuading established corporations to give continued technical assistance through having their own staffs on call by minority or poverty area businessmen; by asking local colleges or other institutions to give special business courses; by giving individual counseling to existing and potential businessmen; by providing contracts to management consulting companies to assist minority and poverty area businessmen.

The federal government should also be making other efforts to provide management and ownership assistance to members of minority groups and residents of poverty areas. Plans to aid small business should be required in all model city plans. The Department of Labor can pay private corporations to provide training and technical assistance to existing and potential minority and poverty area businessmen as it now provides funds to corporations to train the unemployed. The Office of Education can develop special programs to provide high quality management training through scholarships to business schools and through special business school courses. Federal funds can pay for research into new techniques for assisting minority and poverty area businessmen. And the federal government can coordinate and assist the efforts of local programs.

It is of vital importance that the federal government involve our national corporations in this effort. They can provide training, subcontracts and franchises, loans or equity capital, and technical assistance. They can, as the Fairchild–Hillyer Corporation has in the District of Columbia, start manufacturing plants, jointly owned with a neighborhood organization in a poverty area, with the objective of completely turning it over to the community in just a few years. National corporations can as they have agreed to do in Baltimore, provide financial support for a small business investment company controlled by Negroes. All this can occur throughout the country by joining the dedicated efforts of business and government.

These proposals will require appropriations of only $43 million the first year and $337 million over five years for interest subsidies and technical assistance. In addition, $1 billion will be required for the New Fund over five years to provide direct federal loans and as a reserve for guaranteeing private loans, but these funds will be recoverable by the federal government. It is a reasonable estimate that these measures will result in the loan of about $3 billion by private lenders and the federal government to all kinds of businesses in or near poverty areas and for the establishment of many successful businesses owned by members of minority groups and residents of poverty areas.

These loan and technical assistance proposals and my tax incentive program proposed last July will not, of course, solve all the problems of poverty. They are important steps. They will offer a mechanism for bringing new business and jobs into our poorest areas.

But they are but one part of the job we must begin. They must be joined with other equally important effects.

They must be combined and coordinated with present Federal education and manpower training programs. They must also be used in conjunction with other new programs which I have proposed and sponsored in the Senate—an emergency employment program to provide 2.4 million new jobs in public service and private enterprise and the housing program which I sponsored in 1967 to give tax incentives to private industry to build and rehabilitate housing for low-income families.

And most important, there must be full participation of community residents through their own institutions, in the development and implementation of all projects. We must shape our government policies with the active participation of our citizens. What we must seek is not just greater programs, but greater participation—by putting our resources directly into the communities, both urban and rural, where the citizenry can determine how best to use those resources. If we accomplish this, we will have begun one of this nation's great remaining tasks—to make this a land in which equal opportunities are a reality and not a promise, and in which the right to work at a meaningful job and the opportunity to participate fully in the American economy have significance for all Americans.

The Retailers,
the Ghetto,
and the Government

Mildred Hall
and
Bill Williams

This report focuses on the positive: what can be, should be, and is
being done by business, big and small, in cooperation with government and civic officials. Part of the discussion centers around retailer
reaction to the proposal of Senator Robert F. Kennedy (D-N.Y.)
that private enterprise be given tax write-offs and other incentives
to build stores and open new businesses in ghetto areas. Such a
program, according to Kennedy, would persuade the "giant armies"

Reprinted from "The Retailers, the Ghetto, and the Government," *Merchandising Week* (December 11, 1967), pp. 6–7, by permission of Billboard Publications, Inc.

of private enterprise to bring job-creating industries to the slums, stimulating the stagnant ghetto economies.

The report opens by focusing on Washington, D. C., from the downtown retail district to Capitol Hill; shifts to the West Coast for a discussion with two appliance-TV dealers; then moves to the South describing disparate pictures in Nashville and Atlanta.

In the nation's capital, there seems to be a deep reluctance among department store and appliance dealers to talk about building outlets in ghetto areas—with or without government incentives—until other steps are taken first.

The clearest statement, perhaps, came from Richard England, who, along with John W. Hechinger, owns ten stores in the area, which carry everything for the homeowner from tacks to television. Hechinger was recently tapped by President Johnson to head the District's new nine-man City Council, which will try to revamp the ancient administrative machinery of the city.

England's thoughts on the subject are noteworthy, because two of the Hechinger stores—one in existence for forty years—are within the boundaries of ghetto areas. The main hope of both store owners and ghetto dwellers, he claims, lies in "risk removal."

To the store owner, this means, first and foremost, lowered insurance rates and noncancellable insurance policies against all the things that can happen to an inner-city store. A larger and more informed police force is essential; so are the cleaning, lighting, and landscaping of ghetto-area streets, to bring them in line with the beckoning charm of D. C.'s revitalized downtown shopping street and the highly beautiful suburban shopping centers.

One of the biggest problems, said England, is employment. The inner-city dweller is, if anything, even more reluctant to work in the ghetto store than is the outsider. "He is afraid. It is the ghetto dweller who has most to fear, even more than the storekeeper, from the roving bands of young ones, between fifteen and twenty-two, who do most of the rampaging."

What does he think about the principle of generous tax incentives for manufacturers, wholesalers, and distributors—as the Kennedy bill suggests—to encourage inner-city branches staffed largely with untrained slum dwellers? Would this type of tax incentive attract new retail outlets?

England said he has not studied the Kennedy proposal enough

to comment on it. But he did not hesitate to reiterate his belief in the prime necessities of inner-city retailing: better insurance, improved police protection, and a general sprucing up.

At the time of this interview, the celebration of the seventy-eighth birthday of the Metropolitan Washington Board of Trade, along with the pre-holiday rush, monopolized the time of store owners and prevented their personal comment. Two discount appliance dealers contacted through their administrative offices, however, chose not to comment at all on whether any kind of government tax incentive program would lure them into the ghettos. The local Hecht department store management was reportedly involved in two imminent store openings—in suburban locations.

But, if top-level management was shy of comment, the lower staff levels were not. Administrative office personnel in some stores were just plain afraid. They frankly hoped their particular department, discount, or appliance store would by no means get into the inner-city turmoil. Such comments underlined England's point that a primary problem would be employment. Said one staffer: "You take ,your life in your hands when you open your door in those places." Said another: "Things are just going from bad to worse— the stealing and vandalism."

On another front, George Washington University professor and employment analyst Dr. Sar Levitan asks "Will Employers Be Induced to Train the Poor?" His article on the subject was placed in the *Congressional Record* by Senator Winston Prouty (R-Vt.), himself a sponsor of employment-incentive bills.

The professor is sympathetic to, but somewhat dubious about, the effectiveness of the current federal incentive moves to improve the ghetto situation. "Doing business in slum areas involves special costs. This is not only because of higher taxes and higher insurance rates (assuming insurance is obtainable), but also because of the difficulties in training residents of slum areas. . . . The crucial issue is to determine the level of incentive needed to compensate for the extra cost. . . ."

Judging by local comment in Washington, that "level of incentive" would have to be rather high. Insurance seems to top the list of vital needs of ghetto storekeepers—present or prospective.

At the legislative level, lower cost and non-cancellable insurance, backed by government funding, arranged through private companies, is the subject of a number of bills getting the prod on both Senate and House sides of the Capitol. A House banking and currency subcommittee has recommended a Crime Protection Insurance Act to set up insurance and re-insurance for small businessmen. Senator George Smathers (D-Fla.), chairman of the Senate Small Business Committee, would establish a Small Business Crime Protection Insurance Corp.

There are some hurdles to this type of government gifting. Businessmen would have to cooperate in approved programs to reduce criminal activity and increase their own mutual protection in high-risk areas. But the Small Business Administration would be authorized to start a "liberal loan policy" to help community merchants get their minimum safety programs under way.

A set of dismal statistics emerged during Senate Small Business Committee hearings last summer—which would discourage retailers from heading for the ghetto trade unless problems of insurance, policing, and lighting are met head on.

A Crime Commission survey found that only 11 per cent of all business units were insured against glass breakage. Acts of vandalism were grossly underreported, because businessmen took the loss rather than invite higher insurance rates or cancellation. Many Washington retailers told the Senators they would fear for their lives if they reported thefts and vandalism to the police.

Last week, still another Federal low-cost insurance program was introduced in a bill by Rep. Jonathan Bingham (D-N.Y.). Some rugged statistics about insurance costs were advanced by the Congressman: after $40 million was paid out in Watts riot claims, five insurance companies raised their rates three to five times the previous levels. Maximum value allowed was $150,000 for a single piece of property, and there were no policies at all for theft, vandalism, and malicious mischief. In Newark and Detroit, losses of nearly $250 million had a similar effect on private insurance companies serving these areas.

The future seems to lie somewhere between the optimism of sponsors and supporters of helpful legislation and the hesitation and caution of those who are most directly involved at the retail level. A realization that the long, hard grind to reverse the unemployment and erosion in the heart of American cities must have commercial steam is imperative.

Manufacturers and wholesalers—possibly because they are relatively far behind the front lines of assault that the retailer faces in ghetto rioting and crime—are more optimistic and cooperative with the government at this point. The Kennedy bill reportedly received many commendatory letters from manufacturers, including Bendix and Whirlpool, who share the Senator's belief that the new tax-incentive business could have a "multiplier effect"—offsetting the tax loss to the government, increasing employment further by bringing in more retail and service trades to serve the primary plants eligible under the government plan.

Kennedy and other legislators frankly admit that without the help, the know-how, the enterprise of the American storekeeper and businessman, any attempt to simply legislate commercial life and employment into ghetto areas would be doomed to failure.

Typically, at the local Board of Trade celebration, businessmen and new D.C. mayor, Walter Washington, pledged a partnership to improve the city conditions "as a simple matter of self-preservation."

At the same time, however, a retailer seminar and the Retail Bureau of the Board of Trade here, worked for stricter anticrime laws, more realistic penalties, and more safeguards against the risk of "false arrest" charges when a storekeeper catches a pilferer. In the District, the theft rate in retail stores has doubled within the past few years.

One root cause common to all ghetto outbreaks and city erosion has been unemployment. The commercial and psychological need for jobs has outstripped the formerly all-important issues of integration and open housing in city areas.

Another point that seems to have been made most often and fervently as new programs, new government and business partnerships grope for improvement: no business community can improve a slum-enslaved city with half of its merchant members committed and half uncommitted to the common cause.

ON THE WEST COAST: THE MEMORY OF WATTS STILL AFFECTS RETAILERS

Any newsstand along Central Avenue in Watts is cluttered with newspapers and magazines that carry endless advertisements designed to tease and tantalize readers into buying the newest washer-dryer combination or shiny vacuum cleaner. Advertising constantly circulates in Watts, like any other section of Southern California.

In Watts today—two years after the 1965 riots set stores ablaze—one would be hard pressed, however, to actually purchase any of the new products that are advertised so freely. Most of Watts' businesses disappeared after those six hot days in August, and Watts residents are left with little more than pawn shops, liquor stores, and charred foundations.

How do West Coast retailers react to Senator Robert F. Kennedy's proposal, which would seek to revitalize business activity in just such ghetto communities as the Watts district?

"The scope of this thing is tremendous—it's such a big thing," is the response of Jim Bethanis, owner of the three MSI appliance stores in Southern California, all located a comfortable twenty miles from Watts.

Kennedy's proposal, as Bethanis sees it, would only help the "large chains" to move into the ghetto. His own small chain, he feels, has no future in Watts. "I wouldn't be large enough to handle this area. I don't want to open another business in a good area, much less a problem one like that."

According to Bethanis, high insurance rates and the extreme poverty level of the area have discouraged businesses from moving into Watts. "You are dealing with people—whether black or white—who just cannot afford new appliances," he said. "Sometimes they will buy used stuff, if the terms are extended far enough."

Glen Hardin, general manager of the three Handy Andy appliance stores in Sacramento, Calif., disagrees: "There is money to be spent on our merchandise in the ghetto areas; there is still a certain percentage of the population that likes new things and can afford to pay for them."

Hardin feels small businessmen could make the move into areas like Watts as easily as the large chains—particularly businessmen already located in what he calls the "gray areas," those adjacent to the hard-core ghettos.

His own stores in Sacramento, however, do not face the problems of an area such as Watts. "It has been very quiet. Oh, we've had a couple of incidents with racial overtones, but nothing that would draw national attention."

Both of the California businessmen think that Kennedy's proposal could attract business to the ghettos.

The major problem is training, said Bethanis. High insurance rates and the risks involved in moving to the ghetto are "not astronomical" problems, he said. The primary problem is adequately trained people. "There is too much emphasis on everybody having a college education today. Let's face it, not everyone is college material. We need more trade schools."

What Bethanis would like to see is a "concentrated effort" by business and government to train the undereducated poor. "Can you imagine what would happen if we had 100,000 trained Negroes in Los Angeles? It would change our whole economy. You could get things done so much cheaper, and it would save the government money in the long run—cutting welfare rolls."

If he were to expand his business to the ghetto, Bethanis would "definitely want" Negro sales personnel, and, "possibly, a Negro partner" in the store. "You cannot be an absentee owner unless you are a large chain; you must take an active interest in the community," he said.

To Hardin, there is *always* a shortage of trained personnel today— "no matter where you consider opening a business." Would he consider moving into a ghetto area with incentives from the federal government—as in the Kennedy proposal? His first reaction: "No." But, on second thought: "We would definitely give it some heavy consideration. It's a real gamble.

"It would depend on how big a write-off was involved," Hardin continued. Ten per cent? He refused to commit himself as to what would be a sufficient incentive. "A program like this requires heavy and deep consideration," he reiterated.

Bethanis, who is "not too keen on government-supported businesses," thinks Kennedy's plan is "worth working at." There will be nothing more important domestically in this country for the next ten to twenty years.

"I don't think anyone has really tried to go into these areas," he said. "You know, it's the old story of 'business is business.' The businessman entering the ghetto must be a humanitarian as well as a businessman," Bethanis added. "He must be willing to take a loss at first in order to stimulate the economy; he must be 'sort of a pioneer doing something for his fellow man.'"

A sobering thought, however, comes from Frederick D. Sturdivant, assistant marketing professor at the University of

Southern California: "While it is extremely important that factories be built and the disadvantaged trained and employed, are not the improvements minimized when these workers and their families are faced with shopping in areas where prices are higher, credit charges inflated, stores generally deteriorated, and customers often treated badly?"

It is generally agreed among businessmen and the Negroes, in government and the ghettos, that programs like the one proposed by Senator Kennedy are required to solve the growing problems in our urban ghettos. The Senate has not acted on Kennedy's proposal, however, and business continues to bypass areas like Watts. In the midst of a great need, there are still no humanitarian pioneers on Central Avenue.

A SOUTHERN REPORT: DISPARATE VIEWS FROM TWO BIG RETAILERS

"Before you can have any tax write-off, there has to be a profit of some sort. In the ghettos of Nashville, there simply isn't enough disposable income for a profit." This was the conclusion of Fred Harvey, Jr., president of Harvey's department store, the city's largest, with a huge downtown outlet and a suburban location.

"Economics—and economics alone—determines the location of any store," Harvey explained. "All stores are interested in expansion. The question is simply, where can we make money? We can't make it on Jefferson Street—no matter what the incentives may be."

Nashville's Jefferson Street is the primary thoroughfare in the city's most populated ghetto. The vast majority of the city's 120,000 Negroes (in a metropolitan area of 450,000) lives in this general region. (As an interesting economic sidelight, it might be noted that only 7,461 of the total are in owner-occupied homes, the median educational level in the region is eighth grade, and an equal number of wives and husbands are working—all figures of the Metropolitan Planning Commission.)

Harvey said he would be interested in a federal program in which minority salespeople are trained for service and other jobs, but only on an on-the-job basis.

"We've had some bad experiences with some government

agencies," he said. "Our problem is this. The government currently is paying 'X' number of dollars to a lot of minorities to go to school and learn service trades. Actually, it's not much less than what we'd pay them by the hour, and, considering the fact they go to school only a few hours a day, they come out ahead. We've found it difficult to get these people to leave and go to work. They've got too good a thing going. So they stay there until they finish the course. We could have given them good training here, but they're not interested. Then, what happens to them after graduation, I just don't know. They never seem to come around."

The bakery trade, said Harvey, is a good example. "We always need bakers for our pastry department. It seems that all the bakers today are old, and there aren't any young ones coming along. But we can't find them, even though they're trained for the trade at school.

"Now, if the government would set up an on-the-job program, where we could train them, pay them, and keep them, I most certainly would be interested. That would have some merit."

Another Nashville department store official, who refused to be quoted by name, said he was "personally opposed" to any government plan to "push" stores into the ghettos.

"We operate on an economic basis, not a sociological basis," he said. "If stores could show a profit in those areas, they'd be there now, and not waiting for the government to help them. As it is, the ghettos have large neighborhood stores, but the wage-and-hour law is playing hell with them. It's going to run the small people out of business, and then the ghettos will have nothing. Whenever there is government involvement, there is trouble."

One of the "neighborhood stores" in the ghetto is that of Ben Schwartz (Schwartz' department store), who has been in business for fifty-three years, always in the same location. His 30-by-50-ft. store is on Charlotte Avenue, one block off Jefferson, in the very heart of the Negro district.

"Harvey's, Cain-Sloan, Castner-Knott? None of them could make it here," Schwartz said. "I'm just staying in business to pass the time. These people are my friends. I now wait on the grand-children of the people I took care of fifty years ago," he said.

The Schwartz store is stacked with "general merchandise," predominant low-cost clothing items and low-end appliances. "I've never sold anything high-end in my life," he said. "Who can afford it here?"

Schwartz said his business has gradually dwindled because of urban redevelopment. "Eventually, it will die," he said, "and so I'm not interested in growing." He is the owner, proprietor, and sole employee of the store.

Asked what would happen to his customers if his store closes down, he said: "They'll take the bus down to Harvey's, or maybe go to another store in the neighborhood."

Has the wage-and-hour law affected him? "How could it, when I'm the only one here. I don't understand all that stuff, anyway."

In Atlanta, Rich's department store took an approach completely opposite to that of the Nashville spokesmen.

"If we had the right kind of tax write-off, and the incentives were right, I don't see any reason in the world why we couldn't go into a ghetto area," said Kenneth Majors, financial vice president and treasurer of the store.

Majors said the matter has never been discussed internally; but, as long as the stockholder's money could be protected, it certainly deserved serious consideration.

"You can't expect stores to go into the ghettos and dissipate the stockholders' money," he said. "You just can't tell the stockholder he has to accept less. While department stores compete with each other in sales, there also is a keen competition for stockholders, and this can't be tossed aside."

A ghetto-based store, according to Majors, would have to be relatively small, self-service ("it could never really be a full-service store"), with check-out lanes. "This gives better physical control," he said. "Theft would always be a problem in an area of low income."

The Rich's vice president noted that one grocery store chain in the Atlanta area already has taken a step on its own to aid the ghetto regions. "Colonial Bread is taking all of its day-old baked goods into the poverty areas and selling them at half price or less. What isn't sold is given away. "So," he said, "it all comes down to what the government would do."

Majors made some concrete suggestions: "A very fast write-off would be acceptable, if this didn't—after a few years—put the store back into a high tax bracket. It would have to have long-range stipulations. A long-range, low tax rate also would be acceptable. Stores currently paying 48 per cent might be cut to 20 per cent over a long-term period, he said, and the stockholder protected in this manner.

"The concept is good. Everyone wants to help the ghettos," he said. "But we'd have to do a lot of figuring, have some serious internal meetings, find out exactly what the government has in mind, weigh all the advantages and disadvantages, and then see if we can maintain a profit. If the government wants to give short-range help, forcing us to re-invest in a new building every few years, it would not be feasible. But if it seriously has a plan that would protect everyone, then Rich's would be interested.

"The government would be ahead in the long run if it did this," Majors added. "What it loses in the corporate taxes it would more than regain in other revenues."

After the Riots—
A Position Paper
for Retailing

Richard Rosenthall

It is not the intention of this study to add to the bulk of riot docu-
mentaries or sociological tracts. Nor does it intend to provide
another list of protection steps or community action programs.

The report does hope to sketch what retailers experienced this
summer and what is foremost in their activities and thinking as they
seek to cool future summers.

The study is based on interviews with seventy-three retailers in
seven cities affected by racial disturbances this summer and on 195
replies to a questionnaire sent to NRMA [National Retail Merchant's
Association] member stores by *Stores* magazine in September. The
questionnaire response was a remarkable 17 per cent.

Thirty-three of the retailers interviewed were proprietors of
small stores in riot neighborhoods, forty were executives in depart-

Reprinted by permission from "After the Riots—A Position Paper for
Retailing," *Stores,* the NRMA Magazine (December, 1967), pp. 11–20. Copyright
1967 by the Retail Merchants Association, N.Y., N.Y.

ment, chain, and discount stores with neighborhood and downtown units in riot cities.

Ghetto residents, public officials, educators, Negro leaders, and business leaders from fields other than retailing were also interviewed.

Stores is very grateful to these many people for their generous disposals of time and frankness in aid of this study. It also expresses its thanks to all those who returned the questionnaire.

INTRODUCTION

Syracuse retailers speak of the "uprising." A New Haven store executive refers to "that teenager spree." A leading Detroit merchant insists that he witnessed an "insurrection."

Each of the three men was, of course, discussing 1967's long hot summer. The experiences, results, and aftermath in every one of America's riot cities have been unique. This is apparent even to the most superficial observer.

Detroit impresses one with its pockets of flattened buildings, as if the ground had been levelled by artillery.

Newark's Springfield Avenue, with its sea of bare plywood and singed street signs, conveys a picture of extensive fire damage. At night, when its stores are closed, Springfield Avenue is a little like a ghost town, floodlit for the filming of a western.

In Syracuse, it is hard to find damaged buildings.

In New Haven, on Congress Avenue, attackers seem to have been selective. There is considerable damage, but many stores were untouched.

On Joseph Avenue in Rochester, damage is squeezed into a few small blocks. Rochester's plywood is more brightly decorated than on riot streets in other cities, which contributes to a feeling that ravaged stores are hopeful about the future. But there are many abandoned store sites on Joseph Avenue, and one is uncertain if they closed this year, or because of Rochester's 1964 riot, or simply because business is hard for a ghetto store even in a prosperous city like Rochester.

Such differences are more than superficial. Newark and Detroit suffered far more than Rochester and Syracuse; Rochester and

Syracuse more than New York and Chicago. Yet all of these cities are on riot lists.

A distinction must also be made between damage suffered by neighborhood stores and by downtown stores. The overwhelming amount of damage was borne by small stores in ghettos.

But despite the varying severity with which ghetto and downtown stores were hit, few stores in riot cities were unaffected. Indeed, the extent to which NRMA members were affected by the riots has been underestimated.

More importantly, there is little reason to expect disturbances to subside, to occur only during the summer, or to remain concentrated in Negro neighborhoods.

CONCLUSIONS AND SUMMARY

NRMA members with stores in racially sensitive cities are convinced they must protect their stores from riots and help to erase the causes of riots. Stores in riot cities place much greater emphasis on erasing riot causes than on store protection. There are four crucial reasons for this:

1. Retailers, more than other businessmen, have the most to gain from harmonious and prosperous communities and the most to lose from disorder.

2. As citizens, retailers want to correct injustices in their communities.

3. Retailers, unlike most other businesses, cannot protect their premises effectively and stay in business.

4. Leaders from all walks of American life, including moderate and militant Negro leaders, are looking more and more to the business community for leadership. They believe that government, labor, the courts, and professional and religious institutions cannot cope with the current situation and that the "realistic businessman" is the last hope for achieving racial peace.

NRMA STORES INVOLVED. More than one third of NRMA stores replying to the questionnaire were affected by riots. Many were seriously affected. Of the 206 stores replying to the questionnaire:

Seventy-three have units in cities or towns that experienced riots, twenty-five in communities that suffered many casualties and very heavy property damage.

Fifteen have units that were attacked by rioters, twenty-two have units near stores that were attacked.

Twenty-five have one or more units that were forced to close; fourteen were closed for more than a day.

These figures represent only a sample of NRMA stores that were directly affected by riots. Executives of twenty-six NRMA stores that were attacked or forced to close, but whose experiences are not included in the statistics, were also interviewed.

RIOT EXPERIENCES

- NRMA stores were rarely surprised that riots occurred, but emergency plans were often inadequately designed and executed.

- Stores which were well illuminated and protected by conspicuously posted guards had an excellent chance of escaping attack, even in areas controlled by mobs.

- Many looted stores which had taken rudimentary precautions greatly reduced their loss and damage.

- Police protection was generally good downtown but often hesitant and sporadic in outlying areas.

- Except for the early stages of a riot, a store's standing in a community seldom had any bearing on whether or not it was attacked.

- In three of the seven cities visited, NRMA store executives were convinced that the manner of television and newspaper coverage in their community had a bearing on whether the riot intensified or abated.

- Exaggerated reports and unfounded rumors were a hazard in all cities, and in at least one city they induced some businesses to close unnecessarily.

- In most cities, after-riot daytime business quickly returned to normal downtown. Neighborhood stores which promptly repaired damage tended to do well. But in tenser cities, night business is still poor.

- Riots have generally been followed by increases in vandalism and pilferage in both downtown and ghetto stores and also by fire bombings and a rise in the burglary rate in ghetto stores.
- In NRMA stores, post-riot racial incidents involving customers or employees have been rare.
- However, a significant minority of stores reports increasing activity and pressure from black extremist and white backlash groups.
- Post-riot antagonism between ghetto residents and independent ghetto merchants has greatly intensified. Ecouraged by extremists, ghetto residents are also increasingly applying a general antimerchant hostility to downtown stores.
- However, some major chains with units in riot-city ghettos report that relations with Negroes have improved since the riots, particularly in stores which have been modernized and adjusted to the needs of local consumers.
- Many department and chain stores have assigned one key executive to oversee all protection, personnel, display, and community relations relevant to race relations.
- Riots were usually followed by greater retailer participation in civic, business, and government programs designed to ease interracial tensions. The scope and energy of this activity varied, and continues to vary, from city to city.

EXPECTATIONS

- Stores, to an overwhelming extent, expect rioting to worsen or to be equally serious next year, but they do think retailer participation in community programs can lessen tension.
- Executives interviewed in riot cities think police will act more promptly and firmly in the event of future disturbances.
- Some leading stores are concerned about the possibility of planned terrorist acts by either white or black racists.

ACTIVITY

Activity in communities: The majority of retailers think measures to prevent riots should concentrate equally on law enforcement and on programs to improve the lives of Negroes (Q. 10, see page 231).

- Executives with units in riot cities have more confidence in the efficacy of efforts to improve ghetto conditions than in efforts to improve law enforcement.

- The greatest community participation by retailers is in programs heavily supported by businessmen.

- A substantial minority of stores has increased communication with moderate Negro groups, and some stores with militant Negro groups (Q. 12). About 60 per cent of stores in riot cities think Negro groups overstate what business can achieve (Q. 18).

- Business-led programs are making positive steps, notably in the areas of recruiting and training unskilled Negroes, promotion of Negro employees, improved community-police relations, and plans to improve housing.

Activity in store operations: Stores are lowering employment qualifications and adjusting employment testing and interviewing procedures in order to hire more Negroes. Stores are also making special efforts to promote Negroes and recruit underemployed Negroes.

- Leading chains are making special efforts to improve units in Negro neighborhoods, but unprofitable ghetto units are still being closed.

Protection activity: Protection activity is concentrating on improved emergency plans, security coverage, illumination, fire-fighting equipment, and liaison with police and stores nearby (see Qs. 5, 6, and 7).

- Very few stores are investing in elaborate protection equipment, allowing greater access by security people or executives to fire-arms, or altering operations in a manner that might have an adverse effect on a store's image or employee relations (see Qs. 5 and 6).

Riot Experiences

MAJOR PROTECTION LESSONS.   Few NRMA stores were taken completely by surprise when rioting broke out. Most big stores have police-band radio receivers, which were and are constantly attended, and most downtown stores were in touch with police.

However, many retailers concede glaring shortcomings in their preparations.

Protection principles learned from the 1965 Watts riots still apply. Three vital principles that were substantiated this summer are:

1. The importance of constant attention to thorough, realistic emergency plans.
2. The importance of "conspicuous protection." In translation, this means maximum illumination of premises and maximum display of well equipped guards. Illumination, a show of sidearms, and uniforms consistently deterred attackers.
3. The importance of undertaking elementary precautions prior to an outbreak. Such precautions as were taken by attacked stores repeatedly minimized loss and damage, even from organized looters operating in unprotected premises.

EMERGENCY PLANS. Poor preparation and administration of plans to protect people and secure violent or valuable merchandise were evident in many stores. Fortunately, few such stores were attacked.

Most prevalent shortcomings were:

- Poor definition of executive responsibilities and posts.
- Malfunctioning of emergency facilities, such as fire-fighting equipment and emergency power generators.

One New York executive told *Stores* that a recent management inspection disclosed that emergency and stair lights were not working, despite the fact that frequent inspections by maintenance personnel have been regarded as urgent since the New York power failure in 1965.

Some stores discovered at critical moments that no one present could locate the telephone numbers or names of key police officials, local police precincts, or newspapers and radio stations.

Store emergency planning is concentrating on thoroughness and follow through.

As a Buffalo store head put it: "Preparing a plan is like programming a computer. People's responsibilities and locations must be made explicit. It is essential to detail every thing, every place, every step of the way—who is on what exit, who is responsible for what piece of fire-fighting equipment, who is in command of places of refuge and so on. Take nothing for granted. And make sure people really know what they are supposed to do."

CONSPICUOUS PROTECTION. In all cities, both downtown and in ghetto neighborhoods, stores that were brightly illuminated and displayed strength tended to escape damage. Invariably, dark unattended stores were the first to be attacked, lighted well-guarded stores the last. Even in areas they controlled, mobs often avoided stores that were not guarded but were brightly illuminated.

In Newark, stores on dimly lighted side streets off Springfield Avenue were among the first to be looted. But in a clothing store on Springfield Avenue, two men who sat, visible to the street, with guns on their laps succeeded in protecting their store for two days and nights until the National Guard arrived.

In one city, downtown department stores that were approached by rioters but that remained well lighted and patrolled inside by guards escaped damage, even though guards were instructed to shoot only to protect themselves. Dark and unprotected stores nearby were ransacked.

In severe riot cities, gates, strong doors, grills, locks, and alarm systems were often useless. Frequently, vandals regarded such defenses as a challenge and made a point of breaching them. A Detroit executive said, "Negroes hate fortified fronts and have promised to come through them."

Occasionally, however, fortifications induced looters to look for easier pickings.

ELEMENTARY PRECAUTIONS. Looters, including professional looters, are usually in a hurry, even if there is no sign of opposition.

A neighborhood Detroit store which was attacked at night by a disciplined, organized band of looters did not lose a single television or radio set, simply because floor samples were chained and the stock was locked up. Looters did not take the time to locate and break into areas where appliances were stored. However, some of this store's fine jewelry was on the floor and in glass cases and so was stolen.

Looters maintained a sense of use and value throughout even the wildest rioting. In Newark, liquor and jewelry stores were invariably looted but most shoe stores were untouched; Newark looters seemed as aware of shoe inventory problems as retailers.

In some stores looters destroyed accounts receivable records.

PRIVATE PROTECTION.   In areas controlled by mobs it was rarely feasible for store or company security guards to resist looters. Guards were, of course, outnumbered, and most stores wanted to avoid use of firearms.

Neighborhood chain units often were not guarded at all, and no attempt was made to guard them during riots. This was usually store policy. Protection of individual units was not considered worth the risks.

One chain executive said, "We could have sent reinforcements. But the important thing to do was get people out."

Larger downtown stores were less willing to abandon their premises. As one downtown executive put it, "You don't give up $10 million worth of merchandise without a try. Employees and customers come first, but we aren't going to just up and leave at the first sign of trouble."

EXECUTIVE VIGIL.   Usually, one or more key executives remained in downtown stores until disturbances were contained. In Newark, one executive remarked, "Who said retailing hours are getting shorter? I ate and slept here for four days."

Some Newark and Detroit stores still schedule key executives for night duty. These executives have established communications with police and are prepared to take charge of protection activities.

Other stores, however, consider executive night vigil unnecessary and leave matters in the hands of store security people.

During the riots, big stores in Newark and Detroit put their premises at the disposal of the National Guard. One store reports it provided shelter, communication facilities and arms, ammunition, cameras, film, and food from stock.

EXPERIENCES VARY.   Department and chain store units were frequently the targets of well organized looters who displayed expertise in entering stores and keen judgment in selecting the most "fencible" and portable merchandise.

Neighborhood stores tended more to suffer from indiscriminate looting and destruction.

NRMA Questionnaire to Member Stores on Problems of Riots

Percentage replies by companies in cities with riots and,
in parenthesis, all companies replying

1. Has any city in which you have a store experienced riots in the past 3 years:

Yes: 100 (37), No:—(63)

2. Have these riots produced:

Many casualties and heavy property damage: 28 (12)
Few casualties but heavy property damage: 21 (8)
Relatively little damage: 47 (20)
No damage: 5 (60)

3. Did riots induce you to close a store:

More than a day: 19 (7)
Less than a day: 15 (6)
Not forced to close: 66 (87)

4. Did rioters attack:

Your store: 20 (7)
Stores nearby: 31 (12)
Only areas not near your store: 33 (13)
No attacks: 16 (68)

5. Since the riots have you:

Provided more fire-fighting equipment:
    Yes: 37 (37), No: 63 (63)
Strengthened security forces:
    Yes: 34 (29), No: 66 (71)
Increased coverage by private security forces:
    Yes: 30 (22), No: 70 (78)
Made closer contact with law-enforcement officers:
    Yes: 67 (70), No: 33 (30)
Made closer contact with National Guard:
    Yes: 5 (6), No: 95 (94)
Made closer relations with stores nearby:
    Yes: 46 (42), No: 54 (58)
Improved lighting or extended hours lights are on:
    Yes: 45 (40), No: 55 (60)
Obtained or rented watchdogs:
    Yes: 13 (6), No: 87 (94)
Marked any property for later identification:
    Yes: 12 (7), No: 88 (93)
Assigned upper-level executives to prepare or execute emergency plans:
    Yes: 65 (59), No: 35 (41)
Kept valuable merchandise out of windows:
    Yes: 21 (21), No: 79 (79)
Permitted key personnel to keep firearms:
    Yes: 15 (12), No: 85 (88)

6. Do any of these have access to arms:

Top execs.: Yes: 18 (12), No: 82 (88)
Store security head: Yes: 31 (24), No: 69 (76)
Other security personnel: Yes: 18 (14), No: 82 (86)
Private security people when in your premises: Yes: 28 (23), No: 72 (77)

7. If your store were attacked by rioters, would any of these people be authorized to use firearms:

Yes: 33 (29), No: 67 (71)

8. Can retailers do anything in your community, in cooperation with Negro groups to prevent or minimize riots in the next two years:

Yes: 75 (62), No: 11 (11)
No opinion: 14 (27)

9. Can retailers in your community do anything in cooperation with private or government anti-poverty or education programs to prevent or minimize riots in the next two years:

Yes: 81 (74), No: 9 (9)
No opinion: 10 (17)

10. Where should efforts to prevent riots concentrate:

Better law-enforcement: 16 (20)
Education and anti-poverty programs 30 (23)
Both equally: 54 (57)

11. Have you within the past two years established or tried to strengthen relations with:

Groups of private citizens working to prevent disorder:
    Yes: 66 (54), No: 34 (46)
Government or government-supported programs to improve living conditions of
    Negroes:
    Yes: 59 (48), No: 41 (52)
Community programs heavily supported by businessmen:
    Yes: 79 (68), No: 21 (32)

12. Have you or your store recently had direct relations with:

Moderate Negro groups:
    Yes: 48 (38), No: 52 (62)
Activist civil-rights groups that oppose rioting:
    Yes: 29 (20), No: 71 (80)
Militant elements in the Negro community:
    Yes: 18 (10), No: 82 (90)

13. Does increasing percentage of Negro personnel lessen tensions between a business and the Negro community:

Yes: 46 (39), No: 32 (30)
Don't know: 22 (31)

14. Do charges of dishonest practices against some merchants in ghetto areas have substance in:

Any city or town where you have a store: 51 (35)
Any other cities or towns: 26 (36)
No real substance: 23 (29)

15. If so, were dishonest practices a real cause in producing riots in:
Your community: 18 (0)
Other communities: 18 (36)
Not much of a factor: 64 (64)

16. In one city, a neighborhood retail association has set up a committee of Negro and Caucasian merchants to screen complaints against stores; the association intends to exert pressure on any store proved to perpetuate unfair practices with consumers. Do you think such a plan is advisable:
Yes: 65 (58), No 15 (16)
No opinion: 20 (26)

17. Have the riots antagonized Caucasians to the point that a substantial increase in Negro personnel might adversely affect your business:
Yes: 12 (16), No: 74 (66)
No opinion: 14 (18)

18. Many moderate Negro leaders assert businesses should be more active in alleviating conditions in ghettos; are these people overstating what businesses can do:
Yes: 60 (69), No: 40 (31)

19. What is the population of the city in which you have your main store:
Under 50,000: 3 (23)
50,000–250,000: 35 (36)
Over 250,000: 62 (41)

20. What is the approximate annual volume of your store:
Under $2 mill.: 33 (38)
$2–$10 mill.: 36 (37)
$10–$25 mill.: 14 (14)
$25–$50 mill.: 7 (4)
Over $50 mill.: 10 (7)

21. On a national basis, do you think rioting next year will:
Increase: 52 (44)
Decrease: 14 (20)
Be about the same: 34 (36)

22. Do you think rioting in your town next year will:
Increase: 34 (29)
Decrease: 19 (13)
Be about the same: 47 (72)

In some cities, where riots were less severe than in Newark and Detroit, a number of downtown stores actually experienced normal daytime business while rioters and police were battling a half-mile away.

A Newark store executive advises stores to buy media time and space to inform the public if a store must close. At 9:30 A.M. on the third day of Newark's four-day riot, customers, both Negro and white, were found patiently waiting for the store to open despite the fact that the street in front of the store was full of police, National Guardsmen, and armored vehicles.

A STORE'S REPUTATION.   Retailers interviewed disagreed as to whether a store's standing in a city or neighborhood had any bearing on whether or not it was attacked. There is little doubt that once a mob gained ascendancy, a store's fate was likely to be divorced from its reputation. Even Negro-owned stores in good standing with local black nationalists were not immune.

There is, however, evidence that some stores were singled out for attack early in riots, for either of two reasons—a reputation for dishonest practices, or the presence of desirable merchandise.

In some rare instances, when riots did not get out of hand, local residents protected stores that had established warm relations with the community. A Negro in Detroit, who is employed by the Urban League told *Stores* that during a riot in another Michigan city, older Negroes guarded a white-owned store for two nights because the proprietor had a reputation for fair dealing and "seemed to like us."

PRESS COVERAGE.   Some merchants in New Haven and Syracuse believe that responsible reporting by local newspapers and TV stations helped to contain disturbances. Some merchants in Newark, however, felt that the early reporting of Newark's riot by New York television stations inflamed rioters by sensationalizing violence and featuring film of unrestrained looting.

The Aftermath

BUSINESS LOSS.   Business loss following riots was directly related to the severity of the riots and the continuation of disturbances.

Daytime business tended to return to normal rapidly, even in ghettos in severe riot cities. In many cities, however, night business has remained weak downtown and bad in outlying neighborhoods.

In "severe city" riot neighborhoods, most stores now close before dark. However, most units of national chains remain open, despite the fact that there is little night business. Stores that quickly restored their premises have tended to do well. Bleak "plywood" stores are doing poorly.

In most cities, vandalism, pilferage, and breaking and entering crimes have increased in both ghetto and downtown stores, but mostly in ghettos. In Newark, a merchant on Springfield Avenue reported that the riots were followed by so much vandalism and breaking and entering crimes that he hired "a known hoodlum" to sleep in the store and spread the word in the neighborhood. This step, he said, has reduced the number of attacks on his store.

A downtown Detroit store noted that bands of teenage vandals have created increasing difficulty since the riots and have forced the store to increase protection coverage.

Attempts to hide in stores prior to closing are also on the rise.

ABSENTEEISM.   Employee absenteeism was high after the riots but tended to return to normal within a week. In Detroit and Newark executives report that the absentee rate of Negro employees was no higher than whites.

Some downtown stores, however, are finding it difficult to fill night employee schedules. Many employees fear going home after dark. Some stores have organized car pools.

HARMONY.   There was very little evidence of interracial tension in NRMA stores reopening after riots. This applied in both downtown and neighborhood department stores and to both customers and employees. In many stores, top management immediately ordered that no abuse of Negroes was to be tolerated and that any racial antagonists were to be separated. However, incidents were very rare.

THE GHETTO MERCHANT.   The aftermath for ghetto merchants was not so happy. Relationships between Negro residents and white neighborhood storeowners, strained before the riots, deteriorated rapidly afterwards. The hatred between residents and neighborhood merchants can, without exaggeration, be likened to that existing between two opposing armies.

The neighborhood merchant feels betrayed by ghetto residents, larger businesses, and his city government. His business has suffered, he is a likely target of casual and deliberate violence, and he finds it almost impossible to get minimal insurance coverage. He is financially unable to move, improve his store, or go out of business.

Indeed, many small merchants seem emotionally unable to go out of business, despite their fears and bitterness.

Most ghetto merchants are in their fifties and beyond. A young apparel store owner in Newark, who is moving, remarked that fewer Springfield Avenue stores than expected shut down after the riots because "even store owners who have put aside enough to live on cannot imagine not coming to the store six days a week."

LARGE STORES AFFECTED.   This is not the place to examine if, when, or where "the poor pay more." The relevant fact for this report is that the "gouging merchant," like the "brutal cop," has become a symbol of racial oppression to Negroes and an effective political tool for black extremists.

Since the riots, stores of all sizes and in all areas of a city have been bracketed in the minds of ghetto residents. For obvious symbolic reasons, cities' dominant stores are prime targets. Increasingly, Negro antimerchant feelings are being applied to major downtown stores, irrespective of the latter's merchandising, credit, or personnel policies.

Indeed, there are signs that the police brutality issue is being assuaged and that the merchant is becoming the prime scapegoat. As a New England black nationalist leader, noted for political savvy, remarked to this reporter, "Since the riots you have been sending in your black cops and your police community relations programs. But I still have your honkie merchants."

Often, demagogic charges against a downtown store are accepted by people who concede they have never shopped in that store and rarely shop outside their own neighborhood.

Many non-ghetto retailers remarked that antimerchantism is one of the most perplexing and serious problems responsible retailers must face. Some responsible retailers are concerned that we will soon have to contend with terrorism, with leading stores as the first target.

Responsible merchants concede that some irresponsible stores have been operating in low income neighborhoods. Fifty-one per cent of the riot-city retailers replying to *Stores'* questionnaire think that charges of dishonest practices against some merchants in ghetto areas have substance in cities or towns where they have a store (see Q. 14). An additional 26 per cent of riot-city respondents think such dishonest practices exist in some other city or town. And a large majority of department and chain store retailers who were interviewed for this report consider gouging charges to be true of some independent neighborhood food and appliance stores that extend credit.

Few responsible merchants consider such dishonest practices to have been a real cause of riots (Q. 15). But a majority believe it advisable that neighborhood screening committees of white and Negro merchants be established to screen complaints and exert heavy pressure on any store that is proved to perpetuate unfair practices (Q. 16). Such a program has been proposed by the Springfield Avenue Merchants Association in Newark.

SOME GOOD RELATIONS. There are bright spots in ghettos despite the prevalence of antimerchant feeling. Stores which quickly restored their premises have done much more business and suffered much less vandalism than stores which have tried to operate from behind walls of plywood.

Few chain or department store units that had established good relations in neighborhoods had unusual difficulties after riots. During recent years, a number of chain units have been closed in ghettos, mostly for economic reasons. But there are some very reassuring success stories.

An executive of a giant national chain told *Stores* of a modernization program which has been very successful in a unit located in a racially sensitive, midwestern neighborhood.

This chain's formula:

- Modernization of units.
- Attentive housekeeping.
- Participation in community affairs.
- A high percentage of Negro employees and executives.
- Enlightened flexibility in credit screening.
- Efforts to stock sufficient assortments of merchandise that units not in ghettos do not carry in depth. (Such items include half-size dresses, and different styles of greeting cards, pictures, mirrors, hard-surface floor coverings, and cosmetics.)

The results for this ghetto unit: a one third increase in business and a marked decline in vandalism and pilferage.

It should be pointed out that this company is not a low-price chain, that it is in fact widely commended on Wall Street and by competitors for its success in upgrading.

Expectations

Retailers tend to be pessimistic about the outlook for 1968. A substantial majority (80 per cent) of retailers in both riot and non-riot cities expect rioting throughout the country to increase next year or be about the same as 1967 (Q. 21).

Riot-city retailers are pessimistic, but less so about their own communities than about the nation as a whole. Fifty-two per cent of respondents from riot cities expect riots next year to be worse nationally. Thirty-four per cent of riot-city respondents expect riots to be worse in their own communities next year. Forty-seven per cent expect rioting of equal intensity (Q. 22).

However, the pessimism has not been accompanied by hopelessness or inertia. Sixty-two per cent of all stores replying to the questionnaire and 75 per cent of respondents in riot cities think that retailers can prevent or minimize riots within the next two years by cooperating with Negro groups (Q. 8). Seventy-four per cent of all respondents and 81 per cent in riot communities think they might prevent or minimize riots within the next two years by cooperating with private or government antipoverty or education programs (Q. 9).

Though there is definitely a note of uncertainty about it, a sizable minority of respondents think that increasing the percentage of Negro employees really lessens tension between a business and the Negro community (Q. 13). Stores with annual volumes exceeding $10 million are most optimistic about the value of employing greater numbers of Negroes. Some stores make a special effort to employ more Negroes in branches.

TERRORISM. Newspaper reports of planned terrorist action against leading stores have probably been exaggerated.

In one eastern city a black group which advocates violence distributed a pamphlet with a sketch of the city's leading store going up in flames. A police official focussed attention on the pamphlet in order to get more support from the city. But the "plan" to destroy this store seems to have been a political device or a pipe-dream.

Also, it should be noted that Stokely Carmichael and H. Rap Brown, black nationalist leaders who have praised violence, have so far directed most of their inflammatory advice toward action in ghettos.

However, some eminent retailers believe the major riots were not spontaneous but the result of careful planning.

"I looked out my office window," said a leading Detroit executive, "and what I saw was not a 'riot.' It was an insurrection. This thing was planned." It is this retailer's view that most heavy riots are deliberate, not spontaneous, and that the forces directing riots intend to strike in cities that are showing the most progress in easing racial tension.

He thinks New York is a likely target because its city government has established a reputation for maintaining racial peace.

WHITE BACKLASH.   White backlash groups have so far displayed little strength, but executives in Detroit, Buffalo, and New York observed that they have been more active. The prevailing view of retailers is that "backlash" is not necessarily bad if it is confined to a reaction against the lawlessness of riots and is not racist or reactionary.

Only 12 per cent of stores in riot cities indicated on questionnaires that they thought riots have antagonized Caucasians to the point that a substantial increase in Negro personnel might adversely affect their business (Q. 17).

However, there is real concern among many responsible and knowledgeable businessmen. A significant number of leading retailers consider lawless white backlash to be potentially the most dangerous problem produced by the riots. One executive told *Stores*: "A reason we must act promptly to help Negroes is that if the riots do not cease, white extremists may acquire the strength to restrain our progress." Another retailer dreads "a reversion to the riots of fifty years ago, when whites attacked Negroes."

Activity

IN THE COMMUNITY.   The head of a leading Detroit store summed up the thinking of retailers in riot cities: "We have three choices," he said. "We can suppress the minorities. We can continue as before. Or we can solve the fundamental problems."

Retailers in riot cities certainly do want firm police response to rioting. But few believe in the feasibility or morality of suppression. Virtually all retailers in riot cities want to concentrate on attacking the fundamental problems. Achievement and optimism for community action programs vary widely from city to city and appear to have no relation to the intensity of a city's riots.

Fundamentally, two attitudes are prevalent among retailers in racially tense cities. The most prevalent approach to resolving racial tensions is typified in the remarks of a store president in an eastern city. "Businessmen here are trying to improve the housing situation," he said. "Something really has to be done for these people, the way they live, six, eight, even ten to a room. But I don't know how much we can achieve. The more housing units we build, the more the hard core will move into this city. And our city and county governments are squabbling so much we don't get much sense from them."

The remarks of this man are representative of many sincere retailers in many cities. He expressed both concern and futility. And his feelings were manifest in other businessmen in his community. They want to do more, know they aren't doing enough, and fear what they are doing will accomplish nothing.

The attitude of businessmen in such communities usually regresses within months of a riot, from hope to frustration to resignation, and finally to a defensive posture against charges of complacency. Invariably, community improvement programs in such cities have only limited representation from Negro and other groups.

THE POWER STRUCTURE. The second prevailing view was summed up by a leading retail executive in a midwestern city: "Fifty people can come in this store with guns in their pockets and attack the store," he said. "Or the same fifty people can come in with money in their pockets and buy merchandise. We can't keep them out. The 'power structures' have to open their doors. Representatives from business, labor, government, education, organized religion, and both moderate and militant Negro groups must get together, establish leadership and interest, and have faith and determination in what they set about."

It is not possible here to list adequately all that retailers in riot cities are doing. But it is worth noting that the retailer just quoted is very active in the New Detroit Committee and that businesses active in this group are recruiting thousands of hard-core Negroes in ghettos, providing special training for the unskilled, helping Negro high-school students learn how to apply for a job, working to improve public order and confidence in the police, and undertaking scores of other programs vital to the establishment of racial peace.

The New Detroit Committee is an example of what retailers can do. Joseph L. Hudson, Jr., president of the J. L. Hudson Co., is chairman of the New Detroit Committee, and Stanley J. Winkelman, president of Winkelman Bros. Apparel, Inc., is chairman of its Community Services Committee.

Optimism is greatest among retailers in communities where there is an alert, indigeneous business establishment, where the leading store or stores are firmly committed, where businessmen have a reasonable degree of confidence in the city government, and where, as noted, diverse groups in a community are encouraged to participate fully, irrespective of their political orientation.

THE GOVERNMENT.   Government programs have helped in some areas, but both businessmen and Negro leaders tend to agree they have generally been ineffective, inefficient, and plagued by bickering and bungling. Few retailers think government aid or programs can be dispensed with, but they do think strong infusions of business realism are essential.

In some cities there are signs of bickering among retailers. One store head in New York State noted, "Major stores with varying price emphases or locations are allowing these differences to impede cooperation in both community improvement and protection programs."

Community action programs must, of course, take care not to be top heavy. However, occasionally talent and expertise are being missed because large neighborhood stores, discounters, and local merchants' associations are not fully encouraged to participate.

One important ghetto problem retailers and other businessmen are beginning to investigate is the development of Negro entrepreneurs. Moderate Negro groups are coming to place greater stress on helping Negroes start their own businesses. This is significant in that it indicates a shift of emphasis from "integration" to self-reliance. Retailers can help by counseling potential Negro business-men.

Some leading stores are also trying to persuade cities to strength-en code enforcement of housing and marketing laws. And, as noted before, retailers approve the idea of local merchant gripe boards to help answer any charges of gouging or other unfair practices.

IN THE STORE. Most retailers agree that the greatest direct contribution stores can make to racial peace is in the area of job creation and job training, with quick promotion of able and con-scientious Negroes. Of course, every store must face the fact that, unlike the Ford Motor Company, it cannot hope to set aside 6,500 jobs for ghetto residents. Some stores have made strides in job creating and job training areas. Others seem to be progressing slowly.

Often, unskilled hard-core ghetto residents do not respond to job offers or continuing employment. However, where progress has been slow, retailers also have been at fault. It is apparent that store bureaucracy—not bigotry—is a stumbling block in some cases. The problem is translating policy into practice.

Policy occasionally does not become practice because divisional and lower echelon executives lack the authority, time, or tenacity to execute the policy. A vice president in Newark observed, "The only answer is for top management to make it clear throughout the organization that it seriously means its policy to be effected and will tolerate some substandard performance until inexperienced people can be trained."

HIRING. Stores are adjusting their tests and employment quali-fications to obtain more Negro personnel. The approach is to "screen in" rather than "screen out."

One New York store helps ill groomed or unduly aggressive job applicants by referring them to Negro interviewers, who suggest, politely, that they are now only having a preliminary interview and should return with a more restrained dress and manner.

Stores are very eager to hire Negro executive trainees. But they find it difficult to compete with other industries. A Newark retailer said it is "easier to recruit from Harvard than Howard." Some effective recruitment of Negro executives and employees has been achieved by working with local high schools and distributive education programs.

PRESSURE GROUPS.   No matter how hard a store tries to increase its percentage of Negro employees, Negro groups are likely to demand more. The manner of dealing with these groups, of course, depends on their real intentions and the store's progress and position.

One vice president, a veteran of negotiating with such groups, advises a store or group of stores to "get an experienced labor negotiator with a liberal reputation." This vice president also advises stores to make every effort to employ Negroes in office, as well as selling floor, receiving, and stock jobs. Negro groups, he said, are on the lookout for businesses that have few Negro employees and seem to display those few as conspicuously as possible. Negroes are also sensitive to an imbalance in stock and receiving.

CREDIT.   One chain store reported that it plans to adjust credit screening procedures in ghetto stores so as to grant credit to a maximum number of residents. An executive in this chain says stores located in ghettos "must throw the computer out the window."

However, the entire area of credit remains a serious problem. Poor Negroes need credit but fall far short of minimum consumer credit standards. Stores want to extend credit but cannot expose themselves to inordinate defaulting rates. The result is increased tension and high credit and "service" charges by some local merchants.

PROTECTION ACTIVITY.   Protection activity is not intense and does not vary significantly between riot and non-riot communities (Q. 5). Activity is very similar in both riot and non-riot cities with populations exceeding 250,000.

More than 90 per cent of stores with annual volumes exceeding $10 million are firming up communication with the police and are assigning one upper-level executive the task of perfecting emergency plans.

A number of attacked stores which had relied on protection service companies are developing their own protection operations.

There has been an increase of "hot line" communication systems which include stores, other businesses, and the police. The Syracuse Chamber of Commerce has created such a system.

Some stores have adjusted window display schedules to exclude valuable merchandise but most stores reject this idea. A Detroit executive remarked, "We must not compromise our image unless we really expect an attack."

Another store reports it is considering the purchase of an electronically operated iron gate which could enclose a store within seconds.

Many retailers stated that it is important and feasible for stores, particularly chains, to open units in ghettos. The obstacles are immense. And the prevailing difficulties are often magnified by opposition from local merchants and complications from labor unions, financial institutions, and zoning laws.

MINDING THE STORE.   However active stores become in community affairs, there is much that can be done simply by minding the store. As an executive in a major national chain noted, "The entire organization must constantly be alert to the benefits that will immediately and inevitably result from increasing racial harmony. Personnel people cannot be told 364 days a year to trim, trim, trim, and to hire only experienced help, and then on the 365th day be told to hire more Negroes. Credit people can't constantly be told to eliminate risks, and then one day a year be told to get more Negro accounts. Buyers can't be told to have the highest possible stock turn, and then one day a year be told to go out and get half-sizes.

"And," he concluded, "we should remember that the welfare market is a $20 billion market. That sounds like quite a bit to me."

Deception in the Marketplace of the Poor: The Role of the Federal Trade Commission

Mary Gardiner Jones

The war on poverty will be two years old this August. Spurred on by the anachronism of 50 million people living in conditions of poverty and near-poverty in the midst of the greatest affluence which a majority of Americans have ever enjoyed in this country, this crusade against the conditions of poverty represents one of the most

Reprinted from "Deception in the Marketplace of the Poor: The Role of the Federal Trade Commission," an address before the Zonta Club of Washington (June 22, 1966).

While this text forms the basis for Miss Jones' oral remarks, it should be used with the understanding that paragraphs of it may have been omitted in the oral presentation and, by the same token, other remarks may have been made orally which do not appear in this text.

comprehensive assaults on social, economic and political inequality and deprivation which has ever been mounted. Even the social welfare measures of the 1930's do not compare in scope and concept to the long-range and imaginative objectives which characterize this Administration's war on poverty.

The poverty legislation, formally and descriptively titled the Economic Opportunity Act of 1964, specifically singled out the major projects which were to be launched to start the underprivileged and poverty-stricken of this country down the long road to human dignity, self-respect and economic well-being. Job corps, work-training and work-experience programs, employment and investment incentives, work-study programs for students, adult education programs, teacher-training projects, voluntary assistance programs for needy children, urban and rural community-action programs and special programs to combat poverty in rural areas—these marked the specific areas in the life of the poor on which the efforts of the executive departments and the Office of Economic Opportunity were to be immediately directed, in conjunction, wherever possible, with state and local organizations and private groups. As President Johnson put it in his message to Congress on the need for this legislation:

> Through this program we offer new incentives and new opportunities for cooperation so that all the energy of our Nation, not merely the efforts of Government, can be brought to bear on our common enemy.

Less than a year after the enactment of the Economic Opportunity Act, in response to Senator Magnuson's request, the Federal Trade Commission organized its own special Poverty office, designed to zero in on the marketing and credit practices of those who victimize the poor and the underprivileged. In every big city, and indeed in every community where the poor are congregated, there are merchants who make their living primarily by preying on the fears and lack of sophistication of the poor, capitalizing on their needs and desires for a share in this country's bountiful goods and services and exploiting their total inability to apply for or get the usual credit which is the passport of the affluent to participation in the buy now–pay later economy in which we live today.

The Commission's Poverty office received some 400 complaints about sales and credit practices in the District, ranging from misrepresentation of a sales contract as a mere delivery receipt to outright refusals to return deposits made on goods which were never delivered. Many of the complainants have told us that they never even received copies of the final installment contract which they had executed; many were apparently given blank contracts to sign; and several claimed that the prices and service charges finally collected were far in excess of the amounts they had originally been led to believe they would have to pay. Advertisements of used furniture as new or of so-called bargain merchandise which reportedly turned out to be nonexistent or to be of such shoddy quality as to be virtually unusable were frequently the subject of these complaints. Coercive pressure brought to bear by collection agencies, threats of garnishment actions regardless of the validity of the debt, attempts to collect nonexistent debts, collect telephone calls at home and at complainant's place of work, typify other complaints received by the Commission office. Two things become readily apparent: not all merchants servicing the low-income group are engaged in these practices, but too many merchants are; and those that are so engaged employ every conceivable marketing and credit-collection practice which the Commission has ever encountered in its long history of consumer protection, with one significant and devastating difference. While the ordinary citizen can shrug off the loss with comparative equanimity, or where serious economic loss is encountered, can go to court, the poor sink deeper in the quicksand of contractual obligations and long-term debt arrangements from which they have no recourse. Here is a vital area in the life of the poor which demands immediate corrective action. The Commission is uniquely qualified to take this action and stamp out these practices by proceeding directly against these offending merchants, credit agencies and finance companies.

During this same early period of the poverty program's gestation, OEO was also becoming increasingly conscious of the waste and futility of trying to increase the incomes of the poor only to have them drained away by unconscionable marketing practices. Its community-action programs began to stress consumer education and to explore ways and means of establishing alternative sources of credit to lessen the dependence of the poor on the chicanery too often found in the only market place to which they could turn in meeting their own demands for the necessities of life.

In March of this year, President Johnson gave public recognition to this highly important but hitherto less well recognized facet of the war against poverty and pledged "the all-out effort of the Federal government to help our poorest citizens to spend their limited funds more efficiently as we work to enhance their incomes." In doing so, he specifically referred to the Federal Trade Commission's establishment of a Consumer Complaints Office and its program to help states organize their own consumer protection programs as one of the steps taken to further the Administration's concern with consumer interests in general and the impoverished consumer in particular.

While the OEO and the various community-action offices and neighborhood legal service offices concentrated on helping the poor to help themselves, either through education or, in cases of specific fraud, through legal assistance, this approach involves time and the development of a rudimentary marketing sophistication to enable the consumer to be aware of the deception and to be willing to seek help. Even assuming that those consumers are made aware of the frauds and deceptions practiced upon them, they have no means and indeed in all likelihood little confidence in invoking the judicial machinery to defend their rights. Moreover, their fear of the consequences to their job security or welfare assistance of any legal actions taken against them compels them to accept the fraud and go deeper into debt in order to buy off the merchant or finance company irrespective of the validity of the obligation. In many instances the traditional common-law concepts relating to contracts and credit transactions devised in another era for another type of situation are inadequate and inapplicable as an avenue of relief for this group of consumers. Thus, even with improved knowledge of the marketplace and access to legal assistance, and even with the development of new legal tools by which to determine the bona fides of purportedly properly executed contracts and notes, many of the poor will continue to be defrauded and their scanty resources needlessly frittered on many transactions which may remain just within the commercial law governing contracts and installment purchases, but which nevertheless in a real sense have in fact been induced by coercion and deception. We have to recognize that poverty, like wealth, is an inherited condition. Like wealth, it is easy to aggrandize it. Unlike wealth, however, poverty has a clinging quality which makes it difficult to dissipate. It is vital, therefore, that every possible step be taken to help the poor shake off their shackles and at the same time stamp out the practices which drain off what little purchasing power they have managed to acquire.

It is in this vital part of the life of the poor where the Commission's unique experience in attacking deception in the marketplace can be so powerfully brought to bear in the nation's war against poverty. By focusing its attention on those merchants and credit agencies which perpetrate these frauds and deception on our nation's poor, the Commission does not have to wait until the poor have acquired some basic notions of their rights and of the deceptions practiced upon them. While consumer education, access to legal assistance, and revision of many of our legal concepts respecting contract and credit transactions are essential to any long-range solution of the marketplace chicanery practiced on the unsophisticated and poverty-stricken consumer, direct action against the perpetrators of these practices must also go on simultaneously. Surely, no other responsibility of the Federal Trade Commission in the field of deception has any greater importance or public interest than that of ferreting out those deceptions practiced by the quacks and swindlers who specialize in every conceivable device to induce the poor to their doors, to coerce them into making unwanted purchases and to sign them up to long-term credit arrangements which leave them forever at the mercy of their debtors with little hope of ever extricating themselves from the pyramiding tentacles of debt in which they find themselves.

The first problem which confronted the Commission, if it was to be an effective catalyst in this war against poverty, was to secure concrete and detailed information about the practices used to swindle and befuddle the poor and to pinpoint with probative testimony specific instances of actionable deception of the poor. This was a vital need and a peculiarly formidable task in this marketplace where the swindler is adept at concealing his swindle or at keeping his actions colorably within the law and his victims are fearful of talking, frequently unaware or accepting of the deceptions practiced upon them and virtually dependent on those merchants for their daily needs with few known alternative sources of supply which they trust and feel comfortable with.

The reports on the various conferences which have been held on poverty and the ever-increasing literature on the experience of the poor in the marketplace contain heart-rending examples of the countless ways in which the poor are victimized because of their poverty, their fears and their lack of bargaining power and sophistication in the marketplace. There is today a graphic awareness of the general types of deception practiced on the poor as they venture forth into the marketplace or are cruelly pressured by door-to-door salesmen or street peddlers into purchasing overpriced, often shoddy merchandise under claims of "no money down, easy credit terms" which ignore the "small print" of the credit agreement. But this generalized knowledge, while essential in demonstrating the need for action, does not substitute for the carefully documented case which must stand up in the hearing room as an unfair and deceptive practice.

Accordingly, in order to move effectively against these marketers and credit agencies responsible for these frauds and deceptions, the Commission realized the importance at the outset of pinpointing carefully the major offenders and the most typical and devastating practices which should be the object of Commission action. The Commission's available resources which it can allocate to this single aspect of its overall statutory responsibilities are not limitless. It cannot abandon its responsibilities with respect to the increasing trends of concentration in industries and markets throughout the country, disregard its obligations to keep the channels of commerce free from restrictive or discriminatory practices, nor ignore its duties to police the labeling of flammable fabrics, furs, wools, and textiles, to name only a few of the statutory duties which Congress has imposed upon it. Further, the Commission's jurisdiction extends outside the District only to transactions which are interstate in nature. This again sets fairly strict boundaries on its ability to act. However, within these limitations of manpower and jurisdiction, the Commission can and is directing its expertise not only to eliminate these practices wherever possible, but also hopefully to point the way to successful action by other law-enforcing agencies and community-action groups throughout the fifty States who are engaged in the same crusade.

The Commission has worked out a two-pronged attack on the problem of poverty in the marketplace: first, to proceed directly against the merchants within its jurisdiction who are engaging in these practices; and, second, to act as a sort of headquarters of expertise in this area, assembling data on the practices engaged in, on the needs of the poor, on the availability of other sources of goods and services and credit facilities and on the various sources of aid which are emerging under the imaginative guidance of OEO and all of the various public and private agencies which are taking action in this area of the poverty war.

Let me first touch upon some of the problems which we have to deal with in mounting an effective law-enforcement program. In the planning of this program in the District, it was soon apparent that we could not confine our efforts exclusively to the practices and persons complained about in the 400 complaints which came to our consumer complaints office. We could not assume that those complaints were typical, or necessarily encompassed the most vicious practices requiring action, nor even the most frequent offenders in this marketplace. The great majority of the victims in this marketplace are not likely to register their complaints with government agencies. The poor do not sit down and write letters, as is the wont of so many of our more affluent citizenry and which provide us with a large part of our insight into the frauds and deceptions in the ordinary marketplace which require Commission action. Moreover, a great many of the complaints which our poverty office received pertained either to matters which were outside our jurisdiction or involved complainants whose only interest in contacting our office undoubtedly was to get their money back. In those instances we could at least field these complaints to the government or private agency, neighborhood legal service center or United States Attorney's office which could deal with them. We have done so on several occasions and have had the satisfaction of working jointly with these agencies and seeing some individual instances of outright injustice rectified by the company after intervention by these agencies. But these complaints did not necessarily advance our own efforts to uncover and proceed against the major and most frequent unconscionable market practices which sapped the pitiful financial resources which the poor manage to get hold of.

Accordingly, our staff turned to the court records of garnishment and replevin proceedings to pinpoint the most persistent plaintiffs, to get leads to possible instances of fraud and deception and at least to identify potential informants respecting the credit and marketing practices current in the District. The basic need to find a time and place of interview of the garnishee posed a problem of real dimension. In some instances employers permitted our investigators to talk with their employees at work. More often, such permission was refused. Evenings or weekends thus became the only time when our staff could even contact this important source of information—the poor themselves.

Another very fruitful source of information of specific instances of deception were the various community-action groups and neighborhood legal services units funded by the OEO which operate throughout the District and the local district attorneys which in the District is the United States Attorney's office. These groups, which are almost daily in contact with the poor, have gained the trust of the poor and therefore are the recipients of a great variety of instances of marketing and credit injustices which the poor have encountered. Simultaneously with the establishment of our poverty office, therefore, we started to explore means of working out fruitful contacts with these groups. We noted that whenever our representatives attended meetings of block clubs and the like, our own ratio of complaints almost immediately increased, thus attesting to the eagerness of the poor to secure recourse once they appreciate their problems and the availability of help. Realizing that these contacts were of great value both to our work and to the work of these organizations, we are now in the process of working out more formal and continuous relationships with these other workers in the poverty vineyard so that all of our resources of manpower and skills can be coordinated and overlapping efforts reduced.

In this same connection all of our field offices are under instructions to contact the local poverty organizations and legal-aid centers operating in their areas to ascertain if they have received actionable complaints in this area which would be subject to our jurisdiction and at the same time to offer these groups whatever assistance they may need in their work in helping the consumers help themselves as they sally forth into this marketplace. These contacts have been initiated and will be maintained on a continuing basis, so that even in the areas where the Commission may not have jurisdiction to act, its expertise may be made constantly available to groups which can and are acting to stamp out these practices. Parenthetically, I should point out that the Commission is urgently in favor of the enactment of civil consumer protection statutes in the various states which do not as yet have them, so that a legal basis will exist in every state for proceeding against the local retailers and credit agencies which are engaging in deception and unfair practices.

A serious problem encountered by our staff in their investigations was the absence of any written evidence attesting to the fraud or deception complained of. Frequently these informants did not even have copies of the sales contracts. Obviously, they had not retained the advertisement which had lured them into the store. It was not surprising that the witnesses had little specific recall of what the original oral representations had been which had induced them into the purchase or was the source of the deception. The rapid-fire sales pitch of the door-to-door peddler or of the facile salesman in the showroom hardly lends itself to specific recall in the type of pro-bative form which is so essential to prepare a complaint for hearing rather than to merely assemble a narrative of the deception. Most citizens are understandably reluctant to be witnesses in any govern-mental proceeding. With the poor, this reluctance is aggravated by their unfortunately realistic fears of retaliation by the merchant or credit agency on whom they are so dependent, by their inabilities to express themselves in the language of the establishment and by their sense of inferiority, hopelessness and general mistrust of any governmental authority, which they regard not as the protector of their rights, but as the body which puts them into jail, evicts them from their apartment or garnishees their salary. I detail these problems not because they are insuperable but because they consti-tute some of the obstacles which must be overcome by any law-enforcement agency which attempts to mount a full-scale war on eliminating the illegal marketing practices which victimize the poor.

In many situations there will be no substitute for a case by case approach against the law-breaking market marauders looking towards a cease and desist order which if flouted can be followed up by a civil penalty action and the imposition of substantial money fines.

But the Commission is not limited to this single avenue of adversary proceedings and individual cease and desist orders. There are other courses of action which the Commission can take to put its expertise and special techniques of fact-finding and guidance to work in the fight against illegal commercial exploitation in the marketplace for the poor.

The free enterprise system is predicated on an open marketplace where informed and willing buyers and sellers may meet and agree among themselves on the terms and conditions upon which they will enter the stream of commerce. The free enterprise system breaks down when one party to this bargain is misinformed, deceived or defrauded. In an age when it is difficult for well-educated people to make wise decisions in the marketplace, the poor—who must make every dollar count—are least prepared to make those decisions. Lack of knowledge and information often leads them to accept poor-quality merchandise at high prices. It is ironic that those who can least afford to, pay more. The common-law concept of "caveat emptor"—"let the buyer beware"—is unfortunately still much too much with us in 1966. Yet in all too many instances the consumer is not on an equal footing with the seller because he lacks vital information about the product, about the tactics of the marketplace, and, in the low-income market, particularly, about the terms of the bargain which he is purportedly making of his own free will. Without some rudimentary marketing know-how, including as a minimum the know-how as to what questions to ask and what his basic rights as a consumer are, the less advantaged segment of our population is left an easy prey for those who would be unscrupulous. If through a combination of ignorance of the marketplace and elementary marketing know-how, on the one hand, and callous, aggressive salesmanship, deception or outright fraud on the other hand, consumers are thereby coerced into paying exorbitant prices for inferior products, or induced into making unwanted purchases and going deeply into debt in the bargain, then the consumer's meager financial resources are wasted, our national resources are misallocated and respect for law and order and governmental authority is diminished, if not eliminated.

One of the most immediate needs of the poor is to obtain some basic information about the marketplace and to get access to alternate sources of credit and to other sources of goods, or, as the OEO puts it, to have multiple sources of choice available to them when they decide to enter the marketplace. This will not only give them an opportunity to compare prices and terms offered by a variety of merchants but will lessen their dependence on the single merchant who poses as their provider and ends up as their defrauder. The more reputable merchants are beginning to appreciate that the poor, while posing special problems of credit and the like, nevertheless represent an untapped market of considerable proportions and substantial potential. The old shibboleth that the poor are on that account hopeless and unreliable credit risks is simply not the fact. The poor do need credit—a good deal of credit—and probably under more generous terms than some stores have heretofore been accustomed to offer. The poor also need somewhat more flexible credit which will permit them occasionally to miss a payment without calling the entire debt due. The poor may also need a more personalized or sympathetic type of service, at least as respects their initial contact with the information booths in the stores and the credit personnel with whom they must deal. But within this framework they represent a potential market to the reputable store which it should be encouraged to explore. Some of the credit needs of the poor can perhaps be furnished through credit union devices. Some of their fears and insecurities and unfamiliarity with large department store-type service could be alleviated through counselling and other devices.

In any event, there is today a substantial need for concrete information, not only as to the ways by which the poor are fleeced and victimized, but also as to the availability of alternative sources of goods and credit, as to the actual costs of furnishing credit to this segment of the market and as to the business problems in general which may be involved in servicing this group of consumers.

Public airing of the needs of the poor and of the characteristics of the marketplace which the poor now patronize could serve to illuminate entire areas of potential action which should be undertaken in order to combat the deceptions. For example, to what extent can some of the deceptions be avoided in the first instance if specific disclosure of the prices and terms under which the goods are sold and the credit offered were required, and what legitimate problems might be posed by such requirements? Would the exploitation be lessened if restrictions were placed on the types of situations for which garnishment and replevin actions could be instituted? Is it necessary and feasible to work out limitations on the extent to which these retail installment contracts can be factored, either as respects situations in which the seller is on notice that the buyer is challenging the validity of the contract, or in cases where the finance company and the retailer are affiliated? What would be the impact of prohibiting absolutely the practice of tying one installment contract into another so that a default on one will automatically entitle the seller to recover on all, of conditioning any collection proceedings on the possession by the purchaser of the original copy of the executed installment contract, of outlawing the more outrageous unconscionable terms of such contracts? All of these proposals and others should be explored in the fight to eliminate this commercial victimization of this segment of our population. Some of these sanctions might be beyond the power of the Commission to impose. Nevertheless, it is the Commission, with its expertise in the practices of the marketplace which can aid in outlining and illuminating the dimensions of the problem and in analyzing the various means which might be taken to deal with it.

The Commission can lead the way in this broader aspect of the fight against deception in the marketplace of the poor. Through its power to hold public hearings, the Commission can bring together all of the agencies and organizations active in this field with a view to providing a forum where experiences can be shared, ideas exchanged and even in some situations programs of action co-ordinated. The Commission can bring together the representatives of business who are now or may in the future be potential suppliers of this market segment to ascertain in detail their experiences and expertise. The Commission can compel the production of books and records of the merchants now engaged in dealing with these con-sumers in order to ascertain precisely just what the costs of doing business, servicing contracts and extending credit in this area really are. Finally, and most important, these consumers themselves should have a forum where they can explain on their own behalf the problems which they face in trying to supply their needs and the needs of their families in a marketplace which up to now has been so thoroughly oriented to the needs of the more affluent wage-earners.

The thoughts which I have outlined today are not new or original with me. Much of what I am describing to you is the subject of active consideration by many agencies working in this field, including the Federal Trade Commission, which is constantly sharpening and refining its general expertise to cope with the special problems which the poor face in our marketplace today. Much of the Commission's experience and many of its concepts of deception are undergoing changes as the practices which victimize the poor are examined from the point of view of those victims rather than of the more affluent and experienced consumers who are usually the objects of the Commission's scrutiny. What is deception to the poor may never have been deception to a more experienced shopper. Many practices which in some situations may have never been thought to be deceptive must be so regarded when practiced against this less sophisticated and more fearful group of consumers.

Thus, the Commission can and is playing an important part in the overall fight against poverty. It will undoubtedly find other ways in which it can apply its marketing expertise to the problems of the low-income market and the need for increased consumer know-how and education.

Franklin D. Roosevelt said thirty years ago, "The test of our progress is not whether we add more to the abundance of those who have much; it is whether we do enough for those who have too little." It is with this "test of progress" that all of us must continue with our efforts for the protection of the poor, the uninformed and the uneducated against the deceitful and unscrupulous practices in the marketplace which are sapping their hard-earned but frequently pitifully inadequate resources, their self-respect and their confidence in our American way of life.

The Limits of
Black Capitalism

Frederick D. Sturdivant

Unlike black power, the concept of black capitalism has received widespread support from business and political leaders since it gained general currency recently.

Many of the larger corporations with operations in Northern cities have undertaken or joined programs to further entrepreneurship in the ghettos.[1] In the 1968 political campaign, the presidential candidates of both major parties applauded, with equal fervor, the idea of giving Negro communities "a piece of the action."

One of the most significant outgrowths of this sudden interest in black capitalism is the Community Self-Determination bill, which was introduced in the U.S. Senate last July. Its sponsors ranged from Jacob Javits to John Tower, with twenty-five other Senators

Reprinted from "The Limits of Black Capitalism," *Harvard Business Review* (January–February 1969), pp. 122–128, by permission of *Harvard Business Review* © 1969 by the President and Fellows of Harvard College; all rights reserved.
See pages 289 for all footnotes to this chapter.

scattered between these two extremes on the ideological continuum. Its chances for passage on being reintroduced during the Ninety-first Congress appear excellent. Such broad support for the bill is surprising, since it represents a radical change in public policy and, if enacted, would have a profound effect on the welfare of our Northern cities that have heavy minority-group populations.

The objective of Senate Bill 3876 is to facilitate the creation of what amounts to community-owned and community-directed conglomerate corporations that would control the economic and social development of the areas where they exist. Drafted by representatives of the Congress of Racial Equality (CORE), together with associates of the Harvard Institute of Politics, the bill has these main features:

- A federally chartered community development corporation (CDC) could be created by the residents of any disadvantaged community where at least 10 per cent of them have agreed to buy at least one share of $5 par value stock. At least 500 residents sixteen years of age or older must pay in a total of at least $5,000 before issuance of the charter.

- A local election of stockholders determines the makeup of the board of directors and officers of the corporation.

- The CDC would acquire, create, and manage all businesses in its area; other companies entering the area could operate there only under "turnkey" contracts. Under agreement with the CDC an "outside" company would be permitted to develop an enterprise, with the proviso that it would be sold to the CDC as soon as it was capable of operating on its own. (The "outsider" would be given a tax advantage in the sale.)

- The capital for the acquisition of turnkey facilities and other corporate needs would be made available through a series of community development banks. These banks, supervised by the Comptroller of the Currency, would fund themselves by selling debentures guaranteed by the federal government.

- The CDC and its subsidiaries would receive tax incentives determined by a formula based on an index of area unemployment and median income compared with the national average.

- A portion of the CDC's profits would be used to help finance housing, education, recreation, and health services in the community.

Few would question the desirability of finding avenues toward greater participation by disadvantaged minorities in our society. The merits of the CDC concept in furthering that goal are many. On balance, however, the community self-determination program represents a dangerous and shortsighted approach to the solution of the domestic crisis.

In my view, the program would virtually force the community development corporations to perpetuate the inefficient and fragmented retail structures of the slum areas. In addition, it would not stimulate the involvement in entrepreneurial efforts so badly needed in minority communities. Also, the plan would block many avenues of escape from the ghetto that are beginning to develop.

Most important, the bill ignores the great challenge that confronts this nation, which is to find ways to surmount the racial barriers erected by the dominant society and create a truly pluralistic democracy. Any legislation that ignores this objective and enforces a concept of "separate but equal" economic development moves the nation toward apartheid. It would further the aims of the Black Power advocates, who, the Kerner Commission Report warned "have retreated from a direct confrontation with American society on the issue of integration and, by preaching separatism, unconsciously function as an accommodation to white racism."[2]

If *economic integration* involving community-wide participation is to be viewed as a step toward the goal of equal rights and opportunities for all citizens of this nation, then this approach to black capitalism is not the answer. In this article I shall use this dangerous and regressive legislative measure as a springboard for a discussion, with examples, of what I think is a better answer to the problem of ghetto economic development.

DANGERS IN THE BILL

The chief dangers in the community development corporations, as the bill would establish them, are their potential effects on ghetto retailing and manufacturing enterprises, on their owners' independence and freedom of action, and on the opportunities for employment and advancement in "white" businesses.

Barriers to Growth

Community development corporations would perpetuate the inefficient, fragmented commercial and industrial structure of slum areas. Most low-income urban areas are characterized by the virtual absence of a manufacturing base and by a retail community made up largely of small, independent stores.

While the CDC plan might lead to the creation of a small manufacturing base, the bill offers little promise for progress in the retail sector. The articles of incorporation restrict the activities of a CDC to the boundaries of its community, thus greatly lessening the possibility of developing chain organizations capable of reaping the advantages of quantity purchasing, centralized warehousing, management specialization, multiple-unit advertising, and other efficiencies of this form of organization. (Even branches of a community development bank would be restricted to the defined area of its affiliated CDC.)

Since the population of a CDC area may not exceed 300,000, the opportunities for development of chains are quite limited. Not only would the development of efficient merchandising by a CDC itself be impeded, but the entry of "outside" companies with these efficiencies would be discouraged—despite the attractive capital gains tax forgiveness available to them when they sell their ghetto operations to a CDC. The only way for J. C. Penney Company, for example, to do business in a CDC area would be under a turnkey contract. But since Penney's involvement would be restricted to the period required to establish the business and put it on a sound basis, the company would have no prospects for long-range growth in that market.

TAX ADVANTAGES: In addition, community development corporations and their subsidiaries would enjoy important tax advantages over outsiders. While both a "normal" tax and a surtax would be imposed on CDC operations, the rates for both would be reduced by application of the so-called development index. The components of the development index for a community would be:

• The ratio of the percentage of national unemployment, or that within the community's metropolitan area (whichever is lower), to the percentage of the labor force unemployed in the community area.

- The ratio of the median family income in the community area to the median nationally, or in the community's metropolitan area, whichever is greater.

The development index, expressed as a whole number, would be the lesser of these two ratios.

Those companies operating in areas with the highest index would be taxed at a maximum of 22 per cent of taxable income, while those companies with the lowest index would be assessed nothing on the first $50,000 of taxable income. The surtax would equal 26 per cent of the amount by which the taxable income exceeded the surtax exemption, which also would be based on the development index. The lowest exemption would be $25,000, while the maximum would equal $200,000.

By restricting the geographical scope of CDC subsidiaries' operations and by erecting tax barriers against outside competitors, the Community Self-Determination bill promises to perpetuate the inefficient and fragmented business structures in ghetto areas.

Loss of Freedom

Entrepreneurs and would-be entrepreneurs in the ghettos, black or white, would be penalized if they refused to join the CDC and would forfeit their independence if they did join.

The operator of a machine shop or the owner of a men's clothing store would not be eligible for the liberal tax advantages unless he sold a majority interest in his business to the local CDC. Moreover, if he sought funds from the local community development bank, consideration of the loan application would be conditional on his willingness to sign a contract agreeing not to dispose of his interest in his business without first offering it to the CDC.

The bill also would amend the Economic Opportunity Act of 1964 so that, under its provisions, no loan could be made to any small business located in an area served by a community development bank unless it had unsuccessfully applied for a loan from that bank. In effect, therefore, if the machine shop operator should be unwilling to sign the agreement calling for offering his business interest to the CDC in the event he should decide to sell, he could not have his loan application considered and thus would also cut himself off from OEO funds.

If an entrepreneur wanted to sell his business, he might have trouble finding a buyer, as long as the tax incentives were limited to CDC subsidiaries. The bill makes no provision for determining an equitable purchase price in such a situation. The independent businessman faces the prospect of competing in a game where all of the rules favor the CDC.

On becoming the operator of a subsidiary of the local community development corporation, the entrepreneur would face more threats to his independence and freedom of action. The bill would require that each CDC board of directors elect a business management board made up of nine residents of the community. One can imagine the frustrations that would be encountered by a once-independent operator who is now forced to answer to a committee of nine persons trying to manage a corporation for the benefit of the community.

Pressure on the independent businessman to affiliate with a CDC and curtailment of his freedom of action would be especially unfortunate at this time, when encouraging progress is being made in stimulating entrepreneurial activity in black communities. Such groups as the Interracial Council for Business Opportunities and the Negro Industrial and Economic Union have given impetus to this movement by offering capital and advice to black-owned companies. Since the appointment of Howard Samuels as Administrator, the Small Business Administration has been trying to speed up the flow of available funds to aspiring black entrepreneurs. And The Ford Foundation has launched a program to help Negroes establish their own companies and acquire businesses formerly owned by whites.

Clearly, these efforts would be blunted by the passage of legislation granting privileges like tax advantages to community-owned monopolies.

Hampering Advancement

An important part of the social revolution of the 1960's has been the increasing efforts of business to recruit black employees. One important pool of talent in the future could be persons who have gained experience through ownership or management of businesses. Some chain stores operating in ghetto areas, for example, have local residents as managers. This opens the prospect of moving up through the organization's hierarchy.

Few have followed this Horatio Alger path to date, but if the presence of large businesses in these areas is allowed to increase, the opportunities for blacks should multiply rapidly. By blocking entry of such companies, however, the CDC plan would close this narrow, but potentially important, path away from dead-end jobs.

MEETING THE PROBLEM

There are three alternatives in dealing with the problem of the black slums of this nation:

1. Try to disperse their population—that is, achieve total integration.

2. "Isolate" the ghettos from the rest of society, with provision of certain resources and encouragement to develop into prosperous, peaceful, and semiautonomous entities.

3. Try to improve the social and economic welfare of ghettos and increase interaction with "outside" communities, with a view to eventual elimination of the conditions of deprivation prevailing in the ghettos.

However much appeal the first alternative may have to Americans' traditional impatience to deal quickly and decisively with a problem, it obviously is impractical. Our remaining racial and social barriers (against which it is difficult, if not impossible, to legislate) preclude such a move. It also would be enormously expensive. And many, if not most, blacks do not want to integrate in that fashion.

The second alternative is the approach of the Community Self-Determination bill. Creating separate, estranged communities smacks of apartheid and would, I believe, have little appeal to the majority of black or white Americans. It is antithetical to our often violated, but central, idea of this nation as a great melting pot. It runs counter to the dream that Dr. Martin Luther King had for the United States. Perhaps the most damning testimony to the bankruptcy of this concept is the fruitless and wasteful reservation system created for the American Indian.

The third alternative holds the only promise for solving this domestic crisis. Some initial steps have been taken to engage the dominant society in assisting ghetto residents in their efforts to improve their environment. This alternative offers both effective action and the reinforcement of community pride. Notwithstanding the claim that has been made that "whitetown" would oppose programs such as the CDC because of whitetown's obsession with efficiency,[3] I believe that efficiency and self-determination are by no means mutually exclusive. Two examples will illustrate the point:

1. *El Mercado de Los Angeles*—Few ghettos in the United States rival the Mexican-American community in East Los Angeles in size or in the extent to which poverty affects the lives of its residents. But an important development in the commercial life of East Los Angeles—created from community spirit, and action, combined with outside assistance—has given grounds for hope of improvement in its lot.

Early in 1968, El Mercado de Los Angeles opened. El Mercado ("the marketplace") houses forty small businesses under a single roof. Designed to appeal to the Mexican heritage of the area's residents, it features Spanish architecture, mariachis strolling and playing in the patio, and a wide assortment of Mexican wares.

The idea for El Mercado originated with two brothers, Benjamin and Arturo Chayra, who sought the advice of the Small Business Administration. They were able to obtain partial funding under a section of the Small Business Investment Act of 1958 that provides for loans to local development corporations.

Such a corporation uses the funds, along with money raised within the community, to erect facilities for small businesses that participate in the project. Normally a minimum of 20 per cent of the required capital must be raised by the corporation, but in some cases the proportion of funds required from the community may be lower. All the corporation's stockholders must be from the community, and they may not purchase more than $1,000 in stock apiece. Federal loans to El Mercado totaled $1,040,000, while $260,000 was raised in the community.

El Mercado represents an admirable model for the economic and social development of ghettos. The project was community-inspired; it was conceived, planned, and supported locally, and it met a need. Of equal importance, outside involvement was kept in balance; outsiders were used only in a few cases where special resources or training was required.

Because of careful planning of stores and close identification with the local consumers, the marketplace has been very successful. Indeed, although it did not aim to attract shoppers from elsewhere, El Mercado's reputation as an unusual and exciting place to shop has spread beyond East Los Angeles, and it even has become a tourist attraction.

2. *Progress Plaza*—Located in North Philadelphia, Progress Plaza represents a somewhat different approach. The plan for the shopping center was originated by the Reverend Leon Sullivan, a minister well known there for his efforts in behalf of black self-development, and his administrative assistant, Elmer Young, Jr. First they conducted a study to determine the feasibility of and desire for such a venture in the area and to obtain the residents' preferences as to types of stores. On the basis of the study it was decided to move ahead with the project.

The trading area has a population of about 200,000, of which 95 per cent are black. Many of them were very hostile to the existing white-dominated business community, and the idea of a retail center under local direction had great appeal. Less than 2 per cent of those with whom the project was discussed, however, expressed a preference for keeping it all black. In fact, when asked if they wanted outside stores represented in the center, they overwhelmingly favored including units of certain chain stores. Only a relatively small number of militants objected to inviting white businesses to participate in the center.

Progress Plaza has sixteen tenants, including an outlet of a large supermarket chain, a bank, a savings and loan office, and a district telephone office. All the units are managed by blacks, and ten are black-owned. Of those ten, two were ongoing businesses that relocated in the center, the other eight are new. Funds for the center were obtained from First Pennsylvania Banking & Trust Company and The Ford Foundation.

The founders of Progress Plaza are establishing similar centers in other black ghettos and are diversifying into manufacturing activities and apartment buildings. Their confidence in Progress Plaza is based on careful study of the needs of the trading area and awareness of the wishes of the community. Like El Mercado, Progress Plaza draws on the resources and talents of the outside community when necessary, but is otherwise strictly a local endeavor formed in response to local conditions.

Altered Role for the CDC

These examples demonstrate that economic development in the ghetto based on community involvement is possible without creating local corporations that have pervasive economic power in their neighborhood. Such a position for the CDC not only is unnecessary, but also violates the avowed purpose of the Community Self-Determination bill: "to mobilize the talents and resources of the people of this 'nation within a nation' to help them play a more meaningful and rewarding role in building a better, stronger, and more confident America."

To make progress toward achieving these goals, reasonable limits must be placed on this approach to black capitalism. I do not suggest that the concept of community development corporations is devoid of value and should be ignored, community involvement obviously is crucial, and the need is great for locally controlled institutions to direct and coordinate the social and economic development of the ghetto. They can be made effective in this manner:

- Barriers to business development should be lowered by offering tax incentives to *all* businesses opening new facilities or expanding existing facilities in the ghetto.

- Investment capital should be made available through established channels as well as through the community development banks prescribed in Senate Bill 3876.

- Development funds should *not* be restricted to the local CDC and its subsidiaries.

- A national body charged with uplifting the ghettos should be created for the purpose of stimulating and coordinating private and public programs designed to achieve this end.

The high cost of doing business in the ghettos is a main reason why "outside" corporations have shied away from establishing operations there. From many quarters has come the sensible proposal that the federal government offer tax incentives to stimulate investment in deprived areas.[4]

As I have suggested in an earlier HBR article, these incentives should be coupled with an investment guarantee program like that used to encourage corporate ventures in developing countries.[5] These provisions could be terminated if a company were found guilty of violating its community trust (defrauding customers, for example) or at such time as the area's development index reached the national norm.

The entry of outside companies would have to be consonant with the needs and wishes of the local population. Stripped of the stifling and potentially abusive powers now given them in the bill, community development corporations could serve this role effectively. They would stimulate entrepreneurship in their communities, purchase and create their own subsidiaries, and serve as coordinating groups for planning and development.

The national coordinating body would operate as a clearinghouse for the governmental agencies, foundations, businesses, universities, and communities interested in engaging in ghetto projects. There is no reason why carrying out this task would create what is so loathsome to businessmen, a bureaucratic governmental office.

CONCLUSION

Our slum areas show very little evidence of realization of the promises and hopes that were held out for their residents in the early 1960's, when America rediscovered poverty. In Watts, for example, more than three years have passed since the riots, and, except for the Watts Manufacturing Company, White Front (one large discount house that was rebuilt), and a few small stores that have reopened, the business community is more stagnant and inadequate than before.

Clearly, there must be more action. Tax incentives and investment guarantees must be offered; capital for business ventures must be made more readily available; and a more vigorous and better coordinated effort must be made to deal with the crisis. The growing momentum of the activities of the Small Business Administration, the National Alliance of Businessmen, the Negro Industrial and Economic Union, and other groups offers greater promise than ever before that the social and economic conditions of the ghetto can be improved through peaceful revolution.

But our public and private institutions must respond more

effectively if this momentum is to mount into a truly revolutionary force. The architects of Senate Bill 3876 rightly envision the community development corporation idea as an engine to increase that momentum. But the scheme they have chosen to implement the idea is a sure way to slow the momentum.

There is an aspect of political expediency involved, too. The bill offers a radically new approach to the problem—black separatism —without altering the social and economic status quo outside the ghettos. Further, creation of CDCs and their affiliated banks would be relatively inexpensive by Washington's standards: estimates for the first three years of operation indicate annual expenditures of no more than $1.5 billion. The tax incentive and capital availability program that I recommend would doubtless be more expensive.

It would be unwise, indeed dangerous, to pass legislation that stifled efforts within and outside the ghettos to improve the lives of the disadvantaged. Aspiring entrepreneurs within the ghettos must have the chance not only to establish their businesses, but also to enjoy the freedom of action to which they are entitled. "Outside" companies that see an opportunity to make a profit as well as fill an unmet need in the ghettos should be encouraged to join, rather than restrained from joining, in the rebuilding effort.

The essential community involvement can be obtained—as it was in the Bedford-Stuyvesant area of New York, where a local development corporation and outside companies have worked together, and as it was in the cases of Progress Plaza and El Mercado. Community involvement, however, should not be equated with separatism and monopolistic power.

Who opposes self-determination? The vision of poor communities pulling themselves up by their bootstraps with little outside help is in conformance with the American dream. Black capitalism, the label that has been placed on the bill, is an appealing concept. When one moves beyond labels, however, it becomes apparent that this legislation could well deter the economic and social development of ghetto areas and delay by many years fuller participation of their residents in our prosperity. And there is a better way.

Epilogue

It is clear that the interpretations and proposals of the people who have studied the problems of the ghetto marketplace differ. In part, these differences may be attributed to a limited research base. As these readings reveal, relatively little "hard" data are available and those which do exist are characterized by conflicting evidence. The only study to date which approaches a national scope (conducted by the Bureau of Labor Statistics in 1966) focused on comparative prices and was challenged by some because only outlets which consented to be surveyed were examined and these stores received advance notice of the inspection. Most of the other studies have been restricted to one city, and thus the generalizations which can be made are more limited than would be true of a systematic national study. If one reviews the lengthy interview schedule used by Caplovitz, it must be concluded that the settlement house families that cooperated in his study must number among the most patient— and, therefore, perhaps atypical—people in all of New York! The data from Watts were gathered in the weeks immediately following one of the most destructive riots in the nation's history and might, therefore, reflect greater bitterness than otherwise would have been the case. As was noted in the Introduction, a number of the food pricing studies cited in the bibliography completely ignore quality differences and, therefore, lose much of their value.

The studies which have focused on the retailer also have a number

---

See page 290 for all footnotes to this Epilogue.

of limitations. The Caplovitz study and the studies conducted in Los Angeles offer little insight into the cost problems faced by the retailer. Hard data are again missing from the *Food Topics*, *Stores*, and *Merchandising Week* articles. The various retailer groups apparently have made little or no effort to gather such information from their membership. Only the FTC study offers detailed information on the makeup of costs for low-income area merchants; but as the writers of that report themselves note, it is not without its limitations.

Another reason for the rather inadequate research base is the great complexity of the problem. It would be important to have not only a larger geographical framework for future studies with more careful control and inside information in retailer costs but a broader definition of relevant variables. The problem of ghetto marketing clearly is not purely economic. In part, an explanation can be based on economic analysis related to the atomistic structure of retailing communities serving such areas and the income characteristics of the residents. In addition, however, future studies should consider the cultural norms of the people (i.e., the market-basket differences between Mexican-American areas and black ghettos), the history of the trading area, consumer mobility and education, the local power structure, and a host of other variables. In sum, the approach must be eclectic.

In addition to the complexity of the task, the researcher is faced with the growing resentment toward outside investigators, especially in black communities, and the urgency of the problem. Poor people are perhaps understandably tiring of being the research subject for every doctoral candidate, assistant professor, social worker, and federal bureaucrat who comes along. As the well-known psychologist Kenneth B. Clark warned the members of the Kerner Commission:[1]

> I read that report . . . of the 1919 riot in Chicago, and it is as if I were reading the report of the investigating committee on the Harlem riot of '35, the report of the investigating committee on the Harlem riot of '43, the report on the McCone Commission on the Watts riot.
>
> I must again in candor say to you members of this Commission— it is a kind of Alice in Wonderland—with the same moving picture re-shown over and over again, the same analysis, the same recommendations, and the same inaction.

A similar feeling was expressed by a slogan which spread rapidly through Watts in the fall of 1965 by means of campaign-type buttons which proclaimed: "It's Now, Baby!" Indeed, perhaps that should be the title of this epilogue. It would be useful to have more information, and continued research on the subject is certainly to be encouraged. Further studies should be made of marketing not only in the nation's cities, but also among the too often overlooked rural poor. However, enough is known already to begin a systematic private and/or public program to improve the lot of the disadvantaged consumer through the development of an effective distribution system to serve their needs. A number of proposals and ongoing programs were discussed in Part Two of the book. What remains is the task of selecting the most effective methods and accelerating their implementation.

Notes

INTRODUCTION

(See pages 1–11.)

1. James Baldwin, *Nobody Knows My Name* (New York: A Dell Book, 1963), p. 59.

2. See, for example, Jonathan Kozol, *Death at an Early Age* (Boston: Houghton Mifflin Company, 1967) and Joseph P. Lyford, "In My Neighborhood an Adult Is a Dead Child," *Center Diary* (July–August 1966), pp. 1–12.

3. Baldwin, *Nobody Knows My Name,* p. 59.

4. *Report of the National Advisory Commission on Civil Disorders* (New York: Bantam Books, 1963), p. 274.

5. *Ibid.*

6. *Ibid.,* pp. 143–44.

7. Frederick D. Sturdivant, "Business and the Mexican-American Community," *California Management Review* (Spring 1969).

8. David Caplovitz, *The Poor Pay More.* (New York: The Free Press, 1963), p. xxv.

9. U.S. Congress, House, Thirty-Eighth Report by the Committee on Government Operations, *Consumer Problems of the Poor: Supermarket Operations in Low-Income Areas and the Federal Response,* 90th Congress, 2nd Session, 1968, House Report 1851.

10. *Ibid.,* p. 30.

11. *Ibid.,* p. 33.

12. *Ibid.,* p. 29.

13. "The Inner City Poor Found to Pay More for Food than Others," *The Wall Street Journal,* September 6, 1968, p. 1.

14. U.S. Department of Labor, Bureau of Labor Statistics, *A Study of Prices Charged in Food Stores Located in Low and High Income Areas of Six Large Cities* (Washington, D.C.: Office of Publications, 1966).

15. Donald F. Dixon and Daniel J. McLaughlin, Jr., "Do the Inner City Poor Pay More for Food?" *Economics and Business Bulletin* (Temple University), Vol. XX, No. 3 (Spring 1968), pp. 6–12; and Charles S. Goodman, "Do the Poor Pay More?" *Journal of Marketing,* Vol. XXXII, No. 1. (January 1968), pp. 18–24.

16. Kenneth B. Clark, *Dark Ghetto* (New York: Harper & Row Publishers, Inc., 1965), pp. 27–28.

17. Malcolm X, with the assistance of Alex Haley, *The Autobiography of Malcolm X* (New York: Grove Press Inc., 1964), p. 275.

18. See, for example, Clark, *Dark Ghetto,* pp. 28–29.

19. Malcolm X and Haley, *The Autobiography of Malcolm X,* p. 283.

LOW-INCOME LIFE STYLES

Lola M. Irelan and Arthur Besner

(See pages 17–26.)

1. Dotson, Floyd. "Patterns of Voluntary Association Among Urban Working Class Families," *American Sociological Review,* vol. 16, October 1951, pp. 687–93.

2. These four conditions of lower class life were pointed out by Albert K. Cohen and Harold M. Hodges, Jr., in "Characteristics of the Lower-Blue-Collar Class," *Social Problems,* vol. 10, no. 4, Spring 1963, pp. 303–34.

3. Bell, Wendell. "Anomie, Social Isolation, and the Class Structure," *Sociometry,* vol. 20, no. 2, June 1957, pp. 105–16.
Simpson, Richard L., and Max Miller. "Social Status and Anomia," *Social Problems,* vol. 10, Winter 1963, pp. 256–64.
Dean, Dwight G. "Alienation: Its Meaning and Measurement," *American Sociological Review,* vol. 26, no. 5, October 1961, pp. 753–58.

4. Quoted in Cohen and Hodges, *op. cit.,* p. 322.

5. Durkheim, Emile. *Suicide.* Translated by John A. Spaulding and George Simpson. The Free Press, Glencoe, Ill., 1951, p. 253.

6. Merton, Robert K. *Social Theory and Social Structure.* The Free Press, Glencoe, Ill., 1949, p. 128.

7. *Ibid.,* pp. 138, 148–49.

8. Wright, Charles R., and Herbert H. Hyman. "Voluntary Association Memberships of American Adults: Evidence from National Sample Surveys," *American Sociological Review,* vol. 23, June 1958, pp. 284–94.
Leighton, Dorothea, *et al. The Character of Danger.* Basic Books, New York, 1963, p. 384.
Myers, Jerome, and Bertram Roberts. *Family and Class Dynamics in Mental Illness.* John Wiley, New York, 1959, pp. 178–79.

9. Seeman, Melvin. "On the Meaning of Alienation," *American Sociological Review,* vol. 24, no. 6, December 1959, pp. 783–91.
Simpson Richard L., and Max Miller. "Social Status and Social Alienation," paper read at the meetings of the Southern Sociological Society, Miami Beach, Fla., 1961

10. Gould, Rosalind. "Some Sociological Determinants of Goal Strivings," *Journal of Social Psychology,* vol. 13, May 1941, pp. 461–73.

11. Empey, LaMar J. "Social Class and Occupational Aspirations: A Comparison of Absolute and Relative Measurement," *American Sociological Review,* vol. 21, December 1956, pp. 703–709.

12. Bell, Robert R. "Lower Class Negro Mothers' Aspirations for Their Children," *Social Forces,* vol. 43, May 1965, pp. 493–500.

13. Lewis, Hylan. "Culture, Class, and the Behavior of Low-Income Families," paper read at the Conference on Lower Class Culture, New York City, 1963, pp. 26, 34.

14. *Ibid.,* p. 37.

15. Koos, Earl Loman. *The Health of Regionville.* Columbia University Press, New York, 1954, p. 35.

16. Riessman, Frank. *The Culturally Deprived Child,* Harper and Row, New York, 1962, p. 28.

17. Kahl, Joseph A. *The American Class Structure.* Rinehart and Company, New York, 1959, pp. 205–10.

18. Centers, Richard. *The Psychology of Social Classes.* Princeton University Press, Princeton, 1949, p. 62.

19. This controversy is summarized in Hyman Rodman, "The Lower-Class Value Stretch," *Social Forces,* vol. 42, no. 2, December 1963, pp. 205–15.

20. Lewis, *op. cit.,* p. 29. The problem of lower-class attitudes toward "deviant" behavior is currently being researched by Dr. Hyman Rodman of The Merrill Palmer Institute (Cooperative Research Project No. 243, Welfare Administration, U.S. Dept. of Health, Education and Welfare).

21. Miller, Walter. "Lower Class Culture as a Generating Milieu of Gang Delinquency," *Journal of Social Issues,* vol. 14, no. 3, 1958, p. 11.
Rainwater, Lee. *And the Poor Get Children.* Quadrangle Books, Chicago, 1960, p. 52.

22. In research supported by the Welfare Administration (Cooperative Research Project No. 125, Leonard Goodman, principal investigator) it has been found that poor people are more likely, by 13 per cent, to express "strong agreement" with this statement. At less than the .05 level of confidence, the difference is statistically significant.

Economic level and degree of agreement with the statement, "A poor person should never give up hope; there's always a chance that a lucky break will put him on top."

	Per cent indicating—	
Economic level*	Strong agreement	Little or no agreement
Poor (N = 169)	31	69
Not poor (N = 166)	18	82
Per cent difference	13	13

* According to the measure developed by James Morgan *et al.,* in *Income and Welfare in the United States.* McGraw-Hill, New York, 1962, pp. 188–96.

777

777

23. LeShan, Lawrence L. "Time Orientation and Social Class," *Journal of Abnormal and Social Psychology,* vol. 47, 1952, pp. 589–92. An example of this trait is a recent finding by Leonard Goodman (Welfare Administration Cooperative Research Project No. 125): Economic level and agreement with the statement, "Nowadays a person has to live pretty much for today and let tomorrow take care of itself."

Economic level	Per cent indicating—	
	Agreement	Disagreement
Poor (N=169)	48	52
Not poor (N=166)	34	66
Per cent difference*	14	14

* Significant at less than the .05 confidence level

24. Teahan, John E. "Future Time Perspective, Optimism, and Academic Achievement," *Journal of Abnormal and Social Psychology,* vol. 57. November 1958, pp. 379–80.

25. Lipset, Seymour M. *Political Man.* Doubleday and Company, Garden City, N.Y., 1960, pp. 97–130.

26. Bernstein, B. "Language and Social Class," *British Journal of Psychology,* vol. 11, September 1960, pp. 271–76.

27. Miller, S. M., and Frank Riessman. "The Working Class Subculture: A New View," *Social Problems,* vol. 9, Summer 1961, pp. 86–97.

28. Galler, Enid H. "Influence of Social Class on Children's Choices of Occupations," *Elementary School Journal,* vol. 51, April 1951, pp. 439–45.
Morse, Nancy C., and Robert S. Weiss. "The Function and Meaning of Work and the Job," *American Sociological Review,* vol. 20, April 1955, pp. 191–98.

CONSUMER PRACTICES OF THE POOR

Louise G. Richards

(See pages 42–60.)

1. Martineau, Pierre. "Social Classes and Spending Behavior," in Martin Grossack, ed. *Understanding Consumer Behavior.* Christopher Publishing House, Boston, Massachusetts, 1964.

2. Pennock, Jean L. "Who Are the Poor," *Family Economic Review*. Consumer and Food Economics Research Division, Agricultural Research Service, U.S. Department of Agriculture, March 1964.

3. Katona, George, Charles Lininger, and Eva Mueller. 1963 *Survey of Consumer Finances*. Monograph No. 32, The University of Michigan, Survey Research Center, Institute for Social Research, Ann Arbor, Michigan, 1964.

4. Caplovitz, David. *The Poor Pay More,* The Free Press, New York, 1963.

5. Rainwater, Lee, R. Coleman, and G. Handel. *Workingman's Wife*. Oceana Publications, New York, 1959.

6. Holmes, Emma G. "Expenditures of Low-Income Families," *Family Economic Review,* Consumer and Food Economics Research Division, Agricultural Research Service, U.S. Department of Agriculture, March 1955; also LIFE. *Study of Consumer Expenditures: A Background for Marketing Decisions,* vol. 1, Time, Inc., New York, 1957.

7. Katona, George, Charles Lininger, and Richard Kosebud. 1962 *Survey of Consumer Finances*. Monograph No. 32, Survey Research Center, Institute for for Social Research, Ann Arbor, Michigan, 1963; also, Katona, Lininger and Mueller, 1964, *op. cit.*

8. Caplovitz, 1963, *op. cit.*

9. Rainwater, 1959, *op. cit.*

10. Bauer, Raymond. "The Negro and the Marketplace," paper read before the American Psychological Association, Los Angeles, California, September 1964.

11. Rose, Arnold M. "Conditions for Irrational Choices," *Social Research,* vol. 30, no. 2, Summer 1963.

12. David, Martin H. *Family Composition and Consumption*. North Holland Publishing Company, Amsterdam, 1962.

13. Caplovitz, 1963, *op. cit.*

14. Katona, George. *The Mass Consumption Society*. McGraw-Hill, New York, 1964.

15. Mueller, Eva. "A Study of Purchase Decisions," in Lincoln Clark, ed. *Consumer Behavior*. Committee for Research on Consumer Attitudes and Behavior, New York University Press, New York, 1954.

16. Caplovitz, 1963, *op. cit.*

17. Stone, Gregory. "Sociological Aspects of Consumer Purchasing in a Northwest Side Chicago Community," *Unpublished Master's Thesis,* University of Chicago, Chicago, Illinois, 1952.

18. Harp, John. "Socio-economic Correlates of Consumer Behavior," *The American Journal of Economics and Sociology,* vol. 20, no. 3, April 1961, pp. 265–70.

19. Caplovitz, 1963, *op. cit.*

20. Rainwater, 1959, *op. cit.*

21. Sargent, Hugh W. *Consumer-product Rating Publications and Buying Behavior.* University of Illinois Bulletin No. 85, Urbana, Illinois, 1959.

22. Mueller, 1954, *op. cit.*

23. *Ibid.*

24. Katona, 1964, *op. cit.*

25. Caplovitz, 1963, *op. cit.*

26. Katona, Lininger, and Mueller, 1964, *op. cit.*

27. Unpublished data from the author's study, "Cognitive Structure and Consumer Behavior," under a grant from Consumers Union, Mount Vernon, New York, 1961–62.

28. Rainwater, 1959, *op. cit.*

29. Caplovitz, 1963, *op. cit.*

30. Katona, Lininger, and Mueller, 1964, *op. cit.*

31. *Ibid.*

32. *Ibid.*

33. Katona, George. *The Powerful Consumer.* McGraw-Hill, New York, 1960,

34. Caplovitz, 1963, *op. cit.*

35. Katona, 1964, *op. cit.*

36. Katona, Lininger, and Kosebud, 1968, *op. cit.*

37. Caplovitz, 1963, *op. cit.*

38. *Ibid.*

39. Hill, Reuben. "Judgment and Consumership in the Management of Family Resources," *Sociology and Social Research,* vol. 47. no. 4, July 1963, pp. 446–60.

40. Rainwater, 1959, *op. cit.*

41. Katona, Lininger, and Kosebud, 1963, *op. cit.*

42. Caplovitz, 1963, *op. cit.*

43. Katona, 1960, *op. cit.*

44. *Ibid.*

45. Morgan, James, Martin David, Wilbur Cohen, and Harvey Brazer. *Income and Welfare in the United States.* McGraw-Hill, New York, 1962.

46. Willie, Charles V., Morton O. Wagenfeld, and Lee J. Cary. "Patterns of Rent Payment Among Problem Families," *Social Casework,* October 1964, pp. 465–70.

47. Martineau, 1964, *op. cit.*

48. Mischel, Walter, and Ralph Metzner. "Preference for Delayed Reward as a Function of Age, Intelligence, and Length of Delay Interval," *Journal of Abnormal and Social Psychology,* vol. 64, no. 6, 1962, pp. 425–31.

49. Lazarsfeld, Paul. "Sociological Reflections on Business," in Martin Grossack, ed. *Understanding Consumer Behavior.* Christopher Publishing House, Boston, Mass., 1964.

50. Keller, Suzanne, and Marisa Zavalloni. "Ambition and Social Class: A Respecification," *Social Forces,* vol. 43, no. 1, October 1964, pp. 58–70.

51. President's Committee on Consumer Interest. *The Most for Their Money.* A report of the Panel on Consumer Education for Persons with Limited Incomes, Washington, D.C., U.S. Government Printing Office, 1965.

52. Caplovitz, 1963. *op. cit.*

THE MERCHANT AND THE
LOW-INCOME CONSUMER

David Caplovitz

(See pages 61–75.)

1. I am indebted to Robert K. Merton for suggesting the apt phrase, "compensatory consumption." The idea expressed by this term figures prominently in the writings of Robert S. Lynd. Observing the workers in Middletown, Lynd noted that their declining opportunities for occupational advancement and even the depression did not make them class-conscious. Instead, their aspirations shifted to the realm of consumption.

> Fascinated by a rising standard of living offered them on every hand on the installment plan, they (the working class) do not readily segregate themselves from the rest of the city. They want what Middletown wants, so long as it gives them their great symbol of advancement— an automobile. Car ownership stands to them for a large share of the "American dream"; they cling to it as they cling to self-respect, and it was not unusual to see a family drive up to the relief commissary in 1935 to stand in line for its four or five dollar weekly food dole. (The Lynds go on to quote a union official:) It's easy to see why our workers don't think much about joining unions. So long as they have a car and can borrow or steal a gallon of gas, they'll ride around and pay no attention to labor organization. . . . (Robert S. Lynd and Helen Merrill Lynd, *Middletown in Transition* [New York: Harcourt, Brace and Co., 1937], p. 26. See also pp. 447–48.)

It should be noted that the Lynds identify the installment plan as the mechanism through which workers are able to realize their consumption aspirations. Similar observations are to be found in *Knowledge for What?* (Princeton University Press: 1939), pp. 91, 198. Lynd's student Eli Chinoy, also makes use of the idea of compensatory consumption in his study of automobile workers. He found that when confronted with the impossibility of rising to the ranks of management, workers shifted their aspirations from the occupational to the consumption sphere. "With their wants constantly stimulated by high powered advertising, they measure their success by what they are able to buy." Eli Chonoy, "Aspirations of Automobile Workers," *American Journal of Sociology,* 57 (1952), 435–59. For further discussion of the political implications of this process, see Daniel Bell, "Work and Its Discontents," in *The End of Ideology* (New York: The Free Press 1960), pp. 246ff.

2. A frequent practice in extending credit to poor risks is to have cosigners who will make good the debt should the original borrower default. The new arrivals are apt to be disadvantaged by their greater difficulty in finding cosigners.

3. Professor Samuel S. Myers of Morgan State College has studied the credit terms of major department stores and appliance outlets in Baltimore.

Visiting the ten most popular stores, he priced the same model of TV set and gathered information on down payments and credit terms. He found that the cash price was practically the same in the various stores, but that there were wide variations in the credit terms leading to sizable differences in the final cost to the consumer. (Based on personal communication with Professor Myers.)

In his statement to the Douglas Committee considering the "Truth in Interest" bill, George Katona presented findings from the consumer surveys carried out by the Survey Research Center of the University of Michigan. These studies show that people with high income and substantial education are no better informed about costs of credit than people of low income and little education. See *Consumer Credit Labeling Bill, op. cit.,* p. 806.

4. The initials stand for "turn over." The "assistant manager" is ready to make a small concession to the customer, who is usually so flattered by this gesture that he offers no further resistance to the sale. For further descriptions of the "T.O.," see Cecil L. French, "Correlates of Success in Retail Selling," *American Journal of Sociology,* 66 (September, 1960), 128–34; and Erving Goffman, *Presentation of Self in Everyday Life* (New York: Double-day, Anchor Books, 1959), pp. 178–80.

5. The interviewers found that the stores closer to the main shopping area of 125th Street generally had more conservative credit policies than those some-what farther away. This was indicated by the percentage of credit sales the merchants reported as defaults. The higher-rental stores near 125th Street reported default rates of 5 and 6 per cent, those six or seven blocks away, as high as 20 per cent.

6. The referring merchant does not receive his commission right away. Whether he gets it at all depends upon the customer's payment record. He will keep a record of his referrals and check on them after several months. When the merchant who has made the sale has received a certain percentage of the payments, he will give the referring merchant his commission.

7. It is of some interest that the low-income families we interviewed were all familiar with the word "garnishee." This may well be one word in the language that the poorly educated are more likely to know than the better educated.

8. Welfare families cannot, of course, be garnisheed, and more than half the merchants reported that they sell to them. But the merchants can threaten to disclose the credit purchase to the welfare authorities. Since recipients of welfare funds are not supposed to buy on credit, this threat exerts powerful pressure on the family.

9. Not all merchants are paricularly concerned with good will. A few specialize in extending credit to the worst risks, customers turned away by most other merchants. These men will try to collect as much as they can on their accounts during the year and then will sell all their outstanding accounts to a

finance company. As a result, the most inadequate consumers are apt to meet with the bureaucratic controls employed by the finance company. For a description of how bill collectors operate, see Hillel Black, *Buy Now, Pay Later*. (New York: William Morrow and Co., 1961), chap. 4.

10. See *Ibid.,* chap. 3, for a description of the world's largest credit association, the one serving most of the stores in the New York City area.

11. The merchant's access to these networks of social relations is not entirely independent of economic considerations. Just as merchants who refer customers receive commissions, so customers who recommend others are often given commissions. Frequently, this is why a customer will urge his friends to deal with a particular merchant.

12. The local merchants are not the only ones promoting continuous debt. The coupon books issued by banks and finance companies which underwrite installment contracts contain notices in the middle announcing that the consumer can, if he wishes, refinance the loan. The consumer is told, in effect, that he is a good risk because presumably he has regularly paid half the installments and that he need not wait until he has made the last payment before borrowing more money.

13. A systematic study of local merchants and peddlers would probably find that a typical career pattern is to start as a canvasser, become a self-employed peddler, and finally a storekeeper.

14. According to a former customer peddler, now in the furniture business, the peddlers' message will either read "Please *give* Mr. Jones . . ." or "Please let Mr. Jones *pick out* . . ." In the former case, the customer is given the merchandise right away; in the latter, it is set aside for him until the peddler says that it is all right to let the customer have it. The peddler uses the second form when his customer is already heavily in debt to him and he wants to be certain that the customer will agree to the higher weekly payments that will be necessary.

15. One tiny store in the area, with little merchandise in evidence, is reported to employ over a hundred canvassers. The owner would not consent to an interview, but the student-observers did notice that this apparently small merchant kept some four of five bookkeepers at work in a back room. The owner is obviously a "dealer" whose store is his office. As a "dealer," he has no interest in maintaining stock and displays for street trade.

16. Events are sometimes more telling than words. During an interview with a merchant, the interviewer volunteered to help several men who were carrying bed frames into the store. The owner excitedly told him not to help because he might get paint on his hands.

17. In one store in which I inspected this special offer, I was told by the salesman that he would find a chair that was a "fairly close match."

18. Robert K. Merton, *Social Theory and Social Structure,* rev. ed. (New York: The Free Press of Glencoe, 1957), pp. 71–82.

ECONOMIC REPORT ON INSTALLMENT CREDIT AND RETAIL SALES PRACTICES OF DISTRICT OF COLUMBIA RETAILERS

Federal Trade Commission

(See pages 76–107.)

1. These are finance charges as reported by D.C. retailers on their installment contracts. They do not necessarily reflect costs of granting installment credit.

2. Credit unions organized to serve low-income people may be one answer to the problem. More than 400 Federal unions now serve substantially low-income groups. The Bureau of Federal Credit Unions, U.S. Department of Health, Education, and Welfare, is attempting to increase this number through its "Project Moneywise." With proper counseling and organization, credit unions can be successful even with very low-income groups.

3. This report was prepared in response to a resolution adopted by the Federal Trade Commission, July 25, 1966. The text of the resolution is included in the appendix (p. 51) of full report.

4. *Sales Management* magazine, June 10, 1967, "Survey of Buying Power," page D 47, published estimates of the per cent distribution of disposable household income in the District of Columbia for 1966. About one third (32.2 per cent) of District of Columbia households had after-tax incomes of less than $5,000 in 1966. For purposes of analysis, this bottom third of the income distribution will be considered the low-income group. In Chapter IV of this report, the family incomes of a low-income market retailer's customers are tabulated. Three fourths (76.1 per cent) of the sample of customers had before-tax incomes of $6,000 per year or less. This would roughly correspond to after-tax incomes of $5,000 or less. It seems plausible that most of the customers of other low-income market retailers would also have family incomes of less than $5,000 after taxes. We can estimate the total income of such customers for 1966. The total number of households in the District of Columbia was estimated to be 270,500 in 1966. *Sales Management* data indicated 16.6 per cent of these, or 44,900 households, had incomes of less than $3,000 per year. There were 15.6 per cent, or 42,200 households, with incomes from $3,000 to $5,000 per year. If we assume that the *mean* income of households in the under $3,000 category was

$2,000, and that the mean income of families in the next category was $4,000, then the total income of families with incomes below $5,000 would be $259 million.

After-tax income group	Number of households		Mean income		Total income
Under $3,000 income group	44,900	×	$2,000	=	$89.8 million
$3,000 to $5,000 income group	42,000	×	$4,000	=	$168.8 million
All households under $5,000					$258.6 million

5. The Bureau of Labor Statistics conducted a study (*Consumer Expenditures and Income, Washington D.C.,* 1960–61. Bureau of Labor Statistics, Report No. 237–53, February 1964) in 1960–61 of family expenditure patterns in the District of Columbia. We will assume that low-income families spent the same percentage of their income on furniture and appliances as did other families. (Actually the BLS study suggests that low-income families spent a lower percentage of their income on furniture and appliances, but the sample was too small to provide conclusive evidence on this point.)

Household furnishings and equipment accounted on the average for 4.9 per cent of after-tax expenditures. Purchases of television sets, radios, etc., were included in the "recreation" category, which accounted for 4.2 per cent of expenditures. We will assume that half the expenditures in this category may have gone for such appliances. This would give a total of 4.9 + 2.1 or 7 per cent of income spent on furniture and appliances. Multiplying this percentage by estimated total income will give an estimate of the low-income market for furniture and appliances:

$$7 \text{ per cent} \times \$258.6 \text{ million} = \$18.1 \text{ million}$$

6. While most of the sales of low-income market retailers were accounted for by furniture and appliances, other lines of merchandise were sold. The actual proportion of furniture and appliances sales is not known, but examination of survey returns indicates it is about 80 per cent of total sales for low-income market retailers. On this basis, such retailers would account for about 35 per cent of sales of furniture and appliances to low-income customers.

7. Subjecting these differences to statistical analysis indicated that there was only one chance in 100 that they reflected simple random variation. In other words, there is every reason to believe that differences in gross margins of low-income market retailers and general market retailers are systematic.

8. These are cash prices and do not include separately imposed finance charges.

9. These margins for department stores in our survey conform very closely to the national averages compiled by the National Retail Merchants Association, which reported that in 1964 average gross margin for department stores with sales over £1 million per year was 35.3 per cent of sales. *Operating Results of Department and Specialty Stores in* 1964, Controllers' Congress, National Retail Merchants Association, 1965, p. ii.

10. See also discussion Ch. IV, pp. 46–49, *Economic Report on Installment Credit and Retail Sales Practices of District of Columbia Retailers* (Washington: Superintendent of Documents, 1968).

11. Finance charges refer to any extra charges imposed by the retailer when merchandise is sold under installment contract. These charges do not necessarily reflect the true cost to the retailer of granting credit.

12. This add-on rate of 13.5 per cent per year is equivalent to an effective annual rate of finance charges of 25 per cent, calculated by the actuarial method (United States Rule).

13. If no additional charges were made for financing, payments would be $16.50 per month. The six payments plus the original amount down equals $111—compared to the wholesale cost of $109.

14. This add-on rate is equivalent to an effective annual finance charge of 22 per cent.

15. Statistical tests were applied to analyze differences in profit and cost elements for the 10 low-income and 10 general market retailers compared in this section. These tests have limited validity because of the small number of observations and the nonrandom method by which the retailers were selected. They suggest, however, that the differences in profit rates indicated do not justify rejecting the hypothesis that profits are actually similar for both groups of retailers. Similar tests applied to gross margins and other elements of expense, notably salaries, bad debts, and other expenses, appear to justify accepting the hypothesis that expense experience for the two groups of retailers is different.

16. One of the 10 small-volume general market retailers had to be omitted from the net return on owners' equality analysis because of incomplete financial statement information.

POVERTY, MINORITIES, AND CONSUMER EXPLOITATION

Frederick D. Sturdivant and Walter T. Wilhelm

(See pages 118–128.)

1. For examples of the former see, *The Wall Street Journal,* August 16, 1966; *Women's Wear Daily,* July 6, 1966; *Los Angeles Times,* October 8, 1967; and *Los Angeles Herald Examiner,* October 11, 1966.

2. David Caplovitz, *The Poor Pay More* (New York: The Free Press, 1963), p. 179.

3. The Governor's Commission on the Los Angeles Riots, *Violence in the City—An End or a Beginning?* (Los Angeles, December, 1965), p. 63.

4. Interview with Gerald L. Rosen, Staff Attorney, The Governor's Commission on the Los Angeles Riots, January 18, 1966.

5. Caplovitz, *op. cit.*, pp. 90–91.

6. Frederick D. Sturdivant, "Better Deal for Ghetto Shoppers," *Harvard Business Review,* Vol. 46, No. 2 (March–April, 1968), pp. 130–39.

7. Initially, the reader may be disturbed by the small size of the sample. However, it should be noted that *every* television dealer in the low-income areas that met the comparability criteria for the test was included in the study. The comparability criteria could have been relaxed and thus the sample size increased, but such a step would have made it impossible to test the hypothesis.

8. This consistency in retail prices was not attributable to the presence of price tags. In five of the six ghetto stores and one of the control area stores the customers had to rely on sales personnel for price information.

9. The Unruh Retail Installment Sales Act sets the maximum rate a dealer may charge on time contracts in California. A dealer may charge less, of course, but no evidence of this practice was found in the study. For most installment contracts under $1,000 the maximum service charge rate in $\frac{5}{6}$ or 1 per cent of the original unpaid balance multiplied by the number of months of the contract. In revolving charge accounts, such as those used by most department stores, the legal limit is $1\frac{1}{2}$ per cent per month on the first $1,000 and 1 per cent per month on the balance over $1,000.

10. This model Olympic TV set wholesales for $104. Thus, with a retail price of $270 the dealer was already profiting from a markup of 160 per cent.

PRICES IN POOR NEIGHBORHOODS
Phyllis Groom

(See pages 118–128.)

1. For the first appearance in print of the doctrine of let the buyer beware, see Anthony Fitzherbert, *Boke of Husbandrie,* 1534, in W. H. Hamilton, "The Ancient Maxim Caveat Emptor," *Yale Law Journal,* June 1931. The reference was to horse trading.

2. The Office of Economic Opportunity commissioned the housing and nonfood studies and the National Commission on Food Marketing appointed by the President requested the report on food prices, which it published in June 1966.

3. Atlanta, Chicago, Houston, Los Angeles, New York, and Washington.

4. The BLS has developed this definition as a tool for analysis of income and expenditures of poor families to allow for variations in family size. In these terms, an income of $3,000 that provides a given level of living for a 4-person family would be equivalent to $1,500 for a single consumer, about $1,900 for a retired couple, and $4,500 or $4,600 for a family of 6 or more members, including teenage children.

5. *Consumer Expenditures and Income with Emphasis on Low-Income Families* (BLS Report 238–6, July 1964), p. 1.

6. *Consumer Expenditures and Income, Urban United States,* 1960–61 (BLS Report 237–38, 1964), p. 10.

7. For the purposes of this survey, those with less than $3,000 income before taxes in 1959.

8. In the study of rental data, approximate annual family incomes for the year preceding the survey were grouped into three categories: under $3.000; $3,000–$5,999; and $6,000 and over. Monthly rents as of the survey date (1960 or 1961) were grouped by $20 intervals; the lowest segment was "under $40." A fourth of the housing units surveyed in the 1960 census rented for less than $40 a month.

9. London, Thomas Nelson and Sons, Ltd., 1964, pp. 76–106.

10. Data were not available for selecting stores that would be representative of the distribution of the full-line grocery stores within the low-income area. Nor do we know what proportion of the food bought by poor families is bought in their own neighborhood.

11. George Katona, Charles A. Lininger, Eva Mueller, "Installment Debt." 1963 *Survey on Consumer Finances* (Ann Arbor University of Michigan Institute for Social Research, 1964). Monograph 34, p. 60.

12. See Emma Holmes and Minne Belle McIntosh, "Consumer Installment Credit—Patterns of Use and Costs," *Journal of Home Economics,* February 1960, 95–98.

13. David Caplovitz, *The Poor Pay More* (New York, The Free Press, 1963).

14. Ibid., p. 87.

BETTER DEAL FOR GHETTO SHOPPERS
Frederick D. Sturdivant
(See pages 142–157.)

1. *The Intelligent Women's Guide to Socialism and Capitalism* (Garden City, New York, Garden City Publishing Co., Inc., 1928), p. 42.

2. See Alfonso J. Cervantes, "To Prevent a Chain of Super-Watts," HBR September–October 1967, p. 55.

3. The Governor's Commission on the Los Angeles Riots, *Violence in the City—An End or a Beginning?* (Los Angeles, December 1965), pp. 23-24.

4. California Department of Industrial Relations, *Negroes and Mexican-Americans in South and East Los Angeles* (San Francisco, July 1966); these data understate both the income and unemployment problems since they cover the entire area and not just the poorest sections analyzed in this study.

5. David Caplovitz, *The Poor Pay More* (New York, The Free Press, 1963).

6. Ibid., p. 180.

7. See, for example, "Supermarkets in Urban Areas," *Food Topics,* February 1967, pp. 10–22.

THE LIMITS OF BLACK CAPITALISM
Frederick D. Sturdivant
(See pages 257–268.)

1. See Robert B. McKersie, "Vitalize Black Enterprise," HBR September–October 1968, p. 88.

2. *Report of the National Advisory Commission on Civil Disorders* (New York, Bantam Books, 1968), p. 235.

3. See W. H. Ferry,"Whitetown and Blacktown: A Case for a New Federalism," *The Saturday Review,* June 15, 1968, p. 15.

4. See, for example, Robert F. Kennedy, *To Seek a Newer World* (New York, Bantam Books, 1968), p. 40.

5. "Better Deal for Ghetto Shoppers," March–April 1968, p. 130.

EPILOGUE

(See pages 269–271.)

1. *Report of the National Advisory Commission on Civil Disorders* (New York: Bantam Books, 1968), p. 483.

Selected Bibliography

PART I. CHARACTERISTICS AND BUYING PRACTICES OF LOW-INCOME CONSUMERS

"The BLS Interim Budget for a Retired Couple." Margaret S. Stotz. *Monthly Labor Review,* Vol. 83, November, 1960, pp. 1141-1157. Estimates of the cost of a "modest but adequate" standard of living for a man age 65 or over and his wife (living in rented housing), at autumn 1959 prices, in 20 large cities and their suburbs. Includes a detailed list of goods and services considered necessary for retired couples to maintain the specified living standard as determined by levels of living actually achieved in the 1950's; and describes how this representative list was developed and priced.

"Changes in Concepts of Income Adequacy over the Last Century." Helen H. Lamale. *American Economic Review,* Vol. 48, May, 1958, pp. 201-299. An analysis of the relationship over time between actual

Most of the entries in this bibliography are taken from Robert J. Holloway and Frederick D. Sturdivant (editors), *Bibliography on Marketing to Low Income Consumers* (Washington, D.C.: U.S. Department of Commerce, Business and Defense Services Administration, 1969). Professor Holloway of the School of Business Administration at the University of Minnesota is director of a national clearing house for materials related to marketing in low-income areas.

levels of living in the United States and goals or standards of living which have been accepted in different historical periods and for different purposes; and a discussion of the implications in this relationship for present-day concepts of income adequacy.

Characteristics of Families Residing in "Poverty Areas" March 1966. (Series P-23, No. 19), Washington, D.C.: U.S. Department of Commerce, Bureau of Census, August 24, 1966. 5 p. A report presents summary statistics on families in March, 1966 residing in "poverty areas" within standard metropolitan statistical areas (SMSA's) with 1960 population of 250,000 or more. These families are white (57.9%) and nonwhite (42.1%); headed by a male (79.9%), an unemployed person, and semiskilled or unskilled workers; and containing a large number of children under 18 years old.

Consumer Income. (Series P-60, No. 54), Washington, D.C.: U.S. Department of Commerce, Bureau of Census, May 31, 1968. 32 p. Deals with trends in consumer income since 1959-1960, the structure of poor families, the poverty gap. Gives definitions and explanations—and sources and reliability of estimates. Also contains several detailed tables with census figures broken down by various demographic characteristics. These are current population reports.

"Consumer Motivations in Black and White." Henry Allen Bullock. *Harvard Business Review,* Vol. 39, May-June, 1961, Part 1, pp. 89-104; July-August 1961, Part 2, pp. 110-123. A comprehensive study of the differences, distinctions, and dissimilarities between white and Negro consumers. Part 1 contains extensive coverage and analysis of various media appeals, advertising programs, and the behavior of Negroes and whites as consumers. Part 2 presents an "integrated marketing program" most responsive to the Negro consumer. Separate media marketing techniques are regarded as illusory rather than factual.

"Consumer Practices of the Poor." Louise G. Richards. *Welfare in Review,* November, 1966. 24 p. This article is an integrated summary of research findings on consumer practices of the poor conducted by economists and behavioral scientists. It covers mainly how money is spent, shopping behavior, and methods of payments of the poor.

"Consumption Pattern Differences Between Urban Whites and Negroes." James Stafford, Keith Cox, and James Higginbotham. *Social Science Quarterly,* Vol. 49, December, 1968.

"Effects of Income upon Shopping Attitudes and Frustrations." Charles J. Colazza, Jr. *Journal of Retailing,* Vol. 42, Spring, 1966, pp. 1-7. The consumer becomes a more discriminating and particular (mature) shopper as average income increases. The maturity makes it necessary for manufacturers and retailers to determine precisely what the consumer needs and wants which in effect brings more satisfaction to the consumer.

A Guide to Negro Marketing Information. Washington, D.C.: Department of Commerce, Business & Defense Services Administration, September, 1966. 50 p. An annotated bibliography of selected articles and marketing studies which deal with Negro marketing. Also, a statistical summary of population, consumption, and income characteristics presented. Finally the guide includes a directory of National Negro Business Associations and Negro newspapers, and national magazines.

"Intercity Differences in Family Food Budget Costs." Jean C. Brackett. *Monthly Labor Review,* Vol. 86, October, 1968, pp. 1189-1194. An analysis of the effects on food budget cost estimates of using for all cities a single set of weights representing urban U.S. food patterns, or different weights for each city reflecting the food preferences of the region in which the city is located. Also presents a discussion of the conceptual implications of varying the weights in place-to-place comparison of family living costs.

Levels of Living Among the Poor. (BLS Report 238-12) Washington, D.C.: U.S. Department of Labor, August 1965. 28 p. This report gives perspective to the consumer activities of the poor. Some comprehensive tables of expenditures and consumer characteristics included.

The Low Income Consumer: An Exploratory Study. Robert J. Holloway and Richard N. Cardozo (with assistance of Richard Allendorf, Robert Fiske, and Stephen Margrett). Minneapolis: School of Business Administration, University of Minnesota, February, 1969. Results of studies of low-income consumers. General data, retail strategy, consumer aspirations.

Low Income Life Styles. Lola M. Irelan, ed. Washington, D.C.: U.S. Department of Health, Education, and Welfare, 1966. 86 p. A study of the social, cultural, and psychological aspects of poverty. Contains a separate section dealing with consumer practices of the poor. Good bibliography with each section.

"The Marketing Dilemma of Negroes." Raymond A. Bauer, Scott M. Cunningham, and Lawrence H. Wortzel. *Journal of Marketing,* Vol. 29, July, 1965, pp. 1-6. A study based on a dozen surveys, both local and national, depicting the behavior of the Negro in the marketplace. Compares spending habits of Negroes with those of whites.

"Marketing to the Negro Consumer." *Sales Management Magazine,* Vol. 90, March 4, 1963, p. 36. Analysis of the scope, size, and quality of the Negro market. Selected metropolitan areas included.

"More about the Poor in 1964." Mollie Orshansky. *Social Security Bulletin,* Vol. 29, May, 1966, pp. 3-38. This article offers highlights about the poor in 1964. It covers the geography of poverty, the profile of poverty, and the sources of income of the poor.

"Needs, Motivations, and Aspirations of the Low-Income Consumer." Richard K. Allendorf. Master of Science Thesis (unpublished), Minneapolis: University of Minnesota Libraries, December, 1968. 168 p. Report of research carried on among low-income residents of the Twin Cities. Author used a combination of research techniques in an effort to get at aspirations.

"The Negro Consumer." *The Wall Street Journal,* June 30, 1961. Special article dealing with the Negro consumer market, its size, scope, and growth.

"The Negro Market—Growing, Changing, Challenging." Lawrence E. Black. *Sales Management Magazine,* Vol. 91, October 4, 1963, pp.

42-47. A summary of the traits which set the Negro market apart from the general mass market.

"Negro Market—Special Report." *Printer's Ink,* Guide to Marketing 1962, Vol. 276, September 1, 1961, pp. 282-285. Special report of U.S. markets and world markets for 1962 in sections: (1) Total U.S. Market; (2) Geographic markets; (3) Special interest markets; (4) Business—Industry market; (5) International market. Includes an analysis of the special Negro market—its scope, size, and potential growth. Lists publications and marketing research firms which furnish current information on the Negro consumer market.

The Negroes in the United States: Their Economic and Social Situation. (Bulletin No. 1511) Washington, D.C.: U.S. Department of Labor, Bureau of Labor Statistics, June, 1966. 241 p. A comprehensive study of the Negroes in the United States. It covers the topics of Negro population, employment, income, and effects of selected Federal programs on employment. A long bibliography (192 items) and a large number of background statistical tables are provided.

Poverty: American Style. Herman P. Miller, ed. Belmont, Calif.: Wadsworth Publishing Co., Inc., 1966. 304 p. Series of essays dealing with poverty, including two essays concerned with consumer habits of the poor.

"Profile of the Bankrupt." Suzanne Matsen. *Journal of Home Economics,* Vol. 60, January 1968, pp. 33-36. The *Journal* is given to a review of a consumer credit workshop. Pages 33-36 review some credit problems of the poor, and the articles contained throughout the *Journal* may provide ideas in how to aid the poor to better use credit facilities.

Recent Trends in Social and Economic Conditions of Negroes, 1968. (Series P-23, No. 26) Washington, D.C.: U.S. Department of Commerce, Bureau of the Census, 1968. Updates previous publications on social and economic conditions of Negroes.

"Remedies, Enforcement Procedures, and the Duality of Consumer Transaction Problems." David O. Rice. *Boston University Law Review,*

Vol. 48, December, 1968. Critical discussion of legal remedies and enforcement procedures available through private, state, and federal actions.

Report of the National Advisory Commission on Civil Disorders. (Supplemental Studies) Washington, D.C.: U.S. Government Printing Office, July, 1968. 248 p. A supplement to the "Kerner" report. Includes a chapter on black and white attitudes relative to stores and merchants. Data on retailers also included.

Rich Man, Poor Man. Herman P. Miller. New York: Thomas Y. Crowell Company, 1964. 260 p. A statistical analysis of income distribution based on United States Census information. Although consumption habits of the poor are not examined, there is extensive discussion of the economic environment of the poor.

PART II.   CHARACTERISTICS AND PRACTICES OF COMMERCIAL ENTERPRISES IN LOW-INCOME AREAS

"Business Must Act to Keep Ghetto's Distrust of Crooks from Hurting All." Stanley E. Cohen. *Advertising Age,* Vol. 39, April 15, 1968, p. 16. This article concludes that concerned businessmen should support legislation which will rid the ghetto of fraudulent merchants who jeopardize the businesses of all.

The Commercial Structure of Depressed Neighborhood: I. William E. Cox, Jr. Cleveland, Ohio: Bureau of Business Research, Case Western Reserve University, 1968. 146 p.

The Crisis in America's Cities, a Report on Civil Disorders in 1967. Washington, D.C.: American Retail Federation, September 6, 1967. 41 p. A critique of past riots, their causes and effects, and an enumeration of possible retailer response.

"Do the Inner City Poor Pay More for Food?" Donald F. Dixon and Daniel J. McLaughlin, Jr. *The Economic and Business Bulletin,* Vol. 20, Spring, 1968, pp. 6-12. Research in the North Philadelphia Inner

City shows that price differentials, where present, were due to type of store rather than area policy. These hypotheses were examined in the course of the study.

"Do the Poor Pay More?" Charles S. Goodman. *Journal of Marketing,* Vol. 32, January, 1968, pp. 18-24. Examines purchasing patterns of low-income families and prices of low-income area food stores. Based on a survey in a Philadelphia redevelopment area.

Economic Report on Installment Credit and Retail Sales Practices of District of Columbia Retailers. Washington, D.C.: Federal Trade Commission, Bureau of Economics, March, 1968. 52 p. The report presents the results of a survey on sales practices involving household furnishings and credit practices in the District of Columbia. Covers 85% of the D.C. sales of these items.

Organization and Competition in Food Retailing. See chapter "Prices and Margins in Different Income Areas." Washington, D.C.: National Commission on Food Marketing. June, 1966. pp. 335-342. This chapter is directed to an analysis of food retailing in poorer urban communities, generally confined to the central city (data on family income from the 1960 census of population).

"The Other Side of the Poverty Problem." David Caplovitz. *Challenge Magazine,* Vol. 14, September-October, 1965, pp. 12-15. The article points to the unscrupulous methods used by many merchants in their dealings with the legally naive poor. The author's conclusion is that there is a clear need for legal safeguards to supplement poverty programs.

The Poor Pay More. David Caplovitz. New York: The Free Press, 1967. 225 p. A study of a group of low-income families in four New York City housing projects. This book discusses buying patterns, price patterns, credit patterns, family finances, problems of the low-income consumer, practices of merchants, and proposals for dealing with the problems.

"Poverty, Minorities, and Consumer Exploitation." Frederick D. Sturdivant and Walter T. Wilhelm. *Social Science Quarterly,* Vol. 49,

December, 1968. Reports on an experiment involving the use of three low-income couples (Negro, Mexican-American, and Anglo-White) who shopped for identical products in ghetto and non-ghetto stores.

"Prices in Poor Neighborhoods." Phyllis Groom. *Monthly Labor Review,* Vol. 89, October, 1966, pp. 1085-1090. The author's findings are based on three surveys made by the Bureau of Labor Statistics. The author includes conclusions that poor families get poorer housing for equivalent payment; food prices are higher because small independent stores are common in poor areas; and prices of non-food items for the poor are higher for some and lower for others.

Retailing in Low-Income Areas. Real Estate Research Corporation. Chicago, August, 1967. 107 p. A look into the retail shopping habits of Chicago's poor. Contains contrasts with higher income shoppers, as well as a recommendations section. Analysis of retail structure also included.

A Study of the Commercial Structure in Economically Depressed Neighborhoods. Fred Barry, Aaron Kennedy, Carl Koch, Sue Seidman. Cleveland, Ohio: Department of Marketing, Case Western Reserve University, 1968. 21 p. Examination of operations of retailing in low-income areas, especially (1) retailers' reasons for operating in depressed areas, and (2) attitudes of retailers.

A Study of Prices Charged in Food Stores Located in Low and High Income Areas of Six Large Cities. U.S. Department of Labor, Bureau of Labor Statistics, February, 1966. 28 p. No significant differences in prices charged by food stores of similar types and for similar products located in low vs. high income areas were found. However, higher prices are charged by small independent stores which are most common in low-income areas.

A Study of Prices Charged in Food Stores Located in Low and High Income Areas of Six Large Cities for Non-Food Items. Washington, D.C.: U.S. Department of Labor, Bureau of Labor Statistics, February, 1966. 11 p. The study covered 16 non-food items (clothing appliances, drug items, services, household supplies, and cigarettes). No consistent differences in prices charged by various types of stores located in low vs. high income areas were found.

"White Withdrawal: Ghetto Merchants Stay Away from Ties in Areas." *The Wall Street Journal,* Vol. 168, August 16, 1966, pp. 1 and 8. A report on interviews with Negroes and whites in Los Angeles, New York, Chicago, and Cleveland. The article considers the issue of customer relations and withdrawal and isolation of white ghetto merchants.

PART III. CONFLICTS AND PROBLEMS IN LOW-INCOME MARKETS

"Business and the Mexican-American Community." Frederick D. Sturdivant. *California Management Review,* Spring, 1969. Based on an extensive study of the characteristics of low-income Mexican-American consumers in East Los Angeles and the characteristics and practices of retailing enterprises serving that community. In concluding, the article states that while the challenges facing business are great, there are outstanding opportunities to improve the distribution of goods and services to this important segment of the market.

Consumer Problems of the Poor: Supermarket Operations in Low-Income Areas and the Federal Response. Hearings before a Subcommittee on Government Operations, House of Representatives. October 12, November 24 and 25, 1967. 352 p.

District of Columbia Consumer Protection Program. Washington, D.C.: Federal Trade Commission, Legal and Public Records Division, June, 1968. 30 p. A report of the Federal Trade Commission's examination of retailing practices relative to the low-income residents of the area.

"The High Price of Being Poor." *Changing Times: The Kiplinger Magazine,* August, 1968, pp. 39-44. The how and why of economic discrimination in our city slums.

"The Inner City." *Food Topics,* October, 1967, pp. 17-30. Problems of operating a store in an inner-city area, using Detroit, Newark, Baltimore, and Watts as examples.

"Low Income Consumers Pay More Because of Ignorance, Not Chicanery." *Advertising Age,* Vol. 36, May 31, 1965. An annotated speech delivered by Mrs. Esther Peterson, the President's advisor on consumer affairs. She indicated that, in general, the poor pay more because they lack shopping skills and financial resources which make them either buy low quality items or buy from stores that charge higher prices because of credit.

Negro and Jew: Encounter in America. Shlomo Katz, ed. New York: The Macmillan Company, 1967. 141 p. Several articles in this collection of readings discuss the perceptions of Jewish merchants by low-income Negroes. These items consider the roots of anti-Semitism among the Negroes and the role of the Jewish merchant in contributing to these feelings.

"The Negro Entrepreneur." Wilford L. White. *Occupational Outlook Quarterly,* Vol. 10, February, 1966, pp. 19-22. Author discusses obstacles in business that especially plague the Negro entrepreneur.

"The Negro Merchant, a Study of Negro Anti-Semitism." Harold J. Sheppard. *American Journal of Sociology,* Vol. 53, September, 1947, pp. 96-99. Article examines causes of Negro anti-Semitism as they relate to competitive business efforts.

Our Most Urgent Task: To Protect the Consumer Needs. Mary Gardiner Jones. Federal Trade Commission, Legal and Publications Office, April 22, 1966. 31 p. Discussion of the problems faced by the low-income consumer.

The Problems and Opportunities Confronting Negroes in the Field of Business. H. Naylor Fitzhugh, ed. Washington, D.C.: U.S. Department of Commerce, 1962. Report condenses papers delivered before National Conference on Small Business in 1961. Central issues were small business operations and fields heavily influenced by race-relations patterns.

"Riot Report." Bruce Weber. *Merchandising Week,* August 14, 1967, p. 12. A brief article which sets the scene in terms of the frustrations and barriers involved in consumer-business relations in slum areas. It looks at Watts two years after the riots.

PART IV.   PROGRAMS AND
POTENTIAL SOLUTIONS

"After the Riots—A Position Paper for Retailing." Richard Rosenthal. *Stores* (National Retail Merchants Association Magazine), December, 1967, pp. 11-20. An examination of what retailers experienced, both in and outside riot areas, what they learned, what they are doing now, and their expectations for the future.

"Aiding the Poor." *The Wall Street Journal,* Vol. 176, January 4, 1968, pp. 1 and 18. The article cites numerous cases of unethical and fraudulent business practices involving the poor. It also discusses possible social and legal actions aimed at remedying these conditions.

"Better Business Bureau Alters Approach." *New York Times,* October 10, 1967, p. 67. Describes various ways the Better Business Bureau is providing help for the disadvantaged poor before they purchase. Material is also available from the Better Business Bureau main office on a project for establishing B.B.B. operations in Harlem.

"Better Deal for Ghetto Shoppers." Frederick D. Sturdivant. *Harvard Business Review,* Vol. 46, March-April, 1968, pp. 130-39. This paper presents an overview of the findings from a study of business-consumer relations in the disadvantaged areas of south central and east Los Angeles. Based on some 2,00 interviews and observations, the article illustrates the dilemma of the poorest segments of our society being served by the most inefficient and exploitive members of the nation's distribution system. A proposal is offered to revolutionize the economic structure of ghetto areas.

"Is Black Capitalism the Answer?" *Business Week,* August 3, 1968, pp. 60-61. This article summarizes the major provisions of Senate Bill 3876 which is designed to create community development corporations to uplift the economic and social structure of disadvantaged areas through a process of community self-determination.

Business Amid Urban Crisis. The National Industrial Conference Board, Studies in Public Affairs, No. 3, October, 1968. 80 p. Describes what 356 American firms are doing to combat the problems of the cities.

"A Business Development Program for Our Poverty Areas." Robert F. Kennedy. *Congressional Record,* 90th Congress, Second Session, May 29, 1968. Senator Kennedy's program is outlined. The program is designed to attract business investment to slum areas.

"Business Must Put-Up." Leland Hazard. *Harvard Business Review,* Vol. 46, January-February, 1968, pp. 2-12, 168-170. Mr. Hazard makes a distinction between real and relative poverty—the former of which business must deal with before government takes over and does an inept job. He proposes formation of a Council of Business for Social Welfare to explore and direct efforts to eradicate real poverty.

The Businessman and the City. David L. Birch. Cambridge, Mass.: Harvard University, Graduate School of Business Administration, 1967. 220 p. A group of writings addressed to solving urban ills and the role of business and government in attacking these problems. Selected bibliographies are included after each general area.

"Deception in the Market Place of the Poor: The Role of the Federal Trade Commission." Mary Gardiner Jones. An address before the Zonta Club of Washington, June 22, 1966, Federal Trade Commission, Legal and Publications Office. 27 p. This paper reviews the studies conducted by the Federal Trade Commission and corrective actions initiated by that agency.

"Ghetto Needs 'Marshall Plan,' Grocers Told." *Food Mart News,* Vol. 31, April, 1968, pp. 1 and 14. Summarizes talks of the Industrial Appreciation Day at Western Michigan University where several experts in the food industry advocated more involvement by business in ghetto regions.

"The Kerner Report and the Federal Trade Commission." Mary Gardiner Jones. Washington, D.C.: Federal Trade Commission, Legal and Publications Office, April 26, 1968. An address by Mary Gardiner Jones before The City Club of Cleveland, Cleveland, Ohio. What the Federal Trade Commission can do about the problem of sales and credit practices in the inner city.

"The Limits of Black Capitalism." Frederick D. Sturdivant. *Harvard Business Review,* January-February, 1969, pp. 122-128. The article calls for balanced approach to ghetto development involving maximum community participation and interaction with the outside society. Examples of successful programs based on this approach are cited.

The New Mood of the Negro: Some Implications for Market Developers. H. Naylor Fitzhugh. Washington, D.C.: Howard University, September 23, 1963. A study of significant dimensions of the current civil rights program and its impact on the Negro market. Describes specific goals of the program in relation to equal employment opportunities. Cautions Negro market developers regarding unwise use of pressure group tactics. Urges intensive preparation and pursuits of the "new type of nonracially specialized posts."

"The Retailers, the Ghetto, and the Government." *Merchandising Week,* December 11, 1967, pp. 6-7. This article consists of the findings of a series of interviews with retailers in various parts of the country reacting to the kind of program recommended by Senator Robert Kennedy.

"Should Supermarkets Take a New Look at Urban Areas?" *Food Topics,* Vol. 22, February, 1967, pp. 10-22. The article considers the problems of doing business in urban areas (especially low-income neighborhoods) and points to the profit potential in such areas. The opinion is expressed that the private sector had better move into these areas or be forced with undesirable actions by the government.

"The Urgent Need for Consumer Protection for Our Inner Cities." Mary Gardiner Jones. An address at the Ambassador Motor Hotel, Minneapolis, Minnesota, Federal Trade Commission, Legal and Publications Office. An exposition of consumer problems in low-income areas and how business can cure them.

Violence in the City—An End or a Beginning. The Governor's Commission on the Los Angeles Riots, December, 1965. Governor's Office, Sacramento, Calif. 104 p. A report of the commission established by the governor of California to study the causes of the Watts riots. The report reviews the events of the riot and attempts to identify its causes. One section, pages 62-65, deals specifically with the problems of the consumer.

"Vitalize Black Enterprise." Robert B. McKerzie. *Harvard Business Review,* Vol. 46, September-October, 1968, pp. 88-99. Condition of Negro-owned business. Responses to the problem: role of Negro groups, white business, federal government. Strategies for development.

"Is War on Poverty Becoming War on Business?" D. Hencke. *Nation's Business,* Vol. 54, March, 1966, pp. 40-41 and 58-61. An investigation by *Nation's Business* reveals that a national campaign is under way employing poverty program workers to tell consumers what to buy, how much to pay, and how to boycott firms. The author indicates that business has moved to help the poverty fighters; however, this help has been limited.

PART V.   GENERAL WORKS ON POVERTY

The Anatomy of a Riot: Buffalo, 1967. Frank Besag. Buffalo, N.Y.: University Press at Buffalo, 1967. The author concludes that some businesses were hit because they cheated the people with things sold at a higher price than would be paid for the same item in the suburbs.

Beyond the Melting Pot. Nathan Glazer and Daniel P. Moynihan. Cambridge, Mass.: Massachusetts Institute of Technology Press, 1963. 360 p. The point of departure is the recognition that ethnicity is a permanent quality of the American society, particularly the cities.

"Blacks in America." *Social Science Quarterly,* Vol. 49, December, 1968. A double-length issue dealing with the Negro in America. Four articles deal with marketing problems specifically.

Dark Ghetto: Dilemmas of Social Power. Kenneth B. Clark. New York: Harper & Row Publishers, 1965. 251 p. A diagnosis of our ghetto problems, their social consequences, and what Americans must do to deal with them.

The Economics of Discrimination. Garry S. Becker. Chicago: University of Chicago Press, 1957. 137 p. The author develops a theory of discrimination in the market-place that supplements the psychologists' and sociologists' analysis of causes with an analysis of economic consequences.

The Economics of Poverty. Alan B. Batchelder. New York: John Wiley and Sons, Inc., 1966. 214 p. This book presents an economic analysis of poverty in the U.S. It does not deal specifically with the low-income consumer, but does provide a useful framework for analysis and a good bibliography.

New Perspectives on Poverty. Arthur B. Shostak and William Gomberg, eds. Englewood Cliffs, N.J.: Prentice-Hall, Inc., 1965, 185 p. A collection of 18 articles covering poverty, its problems, and recommendations to cure the problems. In contains an annotated bibliography.

The Other America: Poverty in the United States. Michael Harrington. New York: The Macmillan Company, 1962. 191 p. The book that is credited with initiating the war on poverty. It treats the full range of poverty groups in the U.S.

Poverty Amid Affluence. Leo Fishman, ed. New Haven, Conn.: Yale University Press, 1968. 246 p. A collection of original papers presented at the West Virginia University Conference on Poverty Amid Affluence in May, 1965. The major subjects covered are: definition and measurement of poverty; social attitudes, social organization, and poverty; special cases of poverty; and approaches to the elimination of poverty.

Report of the National Advisory Commission on Civil Disorders. Washington, D.C.: U.S. Government Printing Office, 1967. 425 p. The Commission explains what has happened to our riot-torn nation in terms which call for immediate action to implement their recommendations.

The Economics of Poverty. Burton A. Weisbrod, ed. Englewood Cliffs, N.J.: Prentice-Hall, Inc., 1968. 180 p. This book deals largely with the origins and characteristics of the federal war on poverty.

Index